Richard Barltrop is a researcher and consultant who has travelled extensively in Sudan and South Sudan. He holds a DPhil in International Relations from the University of Oxford.

'This book examines the engagement of the international community in Darfur and Sudan more broadly and in greater detail than any other study I have seen. His personal involvement with Sudan has clearly helped in regard to the many interviews he has obtained as well as the numerous unpublished materials he has accessed. The work raises many issues with regard to international engagement in situations such as that in Sudan and will be of great interest to practitioners, as well as academics and a wider concerned readership.'
Peter Woodward, Professor Emeritus, University of Reading, and author of *The Horn of Africa: Politics and International Relations* (I.B.Tauris)

'Conflict mediation and humanitarian aid have usually been discussed separately. In this innovative and meticulous study, Barltrop ably brings these fields together and enhances our understanding of peace processes in southern Sudan and Darfur.'
David Keen, Professor of Conflict Studies, London School of Economics and Political Science (LSE)

'Richard Barltrop's elegantly written, original, scholarly and empirical study of these conflicts and the international response to the resultant humanitarian crisis is exceptional ... Researchers into Sudanese affairs, policymakers and members of non-governmental organisations will find this book is essential reading.'
Ahmed Al-Shahi, Research Fellow, St Antony's College, University of Oxford

Richard Barltrop

DARFUR
and the
INTERNATIONAL COMMUNITY

The Challenges of
Conflict Resolution
in Sudan

New paperback edition published in 2015 by
I.B.Tauris & Co Ltd
London • New York
www.ibtauris.com

First published in hardback in 2011 by I.B.Tauris & Co Ltd

Copyright © 2011, 2015 Richard Barltrop

The right of Richard Barltrop to be identified as the author of this work has been asserted by the author in accordance with the Copyright, Designs and Patents Act 1988.

All rights reserved. Except for brief quotations in a review, this book, or any part thereof, may not be reproduced, stored in or introduced into a retrieval system, or transmitted, in any form or by any means, electronic, mechanical, photocopying, recording or otherwise, without the prior written permission of the publisher.

Every attempt has been made to gain permission for the use of the images in this book. Any omissions will be rectified in future editions.

References to websites were correct at the time of writing.

ISBN: 978 1 78453 205 5
eISBN: 978 0 85773 939 1

A full CIP record for this book is available from the British Library
A full CIP record is available from the Library of Congress

Library of Congress Catalog Card Number: available

Camera-ready copy edited and supplied by the author

CONTENTS

List of tables	vii
Note on transliteration and terminology	ix
Abbreviations	xi
Selected chronology	xv
Acknowledgements	xix
Map of Sudan	xxi

INTRODUCTION	**1**
1. CONFLICT, WAR AND PEACE	**13**
The background to the civil war	13
The course of the war and the Darfur conflict	20
2. MEDIATION	**36**
Good offices and eminent persons	36
Regional initiatives	40
An international initiative	50
Darfur mediation and fragmentation	62
3. RELIEF	**69**
Relief before Operation Lifeline Sudan, 1983–9	69
Operation Lifeline Sudan and relief, 1989–2001	74
Relief, 2001–4	91
The Darfur relief operation, 2004 onwards	96
4. FOREIGN POLICY	**103**
Clientelism and aid, 1983–9	103
Containment and relief, 1989–2001	109
Engagement and relief, 2001–4	122
Engagement and containment, 2004 onwards	131
5. OPTIONS	**137**
Mediation	137
Relief	149
Foreign policy	159
6. CONCLUSION	**169**
The outcomes in Sudan	169
Comparisons and prospects	175
Conflict resolution	181
Notes	191
Appendix	221
Bibliography	225
Index	237

LIST OF TABLES

Table 1:	Examples of attacks and killings of civilians	28
Table 2:	Examples of attacks and killings of civilians in Darfur	32
Table 3:	Examples of security-related incidents	80
Table 4:	Examples of obstruction of relief agencies	81
Table 5:	Examples of exploitation and diversion of relief	82
Table 6:	Determinants of mediation outcomes	138
Table 7:	Possible consequences of humanitarian relief	150

NOTE ON TRANSLITERATION AND TERMINOLOGY

As with Arabic words, Sudanese names may be written in English in a number of ways. For ease of reading, I have tried to use the most common spellings in English, and have avoided the less common, but more accurate, formal Arabic transliterations. I have therefore used, for example, Khartoum, Nimeiri and Omar, rather than Khartum, Numayri and 'Umar; and *sharia*, rather than *shari'a*. In quotations, Arabic words or names are written as given in the sources themselves.

For simplicity, I have often used the term 'relief' rather than the more formal term 'humanitarian action', although in keeping with usage in international relations, I have reserved the term 'humanitarian intervention' to mean armed intervention on humanitarian grounds, rather than conflate it with relief and development (which in the aid world are often called 'interventions'). For simplicity too, I have also sometimes used the term 'civil war' where it might be more correct, but less idiomatic, to say 'internal conflict'.

Given the slender division between the SPLM and the SPLA, I have generally written 'SPLM/A' rather than specifying one rather than the other, except where the context makes it obvious to do so. I have generally written 'the Sudanese government' or 'the government', but on occasions used the abbreviation 'GOS' (Government of Sudan), which became common usage in the 1990s.

ABBREVIATIONS

AMIS	African Union Mission in Sudan: AU ceasefire observer-cum-peacekeeping mission
AU	African Union
CIRF	Commission on International Religious Freedom (US)
CNPC	China National Petroleum Corporation
CPA	Comprehensive Peace Agreement: between government and SPLM/A, finalised on 31 December 2004 and formally signed on 9 January 2005
CPMT	Civilian Protection Monitoring Team: international monitoring body for government–SPLM/A ceasefire from 2002
CSIS	Center for Strategic and International Studies: US think-tank
DCHA	Bureau for Democracy, Conflict, and Humanitarian Assistance: USAID department
DFID	Department for International Development (UK)
DOP	Declaration of Principles
DPA	Darfur Peace Agreement
DUP	Democratic Unionist Party: formed from merger of the National Unionist Party and the People's Democratic Party in 1968
ECHO	European Community Humanitarian Aid Office
EDF	Equatoria Defence Force
EPLF	Eritrean People's Liberation Front
EPRDF	Eritrean People's Revolutionary Democratic Front
ESPA	Eastern Sudan Peace Agreement: between government and Eastern Front, signed in 2006
GONU	Government of National Unity: formed in mid-2006, in accordance with CPA
GOS	Government of Sudan (also sometimes abbreviated GoS: the

	abbreviation became widely used for the government after 1989)
GOSS	Government of Southern Sudan: formed in mid-2006, in accordance with CPA, semi-autonomous from the GONU
ICC	International Criminal Court
ICF	Islamic Charter Front (renamed the National Islamic Front in 1986)
ICRC	International Committee of the Red Cross
IGAD	Intergovernmental Authority on Development (formerly the Intergovernmental Authority on Drought and Desertification, IGADD)
INGO	International non-governmental organisation
IPF	IGAD Partners Forum
IRIN	Integrated Relief Information Networks
JAM	Joint Assessment Mission: joint GOS, SPLM/A, World Bank and UN needs-assessment mission for Sudan, 2004–5
JEM	Justice and Equality Movement
JMC	Joint Military Commission: international monitoring body for Nuba Mountains ceasefire
NCP	National Congress Party
NDA	National Democratic Alliance
NGO	Non-governmental organisation
NIF	National Islamic Front (renamed the National Congress Party in 1998)
NMPACT	Nuba Mountains Programme for Advancing Conflict Transformation
NPA	Norwegian People's Aid
NSIS	National Security and Intelligence Service
OAU	Organisation of African Unity
OLS	Operation Lifeline Sudan
PAIC	Popular Arab and Islamic Conference
PCP	Popular Congress Party
PDF	Popular Defence Forces
RCC	Revolutionary Command Council: established 1989, dissolved 1993
RRC	Relief and Rehabilitation Commission
SAF	Sudan Armed Forces

SCC	Sudan Council of Churches
SDC	Save Darfur Coalition
SLM/A	Sudan Liberation Movement/Army
SPLM/A	Sudan People's Liberation Movement/Army
SRRA	Sudan Relief and Rehabilitation Association
SRRC	Sudan Relief and Rehabilitation Commission: successor to SRRA after 2003
SSIM/A	South Sudan Independence Movement/Army: name adopted in November 1994 by SPLM/A-United faction led by Riek Machar
SSLM	Southern Sudan Liberation Movement
SUNA	Sudan United News Agency
TMC	Transitional Military Council
UNAMID	African Union–United Nations Hybrid Operation in Darfur
UNDP	United Nations Development Programme
UNICEF	United Nations Children's Fund
UNMIS	United Nations Mission in Sudan: UN peacekeeping mission for CPA
UN OCHA	United Nations Office for the Coordination of Humanitarian Affairs
USAID	United States Agency for International Development
USAP	Union of Sudan African Parties
WFP	World Food Programme

SELECTED CHRONOLOGY

1955	Army mutiny in south: **start of conflict leading to first civil war**
1956	Sudan's independence: coalition government under Umma prime minister, Abdullah Khalil
1958	First military take-over: General Abboud takes power
1959	Nile Water Agreement signed with Egypt
1962	Formation of southern rebel guerrilla movement, the Anyanya
1964	'October Revolution' overthrows Abboud: establishment of national and then multiparty government
1969	Second military take-over, the 'May Revolution': Ja'far Nimeiri takes power
1970	Ansar revolt crushed
1971	Communist-backed coup attempt
1972	**Addis Ababa Agreement** between government and Southern Sudan Liberation Movement ends first civil war
1975	Coup attempt
1976	Coup attempt; joint defence agreement signed with Egypt
1977	'National reconciliation' between Nimeiri and northern opposition. Oil discovered at Bentiu, in south, by Chevron
May 1983	Army mutinies and withdrawal of units at Bor, Pibor and Pochalla into the bush and to Ethiopia: **start of second civil war**
September 1983	'September laws': Nimeiri introduces *sharia*
April 1984	Nimeiri declares a state of emergency
April 1985	Overthrow of Nimeiri: Transitional Military Council

	established, led by General Sawar al-Dhahab
March 1986	SPLM and Umma Party issue Koka Dam declaration
March 1986	Combined Agencies Relief Team set up in Juba
	General elections: Sadiq al-Mahdi becomes prime minister of Umma coalition government with DUP and later NIF
April 1986	General elections: Sadiq al-Mahdi becomes prime minister of Umma coalition government with DUP and later NIF
November 1988	DUP-SPLM accord
April 1989	**Operation Lifeline Sudan launched**
June 1989	Third military take-over: Lieutenant Colonel (later General) Omar al-Bashir takes power
October 1989	First operation of OLS (OLS I) terminated by Bashir
November 1989	**Carter peace initiative**
April 1990	OLS resumes (OLS II)
May 1991	Fall of Mengistu in Ethiopia leads to SPLM/A loss of bases in Ethiopia
August 1991	Attempted internal coup against John Garang leads to splintering of SPLM/A and breakaway of factions
May–June 1992	**First Abuja peace conference**
April–May 1993	**Second Abuja peace conference**
September 1993	**Launch of IGAD peace initiative**
April 1996	SSIM and SPLM Bahr el-Ghazal faction sign 'political charter' with government
April 1997	Government, SPLM/A breakaway factions and other minor southern groups sign **Khartoum Peace Agreement**
September 1997	SPLM/A-United faction of Lam Akol signs **Fashoda Agreement** with government
February 1999	Launch of **Egyptian-Libyan peace initiative**
September 2001	John Danforth appointed US presidential envoy for promoting peace in Sudan
January 2002	Government and SPLA sign **Nuba Mountains ceasefire agreement** in Switzerland
July 2002	Government and SPLM/A sign **Machakos Protocol** in Kenya, as result of peace talks under auspices of IGAD, observed by troika (Britain, Norway and

	USA)
2002–2004	Government–SPLM/A peace talks continue in Kenya, producing four further protocols. Separate government–NDA talks are held in Egypt and government–opposition talks in Khartoum
March 2003	Escalation of conflict in Darfur: JEM and SLM/A declare themselves; fighting and displacement escalate rapidly
April 2004	Government, JEM and SLM/A sign **Darfur 'humanitarian ceasefire' agreement** at peace talks in N'djamena, Chad
May 2004	Government and SPLM/A agree protocol on power sharing at peace talks in Naivasha, Kenya
July 2004	African Union peacekeeping mission in Sudan, **AMIS**, deploys to Darfur
November 2004	UN Security Council meets in Nairobi and sets end-of-year deadline for final agreement
31 December 2004	Government and SPLM/A finalise **Comprehensive Peace Agreement** (CPA) in Naivasha
9 January 2005	Government and SPLM/A formally sign CPA in Nairobi; conflict in Darfur and other parts of Sudan continues
February 2005	Beja Congress and Rashaida Free Lions announce formation of the Eastern Front
July 2005	Formation of Government of National Unity and Government of Southern Sudan; death of John Garang
May 2006	Government and faction of SLM/A sign **Darfur Peace Agreement** (DPA) in Abuja, Nigeria
October 2006	Government and Eastern Front sign **Eastern Sudan Peace Agreement** (ESPA) in Asmara, Eritrea
October 2007	Unsuccessful peace talks for Darfur convened in Sirte, Libya
January 2008	AU/UN hybrid peacekeeping operation, **UNAMID**, replaces AMIS in Darfur
May 2008	JEM attack on Khartoum is repelled in Omdurman
July 2008	International Criminal Court prosecutor requests arrest warrant for President Bashir
February 2009	Government and JEM sign goodwill agreement at talks in Doha, Qatar

March 2009	ICC issues arrest warrant for President Bashir
April 2010	General elections held, one year later than scheduled by CPA.

ACKNOWLEDGEMENTS

In a way, the seed of curiosity which led to this book was sown in the early 1980s when, as a child at school, I first heard of famines and humanitarian crises in the Horn of Africa. For the opportunity that then first developed this curiosity, my thanks go therefore to the Winston Churchill Memorial Trust, which awarded me the travelling fellowship that first took me to Sudan in 1995 and that gave me the freedom to explore the country in a manner that has been of lasting value. For the subsequent opportunities for academic study, and for their support for the original research which underlies this book, my thanks go to the Middle East Centre and the Department of Politics and International Relations at Oxford University, and to the Economic and Social Research Council (UK). In Oxford, I would especially like to thank Ahmed al-Shahi. My thanks go also to Peter Woodward, to those who have made comments on seminars and presentations I have given, and to the editors of my various writings on Sudan.

In Sudan I am grateful to the United Nations Development Programme for the opportunities that working with it has given me since I first worked for it in 2002. More broadly, though, I would like to thank the many people in Sudan and elsewhere – Sudanese and non-Sudanese – who have been helpful to me during and since the research on which this book is based. Many people in academia, aid, business, politics and other fields were generous with their time, assistance and hospitality, some especially so. Such kindness is common in Sudan, even in trying circumstances, but I am no less grateful for it. Lastly, for their help and patience in bringing this book about, I am very grateful to Mette Louise Berg, Peter Oliver and Catherine Robinson, and to Joanna Godfrey and Maria Marsh at I.B.Tauris. As always, responsibility for the content and any errors lies solely with the author.

MAP OF SUDAN

Map no. 3707 rev. 10, April 2007, UN Cartographic Section

INTRODUCTION

On 9 January 2005, at a jubilant signing ceremony in Nairobi, Kenya, the government of Sudan and the Sudan People's Liberation Movement/Army (SPLM/A) formally signed what was called the Comprehensive Peace Agreement (CPA) for Sudan. The agreement had been finalised on 31 December 2004 – a deadline set by the United Nations Security Council – and was the culmination of a long peace process which had aimed to end Sudan's two-decade civil war. Fittingly the CPA was widely welcomed, in Sudan and abroad. But the welcome was tempered by concern about what in many quarters had come to be seen as the most pressing issue in Sudan, namely the ongoing conflict in Darfur, Western Sudan, and the humanitarian crisis that this was causing. Despite its name, the CPA made no pretence to cover this conflict.

This book is about the challenges of resolving conflict in Sudan. It arises out of my interest in the question of how outsiders, or the international community (so far as this exists), can best respond to protracted internal armed conflicts that involve major humanitarian crises. In a small way, the title of the book is therefore deceptive, but also a corrective. Although entitled *Darfur and the International Community*, the book concerns the whole of Sudan, as the sub-title indicates, and this is with good reason. The Darfur conflict was part of a wider picture of conflict in Sudan, at the centre of which was the civil war. There were connections between the two conflicts, and the response of the international community to the Darfur conflict was greatly shaped by how it had responded to the civil war, and by the CPA peace process. For these reasons, the book considers the civil war and the Darfur conflict together, and the wider challenges of resolving conflict in Sudan.

The book therefore focuses on conflict-resolution efforts across the span of the civil war and the Darfur conflict, focusing on those peace talks that had international involvement. However, the book also examines the role of international humanitarian assistance, and its interaction with the question of conflict resolution. During Sudan's decades of conflict, the principal and most consistent response of the international community was to provide humanitarian assistance or, to use its short name, relief. Attempts were occasionally made to link relief constructively to the resolution of conflict. But otherwise, for the most part, relief was provided independently of efforts to resolve Sudan's conflicts. The duration, the intractability, and the human and material costs of Sudan's conflicts, raise many questions. But for outsiders who are interested in helping to resolve wars or save lives, one of the most difficult questions that Sudan's conflicts raise is this: did mediation and relief help or hinder the resolution of the conflicts? There are many reasons for asking this question, not least the facts that the CPA was accompanied by the escalation of the Darfur conflict and that during the civil war some observers asked whether relief was not actually prolonging the war.

Mediation and relief are the two main ways in which outsiders (foreign governments, organisations or individuals) try to respond constructively to internal conflicts, short of taking military action; respectively, they embody political and humanitarian action. But from a perspective of overall outcomes, the efforts of outsiders at mediation and relief in Sudan between 1983 and the end of 2009 (the period covered in this book) present a complicated, mixed picture of apparent failure and success. A string of mediation efforts over more than a decade failed to resolve the war. Then, peace talks in Kenya between 2002 and 2004, under the auspices of a joint regional and international initiative, led to a series of agreements culminating in the CPA. At the same time, however, a destructive conflict escalated in Darfur, and significant opposition groups (armed and unarmed) remained excluded from the peace process in Kenya and, ultimately, from the CPA. In parallel with this, throughout the long civil war, international donors and organisations provided humanitarian relief in Sudan on a massive scale – at an average nominal cost of around US$200m per year – saving some lives and helping others. But this relief did little to prevent the recurrence of humanitarian crises (caused by the war or associated with it) in which people continued to die or suffer on an often dramatic scale. The worst manifestation of this was the escalation of the Darfur conflict after 2003, and the accompanying humanitarian crisis. Meanwhile, throughout the civil war and the Darfur conflict, both international mediation and international relief were subject to a range of common problems. Examples included attempts by the warring parties to use ceasefires instigated by peace talks to improve their positions on the battlefield (for example through redeployments during ceasefires), or attempts by the same parties to divert relief that was intended for civilians to their own armies or supporters.

The international dimensions of civil wars or internal conflicts are often complex and are certainly so in the case of Sudan's conflicts. The duration of the civil war and the Darfur conflict, the human and material cost, and the failures of efforts to help end the conflicts and save lives are issues of concern both domestically and internationally. Between 1983 and 2009, the external actors that were involved directly or indirectly in the civil war and the Darfur conflict included neighbouring and regional African and Arab countries, Western and Asian countries, UN development and humanitarian assistance agencies, UN and African Union (AU) peacekeeping missions, international non-governmental organisations (INGOs), and foreign oil companies. External actors were involved in providing economic, military and political support to the Sudanese government, to opposition parties, and to the armed opposition in the conflicts, in particular the SPLM/A and the Darfur rebel groups. International aid organisations tried to provide both emergency relief to save lives and development assistance to reduce poverty. Foreign companies, state-owned and private, entered the country to develop its oil reserves, most of which lay within the war zone. Sudan also impinged on the outside world: successive governments sheltered armed opposition groups from neighbouring countries (which likewise provided bases and sanctuary to armed groups opposed to the government in Khartoum); in the 1990s the government sought to export its own brand of Islamist revolutionism abroad; and during the 22 years of the war between 1983 and 2005, and the Darfur conflict that continued beyond then, large numbers of refugees fled across Sudan's borders to its neighbours and beyond.

The international dimensions of an internal conflict present external actors with a number of important questions. In particular, what can international powers and organisations do to prevent, manage and resolve internal conflict?[1] And what should they do, assuming that they are interested in mitigating or resolving such conflicts? The importance of such questions in international relations has increased with the proliferation of civil wars and conflicts since the end of the Cold War, such as those in Afghanistan, Côte d'Ivoire, the Democratic Republic of Congo, Iraq, Liberia, Rwanda, Sierra Leone, Somalia, Sri Lanka and the former Yugoslavia. Writing in 1995, Roy Licklider argued that more research was needed into the question of under what circumstances 'outside interventions (military assistance to one or both sides, mediation, humanitarian aid) help or hinder a settlement?'[2] More than a decade later, much research has been done, but the need remains substantial, as actors in the international system continue to face major difficulties in dealing with internal conflicts and related humanitarian crises. Sudan is therefore an important case, both in itself, and for the lessons that it can or cannot offer.

Sudan's conflicts and civil war – or wars

Sudan's civil war from 1983 to 2005 is commonly seen as Sudan's second civil war since independence. In some respects, however, it constituted a resumption of the first war, which began by some accounts in 1955 (the year before independence), by others in 1962, and ran until 1972. The Addis Ababa Agreement signed in March 1972 ended the war and provided for a number of measures designed to satisfy the aspirations of Southern Sudanese for local autonomy for the south. This led to a peace which lasted until the government began to revise the agreed power-sharing mechanisms and a series of mutinies occurred, culminating in the resumption of civil war in 1983. From 1983 the war proceeded uninterrupted, through three changes in government – from autocracy to transitional government, then to democracy, and finally to autocracy again – until the government and the SPLM/A signed a ceasefire in 2002 and finally signed the CPA at the start of 2005, officially ending the war.

That the CPA was not 'comprehensive' was evident from its exclusion of the conflict that had escalated in Darfur from March 2003, as well as lower-level conflicts elsewhere in the country, such as in Eastern Sudan and parts of Southern Sudan. In so far as these conflicts were waged between the government and groups other than the SPLM/A, or were confined to non-SPLM/A groups (as in the south), they can be considered not to have been part of the war between the government and the SPLM/A but to have been separate conflicts. But as several points show, this perspective is partly wrong and misleading. Firstly, the SPLM/A itself fought politically and militarily for more than Southern Sudan. Secondly, in practice the war between 1983 and 2004 was neither confined to the government and the SPLM/A, nor conducted only in the parts of the country covered by the CPA. From the late 1980s the war included fronts outside the south, in the Nuba Mountains and Southern Blue Nile; in late 1991 the SPLA made a short-lived foray into Darfur, led by disaffected Darfurians; and from 1996 the SPLA opened a battlefront in Eastern Sudan, in alliance with a number of northern-based opposition groups, some of which continued fighting after the SPLM/A began to reach agreements with the government during 2002–5. And finally, while it may be appropriate to exclude some small, local-level conflicts (such as some inter-tribal conflicts) from an account of the much larger and more persistent war between the government and the SPLM/A, it is hardly appropriate in the case of the Darfur conflict after 2003. The scale of that conflict, not to mention the military and tactical connections between the establishment of a permanent ceasefire between the government and the SPLM/A and the start of the escalation in Darfur, make it inappropriate to represent Darfur as an entirely separate and unconnected war, although it is also true that the conflict developed its own independent momentum and identity.

For these and other reasons that will become apparent in subsequent chapters, in this book I have generally used the term 'Sudan's civil war' in an inclusive sense, covering the totality of Sudan's war or conflicts between 1983 and 2005. Overall, that war was devastating, especially for the people of Southern Sudan and subsequently those of Western Sudan, but ultimately for people from all of Sudan, and for the infrastructure, the economy, and development of the whole country. Before the escalation of the Darfur conflict, the most common estimate was that some one and a half million people or more had died because of the war and related famines, and that a further four million had been displaced. Between 2003 and 2004, the Darfur conflict is estimated to have led to the deaths of a further 100,000–300,000 people and the displacement of two million more. Such estimates are very approximate, but the actual number killed by violence over the whole period almost certainly ran into the low hundreds of thousands.[3] Throughout these conflicts, despite the country's wealth of natural resources, and despite the inception of oil exports in 1999, poverty was widespread and for many was acute.

Mediation

Over the long course of the civil war and the Darfur conflict, the international community involved itself in a variety of attempts to resolve conflict in Sudan. These attempts fall into three broad categories of mediated peace talks, namely (i) peace talks mediated through 'good offices' or by eminent persons; (ii) peace initiatives by regional organisations and neighbouring states; and (iii) internationalised initiatives involving a wider range of international participants. The first category includes, for example, the initiative in 1989–90 by former US president Jimmy Carter, which the US assistant secretary of state for African affairs, Herman Cohen, then tried to build upon. The second category comprises the Abuja peace conferences in 1992 and 1993, mediated by Nigeria under the auspices of the Organisation of African Unity (OAU); peace talks convened from 1994 onwards by Sudan's East African neighbours, through a dedicated initiative of a regional body, the Intergovernmental Authority on Development (IGAD); a joint Egyptian–Libyan initiative, launched in 1999; and the initial peace talks for Darfur in 2003–4. The third category of mediation is best represented by the talks between the government and the SPLM/A in Kenya between 2002 and 2005, which were mediated by IGAD but involved additional international participation, in particular by Britain, Norway and the USA, but also by the EU and the UN. Another, shorter example is the Abuja talks for Darfur in 2005–6, under the auspices of the AU but with wider international participation.

In this long list of internationally supported peace talks, the greatest success was the CPA; all other initiatives failed to produce an effective peace agreement, with the qualified exception of the Eastern Sudan Peace Agreement (ESPA) in 2006, but not the abortive Darfur Peace Agreement (DPA) signed in 2006. Furthermore, as of the time of writing (early 2010, five years after the CPA was signed) it was still far from certain how effective and lasting the CPA peace would be. Such a caveat is usually appropriate for peace agreements, given how often they fail to deliver the peace that they promise.[4] But it is even more appropriate given the history of failed agreements in Sudan and the juxtaposition of the CPA with war in Darfur and the holding of other peace and reconciliation talks (for Darfur, for the east, and with opposition parties), in various local and regional forums during 2005–9.

With the limited exception of a study of the 1992–3 Abuja talks, no full study has yet been made of international efforts to resolve conflict in Sudan.[5] It would seem reasonable to assume that international efforts to mediate peace talks in Sudan have generally helped the search for peace, but this tells us little. Other generalisations about mediation also run into problems when applied to the case of Sudan. International mediation can, as Stephen Stedman says, 'assist negotiations by influencing the subjective perceptions and the objective environment of the disputants'.[6] It may also be true that for success, 'Mediators must speak with one voice and be able to make credible threats and promises.'[7] But in the case of Sudan, international efforts at mediation were repeatedly fruitless, and unanimity or co-ordination among mediators was largely absent. Steven Wondu and Ann Mosely Lesch suggested that some positive lessons were learned from some of the initiatives before 1993, for example the lesson drawn from the experience of the first initiative in 1989–90, that 'holding high-profile meetings without both detailed preparations and agreement on core principles could lead to greater polarization and intensify the armed conflict'.[8] But little work has been done to draw lessons from the many other peace talk and initiatives since then, through the 1990s and early years of the present century. Indeed, there has so far been no answer to the simple question of why, when one initiative after another had failed, the internationalised IGAD talks in Kenya from 2002 to 2005 then produced ostensible successes, tempered by the failure of talks for Darfur during 2005–9 and by uncertainty about the longer-term survival of the CPA or the incomplete peace that it brought.

Relief

One reason why the story of conflict resolution in Sudan has not been fully told is that attention has tended to focus on the humanitarian story, often to the exclusion of political factors and the role of the war in the humanitarian crises. For a mix of reasons that will be explored later in this book, external actors in effect prioritised saving lives over trying to resolve the underlying war. Droughts and famines in Sudan in the 1980s led to an influx of emergency relief, much as occurred in Ethiopia and the countries of the Sahel. In 1989 the UN established Operation Lifeline Sudan (OLS), a framework agreement with the government and the SPLM/A on relief corridors, under which UN and other agencies could bring emergency relief to populations in the war zone who needed assistance. By the end of the 1990s OLS had grown into the world's largest complex of sustained humanitarian operations. When that operation declined, it was superseded by a new complex of humanitarian operations in Darfur, set up during 2004, which exceeded OLS in its costs.

However, even in this humanitarian aim, significant failure was evident. Civilians continued to die from famine and to suffer displacement and impoverishment. Relief and rehabilitation became entangled with the war and, sometimes, with issues of war aims and how to achieve peace. As a result, relief in Sudan became, as Douglas Johnson says, 'a contested example' in debates about the efficacy of humanitarian action.[9] How successful humanitarian action in Sudan was, and what its consequences were, are still subjects of debate. But by the end of the 1990s and the early years of the present century the belief had spread among some who worked in relief, or who observed or studied it, that relief had in some ways sustained the warring parties and perhaps contributed – to an unknown degree – to the continuation of the war. Despite this belief or view, there was little apparent change in the quantity of relief provided to Sudan, or the means by which it was delivered. Instead, high levels of relief continued to be provided through to 2005 (and beyond), exemplified by the large humanitarian response to the Darfur conflict, which echoed the periodic surges in relief in response to emergencies in the 1980s and 1990s.

Difficult questions about relief in Sudan have therefore sometimes been asked, often as part of questions about relief and aid more generally. Douglas Johnson, for example, in his book on Sudan's civil war, raises the questions of whether relief is 'a political rather than a humanitarian issue', and whether 'relief programmes shorten or prolong conflict'.[10] Alex de Waal has previously argued that 'humanitarian action is political action, of a certain kind', and that there are '"successes" and "failures"... but the unexpected consequences of humanitarian action are more significant'.[11]

He notes that observers and relief workers in the Biafran war were reluctant to draw conclusions about the role of relief there. A similar reluctance has surely affected some relief workers in Sudan's conflicts, despite their concerns about the effectiveness and role of relief in Sudan. Questions have also been asked about the relationship between humanitarian action and domestic politics. It has sometimes been argued that relief had a severely anti-democratic effect in Sudan, helping to legitimise the warring parties and reducing pressure on them to be popularly accountable.[12] And Johnson, for example, has suggested that a proposal by IGAD partners in 1999 'to link humanitarian relief to a peace agreement between the government and the SPLA' was harmful to the IGAD initiative.[13] But in general, the role of relief in the civil war and the Darfur conflict is still under-explored. As with mediation, a thorough analysis has yet to be made of how the warring parties reacted to or used relief, and of how (if at all) it affected the prospects of resolving the war.

Foreign policies and strategies

An analysis of conflict resolution in Sudan's civil war and the Darfur conflict would be incomplete without an analysis of the foreign policies and strategies of the governments and organisations that engaged in mediation and relief. Mediation and relief usually fall under the responsibility of different ministries, departments or organisations, although they may involve the same actors or decision makers. Typically these are donor governments and organisations, and foreign diplomats and aid officials, all of whom may be involved in decisions about political and humanitarian responses to internal conflicts. Such decision makers have (or should have) a strong interest in improving their understanding of the problems that, as Brown puts it, 'internal conflict poses for different kinds of policy instruments and the conditions under which different instruments can be used effectively'.[14]

Foreign and international policy towards Sudan from the 1980s through to 2009 received some attention. Until the Darfur conflict, this attention usually revolved around international security issues, such as Cold War competition in the Horn of Africa, and the threat that the war in Sudan posed to regional stability. Sudan's international relations have been examined in the light of the government's support in the 1990s for foreign opposition groups, its hosting of Osama bin Laden between 1991 and 1996, and its alleged involvement in or support for terrorism. But the policy choices and strategies that underlay donor governments' relations with Sudan have in general not been examined in detail. As a result, no answers have been provided to questions about the effectiveness of foreign policies and whether the international community – or at least European governments, the USA and the UN – could have used better strategies in dealing with Sudan.

To some extent, since the 1990s foreign-policy approaches to conflict and conflict resolution have been influenced by new currents in thinking about sovereignty, internal conflict, state failure and intervention. This has been reflected in the establishment of new departments and initiatives, which in some cases have tried to bridge the gap between foreign policy and humanitarian or aid policy. Two examples are the Bureau for Democracy, Conflict and Humanitarian Assistance set up within the US Agency for International Development (USAID) in 2000, and the British government's inter-departmental 'Global Conflict Prevention Pool' strategy introduced in 2001.[15] Two UN examples are the establishment of the UN Peacebuilding Commission in 2005 and, since 1999, the efforts by the country teams of the UN development and relief agencies to include peacebuilding strategies in their country-assistance frameworks and programmes, and to do so with better co-ordination with the actions of the UN Department of Political Affairs and the UN Department of Peacekeeping Operations. However, such initiatives have not led to consensus about new approaches to dealing with internal conflicts, mediation, relief and conflict resolution. And with international actors still struggling to deal with conflicts such as Sudan's and their consequences, it remains valuable to explore questions about foreign-policy choices, and to consider if there are lessons from the case of Sudan, or for it, from other situations of conflict and humanitarian crisis.

Methods and sources

This book is intrinsically historical and analytical, although it engages too with theory and seeks to make a small contribution to it. In dry, quantitative terms, the book is a single-case empirical study. It is so because of the scale of Sudan's conflicts and humanitarian crises, and the relative lack of detailed examination of the war from the perspective of conflict resolution in international relations. The book does not aim to 'universalise' from the one case to many others, which would be a mistake. Nor for that matter does it aim to be comparative, comparing Sudan's conflicts with others in equal detail, although in the course of the book, and in the conclusions, some comparisons are made where they are appropriate or useful. However, it would also be fallacious to insist that no useful lessons or contributions to theory could possibly be drawn from a single case of such scale.

The book draws on a wide range of sources, some specific to Sudan, others from the academic field of international relations and literature on conflict resolution, mediation and humanitarian action. The primary sources include some 80 interviews which I carried out mainly in Sudan and Kenya (including at the CPA talks), but also in Britain, Egypt and the USA, with people whose perspectives on the subject required to be heard. I conducted the majority of these interviews for a doctoral thesis on which this book is based. Other primary sources are official documents and statements, and what is sometimes called 'grey literature', namely official reports and publications from UN agencies and donor governments, as well as some unpublished documents. In addition the book draws on Sudanese and non-Sudanese media reports where appropriate. Where sources in Arabic have been used, a translation of their title is included. Naturally, the book draws also on secondary sources, in particular the small library of scholarship and research on conflict and aid in contemporary Sudan. Further to these sources, the book draws more generally on my experience and understanding of Sudan over the years, from my first visit to the country in 1995 through to the present.

Inevitably, the focus of the book necessitates some exclusions and limitations in areas where some readers may be interested to read more. Examples include detailed analysis of the peacekeeping missions in Sudan and the US advocacy campaign over Darfur, and academic literature on the causes of war or theories of international relations. However, the book does touch on some of the theories about conflict resolution, such as William Zartman's much-used hypothesis about 'ripeness' as a necessary condition for the resolution of a conflict,[16] and claims about the role of external guarantees and commitments. The book is not idealistic. It is focused on top–down, politically led conflict resolution, the sort that external states or international organisations typically involve themselves in; but it recognises that grassroots or 'bottom–up' conflict resolution plays an important role in resolving conflicts. (Indeed, although grassroots conflict resolution is not the key to resolving Sudan's conflicts in the short term, it is certainly important to attainment of longer-term peace.) The book does not assume that 'peace' must be total, nor that war and conflict are things which are peculiar to poor countries, in Africa or the Middle East or elsewhere. Nor does the book have a liberal-idealist view of peace. It recognises that conflict, war, peace and related terms do not have single, universally accepted definitions. All the same, plainly there are certain basic ideas of conflict and peace on which many people will agree.

The structure of the book is therefore straightforward. It is framed around the purpose of investigating the story of conflict resolution in Sudan, for both general and specialised readers, and the aim of drawing lessons from this story, for people who work on the resolution of conflicts, and potentially for Sudan itself. After this introduction, Chapter 1 presents an overview of the relevant history of conflict and peace in Sudan. Chapter 2 then provides a history and analysis of the mediation that led to the CPA and the unsuccessful talks for Darfur. Chapter 3 provides a history and analysis of relief in Sudan, in the wider civil war and in Darfur, while Chapter 4 presents a history and analysis of foreign policy towards Sudan. After this, Chapter 5 explores what the international community could realistically have done to have achieved better results. Lastly, Chapter 6 draws together the main conclusions that emerge from the book, both for the case of Sudan and for approaches to conflict resolution more generally in international relations.

1
CONFLICT, WAR AND PEACE

This chapter sets out the background to the subject and the questions explored in this book. The chapter gives a brief synopsis of the background, causes and course of the civil war and the Darfur conflict. It also looks briefly at the costs of Sudan's conflicts and some of the domestic and regional political dynamics.

THE BACKGROUND TO THE CIVIL WAR

Every internal conflict has its complexities and specificities which pose challenges for outsiders who want to understand or respond to the conflict, let alone for the parties to and victims of the conflict. In the case of Sudan, underlying issues of geography, history and identity pose particularly important challenges and played a role in the country's first bout of war after independence, as well as in the short period of peace from 1972 to 1983, and in bringing about the second war that began in 1983 and the Darfur conflict. The first war, the agreement that ended it in 1972, and the demise of that agreement were also key factors in bringing about the second war.

Challenges of geography, history and identity

Essentially Sudan has a dual identity, that of being both an African and an Arab country. Geographically it is the largest country in Africa and in the Arab world, at almost one million square miles, with land borders with seven African countries and two Arab countries, and a marine border with another, Saudi Arabia. Historically, too, Sudan's identity has been shaped by its geography and location, with the Nile valley and its Red Sea coast making it a gateway between Africa and the Arab world. Reflecting this, it was from Egypt and the Red Sea that the most decisive external forces to enter Sudan in its modern history first came: in 1820–1 Mohammed Ali Pasha launched the Turco-Egyptian conquest, under the command of his son Ismail. This established the territorial basis of what became, after the 1881–5 Mahdiyya

War, the Mahdist state. In turn, after the British invasion and capture of Khartoum in 1898, this became the Anglo-Egyptian Condominium of Sudan, until in 1956 it became the independent state of Sudan.

Politically, a simple manifestation today of Sudan's dual identity is its simultaneous membership, like other northern African countries, of both the Arab League and the AU. Socially – in terms of ethnicity, customs, self-perception and other factors – Sudan displays both African and Arab facets, and questions about the African or Arab identity of the country have long been a focus of contention, especially in the war after 1983.[1] However, African and Arab are far from the only divisions in Sudan's identity, even if, in the subjective perceptions of identity that many Sudanese construct for themselves, 'African' and 'Arab' are sometimes used as overall dichotomous categories. With a population of around 39 million in 2008, Sudan is a mosaic of ethnic, tribal, religious and linguistic diversity, such that inside the country it is much more accurate to talk of Beja, Fur, Rashaida, or Rizayqat, and Azande, Dinka, Nuer, Shilluk and other tribes and ethnic groups, than simply of 'African' and 'Arab'.[2] This is as true in Darfur as elsewhere in Sudan, despite the polarising and simplifying use of the labels 'African' and 'Arab' in external accounts of the conflict after 2003. In a region with many tribal groups (such as Berti, Daju, Fur, Meidob, Rizayqat and Zaghawa) and some intermixing, it was a misrepresentation to represent the conflict as Arabs against Africans.[3]

Similarly, the religious divisions in Sudan are more complex than a Muslim–Christian north–south divide, as shorthand accounts of Sudan have tended to suggest. The most plausible estimates suggest that between 60 per cent and 70 per cent of the population are Muslim, some 25 per cent are followers of local religions ('animism'), and between 5 per cent and 15 per cent are Christian (allowing for a certain amount of double-counting, for example among rural populations where Christians or Muslims may also adhere to local religions).[4] Furthermore, Islam and Christianity in Sudan comprise different sects and churches, and tribal or ethnic groups are not necessarily religiously homogeneous, with groups such as the Nuba comprising Christians, Muslims and followers of local religions.

This complex ethnic, tribal and religious identity is one of Sudan's key characteristics, differentiating it greatly from less heterogeneous Arab countries like Egypt and Saudi Arabia, and to some degree from its African neighbours, such as Ethiopia and Uganda. Differences between Sudanese have been further fostered by discriminatory administrative policies during Ottoman rule and the Condominium (such as the separative policies under which Britain administered the south), and since independence in 1956. As a result, identity has variously mobilised people or been exploited in conflicts both at the local level (between tribal groups) and at the national level, between the government and political movements and parties (armed and unarmed), and regionally based movements such as the SPLM/A, the Sudan Liberation Movement/Army (SLM/A) and the Beja Congress. Factionalism, too, has therefore been all the more common in Sudanese politics. At root, however, Sudan's major conflicts have all been caused by inequalities in the distribution of political and economic power, and consequent imbalances in development across the country.[5] This was true for the conflicts in Darfur and Eastern Sudan, and the wider civil war that officially ended with the CPA in 2005.

The first civil war, 1955 or 1962–72

Sudan's first civil war is often taken to have begun in August 1955, when southern units of the national army mutinied and attacked northern officers and other northerners. Prompted by anger at growing northern dominance and northern politicians' heavy-handed treatment of southern aspirations as the country approached independence in 1956, the mutiny spread to other southern garrisons, and some mutineers fled to Uganda to seek shelter. However the mutiny led to only a sporadic, low-scale campaign, and it was not until 1960–2 when a wave of southern politicians and students left for the bush to join the remaining mutineers that the conflict began to take the shape of a civil war.[6] In 1962 some of these exiles formed the Sudan African Nationalist Union (SANU), while others formed a guerrilla movement which became popularly known as the Anyanya. Represented as bandits by the north and as liberation fighters by supporters in the south, the Anyanya were initially hampered by a lack of arms, and for some years they were limited mainly to launching hit-and-run attacks on government targets. But in 1963 for the first time they captured a government post, Pochala, and in 1965 they obtained their first significant arms when the rebel Simba were expelled from Congo.[7]

With the exception of an unsuccessful 'Round Table Conference' held in Khartoum in 1965, the government made little effort to negotiate a settlement to the conflict during the early years. Instead it preferred to seek a military solution, and it seemed practicable to hold out for this as long as the scale of the conflict remained small. But when the war intensified between 1965 and 1971, the appeal of a political settlement grew. The intensification in the war was the result of a number of factors, in particular the government's increasing Arabism and repression of domestic opposition,[8] and the influx of new military assistance to the Anyanya firstly from Ethiopia and Israel in the wake of the 1967 Arab–Israeli war, and then from Uganda after the overthrow of Milton Obote in 1970 (which brought to power a Ugandan government that was more favourable to the Anyanya).⁹ Amidst these developments, in May 1969 the Sudanese government was overthrown in a military coup led by Ja'far Nimeiri. Looking to shore up his rule, Nimeiri quickly announced that the war would be solved by political rather than military means, and issued a declaration outlining plans for regional government, which would be an important feature of any settlement of the war.

By itself the declaration was not enough to bring about successful peace talks, but over the following two years two challenges to Nimeiri's rule – a revolt by the Ansar sect in 1970, and a communist-backed coup attempt in 1971 (led by former members of Nimeiri's cabinet) – increased his need to find domestic allies. At the same time, at the start of 1971 Joseph Lagu and other southern Anyanya leaders formed a new anti-government front, the Southern Sudan Liberation Front – which was later renamed the Southern Sudan Liberation Movement (SSLM) – and demanded that the government recognise it as an equal negotiating partner. As Johnson argues, when the government gave this recognition and offered talks in Addis Ababa, 'the conditions for negotiation appeared to be far better than they had ever been before'.¹⁰ Prospects were helped by the involvement of external mediators, in particular the World Council of Churches and the Ethiopian emperor, Haile Selassie, and by the perception of Addis Ababa as an appropriate venue for talks, because Ethiopia was ostensibly neutral in the conflict.¹¹ In addition, in 1971 Abel Alier, the government minister for southern affairs, told church organisations and NGOs in Europe that the Sudanese government was prepared to talk with the southern rebels, believing that if they were convinced that the Sudanese government was taking 'a genuine initiative towards a peaceful settlement', they would tell the southern rebels, who would then be likely to believe it.¹²

The Addis Ababa Agreement

Talks in Addis Ababa opened in mid-February 1972 with only one precondition: a united Sudan. While some southerners were unhappy about abandoning the goal of independence,¹³ the SSLM delegation proposed a federal structure designed to give autonomy. Working from proposals that each side had prepared in advance, the talks progressed quickly, and at the end of the month the parties initialled a final agreement which was witnessed by representatives of Haile Selassie, the World Council of Churches, the All Africa Conference of Churches, and the Sudan Council of Churches.¹⁴ A month later the agreement was formally ratified at a ceremony in Addis Ababa. The agreement provided for a ceasefire and for a number of measures designed to satisfy southern aspirations for local autonomy for the south, in particular the establishment of what became the Southern Regional Government, headed by a Regional President, an Executive Council and a Regional Assembly. The agreement also provided for the incorporation of the Anyanya forces (some 12,000) into the national army's southern command, and guaranteed that while Arabic would remain the official language, English would be the common language and would be taught in schools in the south.[15]

The agreement was widely acclaimed, both in Sudan and abroad, and some talked optimistically of it as a model to be replicated in other conflicts in Africa and the world. As one account in 1973 put it, the agreement was a solution which had neither been imposed from outside 'by great powers, nor arranged by disinterested international organizations'.[16] In the words of one Sudanese scholar writing in 1975, 'it was not only a Sudanese triumph but also an African one'.[17] Mohamed Omer Beshir, who had been the secretary at the unfruitful 1965 Round Table Conference, argued that the agreement was reached because those making peace had understood the 'problem' fully, had made and implemented decisions, and had been imaginative in finding solutions. 'No books dealing with a situation like that of Sudan existed', said Beshir. '[Solutions] could only be found and reached by those involved in the events.'[18]

Plausible though these reasons were, they overlooked what was almost certainly the most important reason why the agreement was reached, which was the combination of political and economic pressures on Nimeiri. As Beshir noted, the dimensions of the conflict were larger by 1971–2 than in 1965.[19] Detailed information about the cost of the war was scarce, partly because of the isolation of the areas of fighting, and partly because successive governments tried to draw a veil over what was happening. But the human and economic costs of the war had mounted – by some guesses or estimates, by 1972 as many as half a million people had died in the war and related humanitarian crises behind the 'grass curtain' of silence about the war.[20] All the same, more important for Nimeiri was his need for new allies. The thwarted coup attempt in 1971 had forced him to turn away from Sudan's principal external patron, the Soviet Union, which had supported the coup attempt, and instead turn to the USA for support. The combination of the shift to US patronage and the need to build a 'new domestic coalition' at least made a negotiated settlement to the civil war expedient, even if it did not actually make it inevitable.[21] In Lagu's words, Nimeiri needed 'a period of peace', while the decisive factor for the Anyanya was the loss of its bases in Uganda in 1972.[22]

The demise of the Addis Ababa Agreement

In the 1970s and 1980s, the Addis Ababa Agreement was a rare example of a successfully negotiated settlement to an African insurgency.[23] Nonetheless, the agreement brought peace for only just over a decade, from 1972 until 1983, when the agreement was decisively repudiated by Nimeiri and Lagu, its two main beneficiaries.[24] That the agreement failed to prevent a return to war was the result of a combination of shortcomings in the agreement itself and its implementation, and changes in the domestic political scene.

The main shortcomings in the agreement came in its provisions governing regional autonomy and border and wealth-sharing issues. These issues were complicated by the discovery in 1977 of oil in the south, and by the Jonglei Canal scheme, a project to build a 360-km canal to ease the flow of White Nile waters through the south, which some southerners believed would harm the south. However, more important than the shortcomings in the agreement itself were the shortcomings in its implementation. As Alier has written, 'The main concern following the agreement was how to implement it',[25] but the agreement did not provide clear provisions and mechanisms for monitoring implementation, nor did it have international guarantors. As a consequence, there was no independent guarantor or monitor who could intervene when, for example, referendums scheduled by the agreement were not held, or when Nimeiri began to change the administrative arrangements for the south and to make concessions to other political parties that were to the detriment of the agreement.

The weaknesses in the agreement were compounded by decisions made by Nimeiri, in particular his decision to abolish the Southern Region and divide the south into three regions, under the official guise of decentralisation. In the south, these changes were controversial and unpopular, but their introduction was hastened by differences and rivalries among southerners and their leaders (exemplified by those between Joseph Lagu and Abel Alier). The division of the south also coincided with and was encouraged by Nimeiri's reconciliation with northern opposition parties in 1977. After two attempted coups in 1975 and 1976 (the first led by Islamist army officers, the second by the Umma Party, backed by Libya), Nimeiri engineered a 'national reconciliation' with a front of northern-based parties, bringing their leaders into government. In return he hoped to secure an end to attempts to overthrow him by instead having the support of the front, which was a loose alliance of the DUP, the Umma Party and the Islamic Charter Front (ICF), the party of Sudan's Muslim Brotherhood. Following the reconciliation, a number of northern leaders joined the government (though the Umma leader, Sadiq al-Mahdi, soon left), and from their new positions began to influence policy. In particular, the leader of the ICF,

Hasan al-Turabi, eventually became attorney-general and lobbied for Islamic reforms of the legal system.[26] It was as a result of pressures such as these – and his own whim – that Nimeiri eventually decided in September 1983 to introduce new laws (subsequently often referred to as the September Laws) which included the imposition of *sharia* law on the whole country and the introduction of the *hudud* criminal punishments (amputations).

Despite the threat that these various changes posed to the Addis Ababa Agreement, little opposition to them was voiced abroad. This was primarily because no-one was trying to monitor or guarantee the agreement, but for Egypt and the USA it was also because of their wish not to rock relations with Sudan. Egypt had signed a joint defence agreement with Sudan after the coup attempt in 1976, and by the late 1970s the USA saw Sudan as an important ally for counterbalancing Libya and Soviet influence in Ethiopia. The USA was therefore reluctant to undermine Nimeiri in any way, seeing him as 'a useful ally in the region, and betting on his survival against the possible Sudanese backlash for helping to keep him in power'.[27] As a result, although the US government expressed concern in advance about the consequences of abolishing the Southern Region and introducing *sharia* law, Nimeiri was confident that when he proceeded to do both those things, he would not lose US support.

Domestically, however, the division of the south, the 'national reconciliation', and the joint defence agreement steadily increased southern discontent and dissatisfaction with the Addis Ababa Agreement. In turn, the growing discontent increased support for the remnants of the Anyanya in the south that had refused to accept the agreement and who, after 1976, began to receive support from the new Ethiopian government (in response to Nimeiri's support for the Eritrean People's Liberation Front). As political unrest in the south grew, new groups of southern guerrillas formed and became more active (after 1980 these came to be referred to collectively as the Anyanya-2) and through the early months of 1983 a growing number of police and soldiers deserted to join the rebels. Measures ordered by the government and army headquarters were resisted, and this culminated in a large-scale mutiny at Bor, near Juba, in May 1983, and the formation shortly afterwards of the SPLM/A, led by John Garang – a 38-year-old army colonel from Bor, with a PhD in agricultural economy from Iowa State University. Weeks later, in early June, Nimeiri issued a decree dissolving the institutions of self-government in the south and dividing it into three regions, effectively abrogating the Addis Ababa Agreement. In this period and the following months, as the proximate causes of the revolt receded and conflict escalated, the aims of the SPLM were gradually framed around opposition to Nimeiri and the 'notorious policy of "divide and rule"', which

Garang saw as having blighted Sudan, and around the slogans of national unity, socialism, autonomy ('where and when necessary'), and religious freedom.[28] These goals soon developed into the goal of liberating the whole of Sudan and creating a 'new' and democratic Sudan, of equality, freedom and justice.[29]

THE COURSE OF THE WAR AND THE DARFUR CONFLICT

The war that began in 1983 ran uninterrupted through four governments – for less than two years under Nimeiri until his overthrow in a popular uprising in April 1985; through the one-year rule of the Transitional Military Council (TMC), headed by General Sawar al-Dhahab; through the three years of the democratically elected government led by the Umma Party and with Sadiq al-Mahdi as prime minister, to which the TMC handed power in April 1986; and then for 15 years under the government of Omar al-Bashir, the army officer who overthrew the government of Sadiq in a military coup d'état in June 1989, and who remained in power at the start of 2005 when the CPA was signed.[30]

A full account of this long span of conflict is neither appropriate nor possible here.[31] But as background to the subsequent chapters, and for understanding the context of the Darfur conflict, it will be helpful to outline the main developments in the war and the domestic and regional political scene, and the main patterns and aspects of events over the course of the war from 1983 to 2005 and the Darfur conflict.

The development of the war, 1983–1989

Unlike the first civil war, the second war escalated rapidly. This was because the SPLM/A was much larger than the Anyanya and received substantial military support, factors matched by the determination of the successive governments in Khartoum to resolve the conflict militarily. As well as support from Ethiopia, between 1983 and 1985 the SPLA received large quantities of arms from Libya, thanks to the hostility of the Libyan leader, Colonel Qadhafi, to Nimeiri. To counterbalance this, Nimeiri looked to Egypt and the USA for military assistance, which they provided with dwindling enthusiasm. After the overthrow of Nimeiri in 1985, Libya promptly terminated its support to the SPLA and began to supply arms to the Sudanese government, which it continued to do when the TMC handed over power to the government of Sadiq in 1986. Nonetheless, even after 1985 the government was unable to prevail over the SPLA, which was training more and more men in camps in Ethiopia, so that by 1989 it was estimated to have some 70,000 troops, compared with around 65,000 members of the national armed forces.[32]

The war initially took the form of a countryside- or bush-based guerrilla insurgency, with the government holding all the towns and transport routes in the south, while the SPLA benefited from the shelter and protection of Ethiopia and exploited the government's weak control of territory beyond the vicinity of most towns, roads and rivers in the south. From the outset, tribal militias played a role in the escalation and spread of the conflict, as first the regional government of Equatoria and then the national government sought to mobilise and arm militias against the SPLA – a tactic which all subsequent governments continued.[33] Prominent among such militias were the Murahilin ('nomads'), a militia drawn from the Misiriyya and Rizayqat herding tribes concentrated in Kordofan, who increasingly raided Dinka villages in neighbouring Bahr el-Ghazal and attacked relief convoys and southerners who had fled their homes.

Over time the SPLM/A's power grew. Although it was not until 1985 that the SPLA captured and held its first towns in the south (Boma and Yirol, which were little more than villages some 300km apart), these were followed by marked progress in capturing and controlling territory outside the major towns in the south. In November 1987, with help from the Ethiopian army, the SPLA took the strategically important towns of Kurmuk and Qaissan in Blue Nile state, outside the south. The government soon recaptured the towns, but the SPLA meanwhile captured and held on to Kapoeta, a town in Eastern Equatoria. In 1988 the SPLA took control of more territory, and in the first half of 1989 the SPLA captured Nasir in Upper Nile and a number of other settlements. As a result, by June 1989 the SPLA held three former provincial capitals (Bor, Nasir and Torit), some 14 'district' towns and some 19 'village council' towns, and a swathe of territory reaching from the Ethiopian border through to northern Bahr el-Ghazal, which amounted to around four-fifths of the south.[34]

The human cost of the early years of the war was high. Detailed data are not available, but a plausible estimate is that 10,000 government and rebel troops were killed, and that a similar number of civilians were killed violently. However, the larger toll of the war was the number of deaths caused by conditions induced by the war, such as food shortages and disease outbreaks (leading to increased malnutrition and mortality rates): by the start of 1989, this death toll had reached perhaps the low hundreds of thousands or, according to some estimates, more than half a million.[35]

Estimating or assessing this wider toll of the war is complicated by the fact that humanitarian crises occurred both inside and outside the war zone, and while elements of the crises outside the war zone were independent of the war, others were not. The main reason for this was that the war displaced large numbers of southerners, some of whom moved and settled in new areas in the south and the north, often (but certainly not always) in camps for internally displaced persons (IDPs), while others fled across Sudan's borders into Ethiopia, Kenya, Uganda and Zaire.[36] The picture was further complicated by the presence of large numbers of Ethiopian refugees in Sudan, many of whom were settled in camps in the east, near the border with Ethiopia. It is therefore difficult to disaggregate from the overall death tolls of food and health crises which deaths were attributable to the civil war, and which were independent of it.

Nonetheless, there is no doubt that the war was responsible for enormous loss of life. In the south the war brought insecurity and the disruption of important transport routes, leading to deteriorations in the economy and in access to food and basic services for both rural and urban populations. Outside the south, the displacement caused by the war led to increased pressure on limited land and food resources, again in both urban and rural areas. The war therefore accounted for much loss of life in the south and some of the loss of life in the major famines in the north, such as the famine in Kordofan and Darfur in 1984–5, which is estimated to have cost between 100,000 and 250,000 lives.[37]

Accurate data for the economic and financial costs of the war are not available, but the financial burden on the governments of Nimeiri, the TMC and Sadiq was certainly high and did no favours for their budgets for public services.[38] However the costs of the war – of whatever kind – were not enough to cripple the governments, or to push them decisively to seek a peaceful settlement to the conflict. Indeed, as the continuation of the war after the coup in June 1989 showed, the cost of the war remained bearable for the government of Bashir too. Meanwhile domestic politics in this period revolved around the successive changes of government, from Nimeiri to the TMC and to Sadiq, and the frequent changes in the coalition of parties which made up Sadiq's government from 1986 to 1989. The degree to which the war impinged on politics was limited.

In the first two years of the war, neither the government nor the SPLM/A showed any interest in negotiating an end to the war. Nimeiri believed that the SPLA could be defeated, and the SPLA appeared to believe that it could achieve a rapid victory. Little changed under the two governments that followed Nimeiri, both of which aimed for military victory and showed little commitment to making peace. The head of the TMC, Sawar al-Dhahab (who had been Nimeiri's defence minister until 1985), sought and obtained military assistance from Libya, and this assistance continued under

Sadiq. Dhahab's prime minister, Al-Jazuli Dafallah, offered to revive the Addis Ababa Agreement, but refused to repeal the September Laws, as the SPLM/A demanded.[39] The SPLM also refused to accept a ceasefire until a constitutional conference had been held, and it refused to participate in the 1986 general elections. In March 1986, just before the elections, the SPLM and an alliance of northern parties, including the Umma but not the Democratic Unionist Party (DUP) or the renamed ICF, the National Islamic Front (NIF), promisingly issued a joint declaration at Koka Dam in Ethiopia, proposing a constitutional convention. But although Sadiq then met with Garang in Addis Ababa after the elections, he too refused to repeal the September Laws, and when the SPLA shot down a civilian airliner in August 1986, he accused the SPLA of terrorism and broke off contacts.[40]

Subsequently, various unsuccessful attempts were made to bring the warring parties to the negotiating table, including initiatives by the presidents of Kenya and Uganda, the former president of Nigeria, Olusegun Obasanjo, and a former Sudanese diplomat, Francis Deng.[41] However, after a series of private talks, in November 1988 the DUP (a partner in the governing coalition headed by Sadiq and the Umma party) signed an accord with the SPLM in Addis Ababa. The accord was a modification of the Koka Dam declaration, with the SPLM dropping its demand that the government dissolve itself, and requiring only the suspension of *sharia* (rather than the full lifting) while a constitutional conference was convened.[42] However, approval and development of the DUP–SPLM accord was frustrated and eventually blocked by the Umma Party and the NIF, who used their combined majority in parliament to reject the accord in December 1988.[43] The DUP then withdrew from the government to join a coalition of opposition parties supporting peace. At the end of February 1989 the army chief of staff issued an unprecedented memorandum stating that the war could not be won by military means. This led the government to resign on 11 March and four days later the parliament approved the DUP–SPLM accord. A new government was then sworn in, which included the DUP and the peace coalition but excluded the NIF, which was determined to prevent a peace settlement that did not fit with the party's Islamist policies. Talks between Sadiq and Garang were then scheduled for July in Addis Ababa. But before the talks could happen, a group of army officers, backed by the NIF, overthrew the government in a coup on 30 June 1989.

Internal though it was, Sudan's conflict – and the changes in government in Khartoum – impinged on Sudan's relations with its neighbours and in the region. While Ethiopia and Libya were hostile to Nimeiri's government and therefore supported the SPLM, Sudan's main Arab allies (to whom the government had often looked for economic, military and political support) generally did not welcome the war, though they continued to support the government in Khartoum, subject to reservations about who was in power. Out of all the countries in the region, Egypt took the closest interest in developments in Sudan, because of its over-riding strategic and security interest in the control of the Nile waters. For this reason, Egypt had undertaken to fund the construction of the Jonglei Canal.[44] On top of this, as of the early 1980s, Sudan was a useful ally to Egypt on several fronts, in particular for resisting Libyan hostility (which had been a problem for Egypt and Sudan ever since the final demise of the tripartite Egypt–Libya–Sudan union in 1972), but also over the Camp David agreement, and for countering Soviet influence in Ethiopia (interests that the USA shared).[45]

Against this background, Egypt did not welcome the outbreak of the war (which stopped work on the Jonglei Canal in 1984) or Nimeiri's courting of the ICF and his last-ditch efforts in 1985, shortly before his overthrow, to secure a rapprochement with Libya. Thus, when Nimeiri was finally overthrown, Egypt at first welcomed the TMC, hoping that it would be a more stable and politically compliant government. The TMC made decisions which Egypt reluctantly accepted, such as signing a military protocol with Libya and receiving Libyan military aid.[46] But in the absence of a better alternative, the Egyptian government was broadly pleased with the TMC and would have been glad to see it remain in power for longer, rather than risk seeing the ICF/NIF or another party (such as Sudan's Ba'athists) taking power.[47] Egypt was therefore disappointed when the TMC handed over power in 1986 to a government led by Sadiq and the Umma Party, which historically had poor relations with Egypt and which proceeded to cultivate closer relations with Libya over the next three years, principally for the sake of arms and as an alternative to close relations with Egypt.

Sudan's Saudi and Gulf allies and patrons were similarly displeased by developments in Sudan after 1983. The Saudi government feared that the rise of the ICF/NIF in Sudanese politics might encourage anti-government Islamist movements in Saudi Arabia. It disliked the rapprochement between the TMC and Libya and it especially disliked Sadiq's attempts to balance relations with Iran and Iraq (and even to mediate in the Iran–Iraq war), rather than siding with Iraq as Saudi Arabia and the Gulf States were doing.[48] This disquiet was shared by the Gulf States, which, although they had no direct political interest in Sudan, had invested substantially in Sudan in the 1970s and early 1980s as part of the vision of making Sudan the 'breadbasket' of the Arab world. Although these investments were concentrated in northern Sudan, a few lay in the war zone and many were jeopardised by the economic crises and famines of the mid-1980s, as well as by problems of mismanagement and economic viability.

Sudan's African neighbours generally had smaller and less visible interests in Sudan than did Egypt, Saudi Arabia and the Gulf States. Nonetheless, some of these interests were affected by developments in the war between 1983 and 1989. Most important was the Ethiopian government's interest in countering Sudanese support for the Eritrean People's Liberation Front (EPLF) and the Oromo Liberation Front in its own internal conflict. This interest was the primary reason why Ethiopia gave the SPLM/A military assistance and shelter, enabling the SPLM to maintain a presence in Addis Ababa and the SPLA to organise the recruitment and training of soldiers drawn from the Sudanese refugee camps in south-western Ethiopia. Following the same pattern of supporting one's neighbour's opponents (the pattern of reciprocal destabilisation so often seen between neighbouring countries), Uganda began to give military support to the SPLA after Yoweri Museveni came to power in 1986. This was done primarily to help combat the remnants of the Uganda National Liberation Army (UNLA) who had served the former Ugandan regime and then fled to Southern Sudan after Museveni came to power: the Sudanese government had begun to support the UNLA remnants, fearing that the good relationship between Museveni and Garang would lead to Ugandan support for the SPLA.[49] As a result, in May 1987 Ugandan troops entered the south, where they remained through to 1989 (and beyond), giving significant material and logistical support and sometimes even fighting alongside the SPLA.

The continuation of the war, 1989–2005

The coup in 1989 undid what little progress had been made in the preceding years towards a negotiated settlement of the war. Indeed, in large part, the coup was intended to halt negotiations with the SPLM about a constitutional conference planned for September 1989.[50] Sudan's new leader, Omar al-Bashir, rejected the 1988 DUP–SPLM accord and convened a 'National Dialogue Conference on Peace' in place of the planned constitutional conference. However, the government controlled participation in the conference, ensured that it concluded by rejecting the Koka Dam and DUP–SPLM accords, and recommended maintaining *sharia*.[51] Subsequently, and over the course of the 1990s, peace talks between the government and the SPLM/A were intermittently held. In 1997 two agreements (the Khartoum Peace Agreement and the Fashoda Agreement) were reached between the government and breakaway SPLM/A factions and minor southern groups. However these agreements failed to last, let alone stop the war, and it was not until 2002 that the first significant agreements were reached between the government and the SPLM/A proper. These agreements – the Nuba Mountains Ceasefire in January 2002, the Machakos Protocol in July, and a renewable ceasefire agreement in October – were followed by further protocols in 2003 and 2004, culminating in the CPA.

During this long period from 1989, the war continued with little interruption and in fact widened, so that by the start of 2002 it incorporated fronts in southern, central and eastern Sudan. Fighting in the Nuba Mountains (South Kordofan State, in central Sudan) – which had begun in the first half of 1989 – increased and continued through to the start of 2002. In November 1991 the SPLA began operations in Darfur, but these stopped only three months later, after the capture and execution of Daud Bolad, the SPLA leader in Darfur.[52] Fighting in southern Blue Nile State, in central south-eastern Sudan – which had begun under Sadiq – also became entrenched. Finally, during 1995 and 1996 the SPLM/A began operations in eastern Sudan, in partnership with the National Democratic Alliance (NDA), an umbrella grouping of opposition parties which brought together the DUP, the Umma Party and other opponents of the government.[53]

Despite the overall enlargement of the war, each side repeatedly gained and lost territory, and fighting typically ebbed and flowed, partly with the coming and going of the wet and dry seasons (which affected conditions for fighting) and partly with the flow of arms supplies. For the SPLM/A, the biggest setback in the war came when the fall of Mengistu Haile Mariam in Ethiopia in May 1991 brought an end to Ethiopian support, causing it to lose its bases inside Ethiopia and laying the grounds for an internal coup against Garang in August 1991 and the splintering of the SPLM/A.[54] Encouraged by this split (which it also helped to nurture), the government launched new offensives against the SPLM/A and made significant advances until the end of 1994, when the SPLM/A began to recover from its earlier loss of unity. Then, in 1995–6, the SPLM/A launched its first offensive in four years, and by March 1996 it had recovered ground it had lost in Eastern Equatoria in 1992.[55] Around this time the position of the SPLM/A also began to be strengthened by its alliance with the NDA. The SPLM/A had agreed to ally with the NDA in 1990, but it was only in 1995, after an NDA conference in Asmara, that the alliance began to have a direct military impact. Two armed groups that were members of the NDA, the Sudanese Allied Forces and the Beja Congress, began to train in camps inside Eritrea and mount raids across the border.[56] By December 1996 operations were being co-ordinated between Beja Congress, Sudanese Allied Forces and SPLA forces, with the additional participation of DUP and Umma militia, though the tangible contributions of all but the SPLA and the Beja Congress were meagre. All the same, during the next five years the NDA – with SPLA participation – took and partially kept control of the Hamesh Koraib region in eastern Sudan, on the Eritrean border.

Within the south, in the late 1990s what was tantamount to a new front in the war developed in western Upper Nile and Unity State, as a result of the government's efforts to develop the oil fields which lay in this region. To develop the oil fields, the government needed to take control of rural areas which were either under SPLM/A control or vulnerable to attack. It therefore stepped up its own offensives against the SPLA and civilians in the region, and cultivated local militias by providing money and guns to leaders who were willing to defect from the SPLM/A. This was an extension of the tactic it had used elsewhere, and capitalised on the 1991 split in the SPLM/A, which had been followed by a further split between Riek Machar and Lam Akol, the leaders of the SPLM/A breakaway faction known as SPLM/A-Nasir (and later as SPLM/A-United). Determined to secure the oil fields, the government's offensives were very destructive: scores of villages were destroyed, and tens of thousands of civilians were displaced; warlord-type militia leaders emerged and fighting between militias across the area became common and persisted through to 2005 and beyond.[57]

Between 1989 and 2005, and in Darfur after 2003, the civil war and the Darfur conflict caused enormous loss of life and suffering. For the most part, detailed or reliable information on the human and economic costs of the war was not available. Notwithstanding this, by 2005 the civil war was commonly said to have been responsible for a cumulative death toll of between 1.5 and 2 million. This estimate was based largely on an extrapolation of an estimate made in 1993 and updated in 1998; it did not include the various separate estimates that were made of the death toll in Darfur in 2003–4 (typically ranging from 100,000 to 300,000).[58] The accuracy of the 1.5 to 2 million estimate was very questionable, but it was rarely questioned, faced with the evidence that the war certainly was responsible for great loss of life and suffering.[59]

As had happened in the early years of the war, the largest loss of life was almost certainly of civilians, as a result of increased mortality rates caused by the war. This could affect people living inside or outside the war zone, whether in villages, towns or IDP camps. Such loss of life continued even when headline-making famines such as the 1990–1 famine in the north and the 1998 famine in Bahr el-Ghazal in the south had passed. Furthermore, the war also killed many thousands directly, with civilians accounting for the majority of those killed violently, and many soldiers on both sides also being killed. In the fighting, the government's armed forces, its militias and the SPLM/A all killed civilians (as the few examples in Table 1 show), though the government's military tactics, and in particular its use of indiscriminate aerial bombings and militias against civilian targets, meant that it killed many more civilians than did the SPLM/A. Such tactics served military purposes and the objective of displacing people and preventing 'displaced persons from settling and becoming self-sufficient'.[60] When these tactics appeared to be targeted against a particular ethnic group and there was large-scale loss of life by violence and displacement, accusations of ethnic cleansing and genocide were sometimes made – notably about the government's campaigns in the Nuba Mountains during the 1990s, and about its campaigns in Darfur in 2003 and after.

Table 1: **Examples of attacks and killings of civilians**

Date	Details
1992	Government alleged to have carried out 230 extrajudicial killings in Juba.[61]
Mid-1992	Government extrajudicially executes 40–50 Nubans it accuses of co-operating with the SPLM/A.[62]
February 1994	Aerial bombardment of market in Kajo-Keji kills 17 people and injures others.
June 1994	SAF troops attack and set fire to village of Lanya, near Juba, reportedly killing around 70 people including women and children.[63]
July 1994	SPLM/A-Nasir forces attack and capture villages in northern Bahr el-Ghazal, killing at least 200 civilians in the fighting.[64]
August 1996–July 1997	Confirmed reports of 56 separate aerial bombardments of civilians in 30 locations. In one incident, helicopter gunships strafe a village in Western Equatoria, killing six people, injuring 41, and destroying 30 houses and two churches.[65]
March 2002	SPLM/A attack and burn down Tuhubak village, near Torit, killing 24.[66]
May–June 2002	Aerial bombardments in western Upper Nile reported to have killed 15 people in Mayam and Manken, 11 at Rier, 18 at Lil, 24 at Madier, and injured more than 100; bombardments in Bahr el-Ghazal reported to have killed at least seven people.[67]
January–April 2004	SAF and pro-government militias attack villages in Shilluk land, Upper Nile, displacing between 50,000 and 120,000 people.[68]

In addition to the loss of life through fighting and war-induced conditions, the war also involved widespread and sometimes rampant human-rights abuses. In 1994 the UN special rapporteur on human rights in Sudan, Gaspar Biro, concluded that abuses affected 'almost all aspects of life' and 'potentially all categories and strata of the population', with violations of human rights being committed by the government and all parties to the conflict.[69] Despite ostensible efforts by the government and the SPLM/A to improve their conduct, by 2002 the situation had scarcely improved, as the government continued to impose states of emergency and press censorship, and its security officials continued to benefit from 'virtual impunity'.[70]

Domestic politics during this time displayed some continuities with the past and some differences. The coup in 1989 was the fourth time since independence that the military had taken over power in Sudan. As Nimeiri had at first done in 1969, Bashir's government claimed to be leading a revolution, which it called the National Salvation Revolution. The government was led by a Revolutionary Command Council (RCC), headed by Bashir, until the RCC was dissolved in 1993 and Bashir was formally sworn in as president. Behind the military front, however, the coup was planned and instigated by the NIF, which effectively became the ruling party after the government officially banned political parties. At the instigation of the NIF, its leader Hasan al-Turabi, and its members and supporters in the army and security service, the government adopted a fundamentalist Islamist ideology. However, during the 1990s its attempts to implement this ideology across domestic and foreign policy proved widely unpopular and problematic, causing the government to come under mounting pressure at home and abroad. Ideology thus failed to mask the government's lack of popular or democratic legitimacy.

The government responded to the international pressure that its ideological agenda provoked by tempering its foreign policy from around 1996 onwards. Under continuing domestic pressure, in the late 1990s it also began to soften its ideological stance in domestic policy. It lifted the ban on opposition parties and set about trying to find new allies, in order to bolster its support. In 1998 the NIF was renamed the National Congress Party (NCP) and at the end of 1999 tensions within the NIF/NCP culminated in the expulsion of Turabi from government and from the party in early 2000, whereupon he formed his own political party, the Popular Congress Party (PCP). Significant though these changes were, they did not bring real democratisation. Elections were held in December 2000 but were neither free nor fair, and were boycotted by the main opposition parties. At root the government remained autocratic and authoritarian – controlled by the NIF/NCP, the government's security apparatus, and President Bashir, whose grip on power strengthened over the years.

During the 1990s, the government's Islamist ideology and policies inflamed the war, especially after the government declared the war to be a *jihad* or, in short, a holy war or struggle. Particularly controversial was the government's 'Comprehensive Call' programme, which embraced the encouragement of Islamic charities, Islamic proselytisation and the prosecution of the war under the banner of religion. In addition it established a national militia movement, the Popular Defence Forces (PDF), and tried to Arabicise the curricula in the school and university system.[71] As a consequence of these policies and actions, religion, *sharia*, and questions of identity became more contentious, among civilians and combatants, in politics, and at the negotiating table, when talks between the government and the SPLM/A were held.

At root, however, the fundamental causes of the war continued to lie in southern discontent with northern political dominance, and this was more or less reflected in the SPLM/A's political programme and aims. Over the years these evolved and broadly settled on two core aims: the establishment of a 'New Sudan', which was governed fairly and in accordance with the country's diversity; and the right to self-determination for the south. Problematically, there was never a united view in the SPLM/A about these aims, especially because in the 1990s many southerners increasingly favoured aiming only for self-determination.[72] However the aim of a 'New Sudan' had been championed by Garang from early in the war (and had drawn non-southerners and Muslims to join the SPLM/A from the early years).[73] To the extent that the idea of a new Sudan could be shared by other parties and movements, it facilitated the expansion of the war outside the south, and the formation of alliances such as the NDA, and even a fruitless initial agreement between the SPLM/A and the PCP in 2001. Nonetheless, fundamentally it was perceptions of political and economic marginalisation, and resentment at the domination of politics by a narrow elite (and the NIF), which motivated the many rebel groups that sprang up around Sudan, such as the Beja Congress and the Rashaida Free Lions in the east, and the Justice and Equality Movement (JEM) and the SLM/A in Darfur.[74]

The Darfur conflict

The escalation of the Darfur conflict from February 2003 onwards was another example of conflict caused at root by perceptions of political and economic marginalisation. In basic respects the conflict in Darfur was separate from the conflict between the government and the SPLM/A, in that there was no official alliance or relationship between the SPLM/A and the main Darfur rebel groups, JEM and the SLM/A. But there were connections that made it wrong to dissociate the conflict in Darfur from the wider civil war, and the conflict was neither entirely new nor unforeseeable. Besides the SPLM/A attempt to open a front in Darfur in 1991, the region had also seen an escalation in conflict in 1998–9 between government forces and allied militias, and people from the Masalit, Fur and other tribes in Darfur. In 1997 a Fur resistance organisation calling itself the Sudan Federal Democratic Alliance joined the NDA and began military training in Eritrea,[75] and in February 2001 Hasan al-Turabi's PCP – which had links with the future JEM – signed a memorandum of understanding with the SPLA, which briefly encouraged plans to start an insurrection in Darfur.[76] It appears too that the SPLM/A secretly provided some policy and military assistance to the Darfur rebels in 2003–4, seeing Darfur as potentially a new front for the civil war.[77]

Darfur itself was ripe for conflict. In the 1980s the war in neighbouring Chad had spilled across the border into Darfur, and Libyan armed forces and Chadian rebels operated in the area for some years with the approval of the Sudanese government, up until 1990. The spill-over of that conflict entailed repeated influxes of arms and soldiers, and repeated displacements of civilians. Meanwhile one government after another in Khartoum sought to manipulate the regional and local authorities in Darfur to their political advantage. This pattern continued under President Bashir's rule in the 1990s, when the government sought to weaken the support bases of opposition parties such as the Umma Party, which historically had strong support in Darfur. As part of a national redrawing of state boundaries in 1994, the government divided Darfur into three states (Northern, Southern and Western Darfur), in the process weakening the political position of the Fur relative to that of Arab Darfurian tribes. At the same time, the Arabising policies of the government encouraged the transfer of power and advantage to Arab Darfurians, which some had been seeking since the 1980s when the 'Arab Alliance' (a militantly 'Arab' Darfurian movement) was set up, itself influenced by Libyan pro-Arab policies.[78] Lastly, in addition to these political developments and factors was the fragile balance between the environment and the livelihoods of many Darfurians. Like other Sahelian regions, Darfur suffered from food and famine crises in the 1980s. Even allowing for uncertainty about longer-term trends in rainfall and land degradation and recovery, through the 1980s, the 1990s and beyond, large numbers of Darfurians were vulnerable to short-term declines in rainfall and localised competition over access to arable and grazing land.[79]

Against this background, discontent in Darfur grew through the 1990s, and the level of armed violence became more severe. The government colluded with Arab militias (including the nascent Janjawid), generally supporting their growth and their actions, while at the same time representing the violence in the region as a problem only of local tribal conflicts and banditry. In an upsurge in fighting in the late 1990s, some 100,000 civilians – mainly Masalit – fled to Chad. During this time, Fur, Masalit and Zaghawa opposition to the Arab militias and government policy began to coalesce into new Darfur-based political movements, armed and unarmed. In 2000 a booklet called *The Black Book* was published anonymously, arguing that Darfurians had long been under-represented in Sudan's central governments, and in 2001 JEM – the authors of *The Black Book* – announced the formation of the movement. Soon after, the Darfur Liberation Front announced itself with a series of attacks on small government targets in Darfur in 2002 and early 2003, before it changed its name to the SLM/A in March 2003.[80] In the same month, JEM announced that it was operating 'in alliance with the SLA'.[81]

The subsequent course of conflict in Darfur was dramatic. Fighting escalated rapidly in 2003, especially following a high-profile attack by the SLA on El Fasher airport in April 2003. The strategy of the government was to try to crush JEM, the SLM/A and their supporters, and to bolster its own supporters in the region. Thus it used almost exactly the same tactics that it had used against the SPLM/A – namely using militias, carrying out aerial bombardments, deliberately displacing civilians, and restricting access for relief organisations. In the most intense period of fighting, in 2003 and 2004, it was as though Darfur was a tinderbox that had been set alight. Villages were destroyed and inhabitants were killed or displaced, on a scale that exceeded the levels of violence seen in Darfur in the 1990s (for examples of violence, see Table 2). The number of displaced people rose to around 200,000 by mid-2003, to 600,000 at the end of 2003, and then to 1.8m by the end of 2004. Added to this were Darfurian refugees in neighbouring Chad, whose numbers had reached around 200,000 by the end of 2004. The number killed by violence in 2003–4 was perhaps in the low tens of thousands, while the number of people who died because of increased mortality rates caused by the conflict and displacement was perhaps higher – with estimates based on short-term data and limited samples suggesting anything between 100,000 and 300,000.[82]

Table 2: **Examples of attacks and killings of civilians in Darfur**

Date	Details
July–August 2003	SAF and Janjawid attack Shoba villages in North Darfur, killing 42 people and destroying the villages. Aerial bombardment of Habila village and market kills 30 civilians.[83]
October 2003	JEM attack Kulbus, West Darfur, killing 42 soldiers and 17 civilians, and injuring 50 civilians.[84]
2003–2004	Hundreds of villages are destroyed. International Commission of Inquiry on Darfur finds that majority have been destroyed by SAF and Janjawid and belong to Fur, Masalit, Zaghawa and other African Darfurian tribes.[85]
January 2004	SAF and Janjawid attack Surra, South Darfur, killing more than 250 people, including women and 'a large number of children'.[86]
February–March	SAF and Janjawid attack Anka village in North Darfur, burning

2004	the village, killing 15 civilians and driving out inhabitants and 30 SLM/A members. Rebels attack Buram and Hufrat an-Nahas in South Darfur, killing policemen and soldiers.[87]
March 2004	SAF and Janjawid surround Deleig, round-up many men, and execute over 120 or more (reportedly mainly intellectuals and leaders). SAF and Janjawid attacks on Kailek kill many.[88]
January 2005	SAF and militia attack on Hamada village kills 'large numbers' of women and children.[89]
March 2005	Janjawid attack Sula, Bala Farak and Doli villages in West Darfur; in South Darfur SLA attacks Haraza and Wazazen villages, and JEM attacks Rahad el-Fateh, killing small numbers of civilians.[90]
November 2005	Clashes between Fallata and Masalit in South Darfur; attacks by militias (reportedly with SAF) on villages near Gereida, South Darfur, kill about 60 people and displace 15,000.[91]
May 2006	SAF kill at least seven people in Karbaba, Nyala; militia attack Malwi, near Gereida, displacing about 8,000 people; Janjawid attack Natiga and Baju Baju villages, killing 35 civilians; militia attack IDP camp at Gua, reportedly killing eight people.[92]
August–September 2006	Intensification in fighting between signatories and non-signatories of DPA; SLM-Minnawi accuses government and Janjawid of breaking DPA ceasefire; SAF, allied militia and air support launch attack on DPA non-signatory groups in eastern Jebel Marra area.[93]
August–September 2007	Fighting between Terjem and Rizeyqat tribes lead to deaths of 100 civilians in South Darfur; clashes between Ma'aliya and Zaghawa supporters of SLM-Minnawi kill 30 and displace about 10,000. Heavy fighting between SAF and JEM around Haskanita, South Darfur; attack attributed to JEM kills 12 AMIS soldiers.[94]
November 2007	SAF aircraft bomb village north of Garsilla, killing 'large numbers of civilians'.[95]
August 2008	Government forces kill 32 and injure at least 85 in the Kalma displaced persons' camp in South Darfur.[96]
February–March 2009	Clashes between Mima tribe and SLA-Minnawi lead to death of at least 45 people; clashes between Fallata, Habaniyya and Rizayqat lead to death of some 248 people in total.[97]

In 2005, the intensity of the conflict declined as a result of a number of factors. To some extent government forces and rebels had all reached the limit of what they could achieve. At the same time, international attention to the conflict had grown sharply in 2004 and 2005, manifesting itself in a series of UN Security Council resolutions, the deployment of the AU Mission in Sudan (AMIS), an International Commission of Inquiry on Darfur, a dramatic scaling-up of humanitarian relief for Darfur, and greater international engagement in peace talks for Darfur. Nonetheless, the SAF, allied militias and the rebel groups and factions continued to clash intermittently, and the pattern continued after an abortive Darfur Peace Agreement (DPA) was signed in May 2006. For example, fighting in early 2006 in South Darfur displaced some 70,000 people; in a bout of fighting in July and August 2006 around Jebel Moon in North Darfur, some 50,000 people were displaced; and between December 2006 and February 2007 fighting in the eastern Jebel Marra area displaced some 35,000 people. Thus the total number of internally displaced at first changed little between 2005 and mid-2006, but then rose in the second half of 2006 and during 2007 up to around 2.5m (according to relief organisations' estimates).

During this time, tensions between Sudan and Chad grew and fluctuated, with each government accusing the other of supporting rebels against it. Chad accused the Sudanese government of being behind Chadian rebel attacks on N'djamena in April 2006 and February 2008. The Sudanese government returned the accusation in May 2008 when JEM carried out an audacious but ultimately unsuccessful armed raid on Omdurman, the twin city of the capital Khartoum. At the end of 2007 AMIS was merged into a new joint AU–UN 'hybrid operation' in Darfur, UNAMID, which gradually scaled up its deployed forces during 2008 and 2009. In parallel, an EU-led peacekeeping mission in eastern Chad, EUFOR, was scaled up into a smaller UN peacekeeping force for eastern Chad and the Central African Republic.

Meanwhile, in the years after 2005, while the conflict in Darfur continued, the CPA was maintained and implemented, albeit with difficulties. These included the death of John Garang in a helicopter crash in July 2005, and missed deadlines and disagreements about troop redeployments, the boundaries of the disputed area of Abyei, the allocation of cabinet positions, and the conduct of a census and general elections, which were required by the CPA. However, the major parts of the agreement – including the formation of a Government of National Unity (GONU) and a Government of Southern Sudan (GOSS), and oil revenue sharing – were upheld, as suited the basic interests of the NCP and the SPLM.

Regional and international responses – and questions

Between 1989 and 2009, Sudan's African and Arab neighbours, and regional and international actors more widely, responded to the civil war and the Darfur conflict in a variety of ways. In terms of political action to resolve the civil war, a number of internationally mediated peace initiatives were attempted – notably the initiative of former US president Jimmy Carter in 1989, the Abuja talks mediated by the OAU and Nigeria in 1992 and 1993, and the IGAD talks begun in 1994, which eventually became the CPA peace process. For Darfur, talks were convened at first in Chad and then in Ethiopia and Nigeria, under the auspices of the AU, and later in Libya and Qatar. In terms of humanitarian action, the international response to the humanitarian crises in the civil war consolidated in the form of OLS and the sustained delivery of relief in northern and southern Sudan. In Darfur after 2003 a new complex of humanitarian aid was set up, one that resembled OLS in its scale and for a time was the largest humanitarian aid operation in the world. These responses were part of a larger picture of foreign policy towards and relations with Sudan.

As indicated in the introduction, it is against the background set out above that this book investigates the story of the international community's responses to Sudan's civil war and the Darfur conflict. How successful were the international community's efforts to resolve conflict in Sudan? What determined the outcomes of peace talks? And what, if anything, could have been done to end conflict sooner or more effectively?

2

MEDIATION

Over the span of the civil war after 1983, through to the CPA in 2005, a variety of peace initiatives and talks were attempted with international assistance. These fall into three broadly distinct categories of mediation, namely (i) *ad hoc* talks arranged through 'good offices' and initiatives by eminent persons; (ii) regional initiatives, such as those undertaken by the OAU and IGAD; and (iii) international initiatives involving a number of parties not restricted to neighbouring states or organisations. For Darfur, a mix of these approaches characterised peace efforts from 2003 onwards. This chapter explores what determined the outcomes of these various talks (for example, how much processual or contextual factors such as 'ripeness' mattered), and what affected the prospects of any eventual peace settlements.

GOOD OFFICES AND EMINENT PERSONS

Talks convened through 'good offices' and at the initiative of eminent persons often occur in inauspicious circumstances. Typically, such initiatives have modest goals, such as to start talks where there are none, or where there has been only failure before. In theory, such mediation has a good chance of achieving its goals, by virtue of the goals being low and/or the mediator having high personal standing but few or no political interests in the situation. In Sudan, the Carter and Cohen initiatives, and a number of other attempts at mediation by prominent figures, were examples of this type of mediation.

The Carter initiative

The Carter initiative came about when Jimmy Carter visited Khartoum in mid-November 1989 and offered on behalf of the International Negotiation Network of the Carter Center in Atlanta to mediate in the war. Bashir accepted, thereby opening the way for the first substantial external mediation in Sudan's war. All previous peace talks had been held without the use of mediators, even though most of the talks had been held in Ethiopia. And in the immediate aftermath of the coup in 1989, the first talks between the new government and the SPLM had also been held in Addis Ababa (on 19–20 August), but without the participation of a mediator. To no one's surprise, those talks had produced no positive results: the new government had come to power partly to thwart the peace initiative that had grown from the 1988 DUP–SPLM accord.

When Bashir accepted Carter's offer, there was little to show that the climate for talks was more auspicious than in August 1989. Bashir was on record as having also asked Egypt to help to bring the SPLM/A to the negotiating table,[1] although the request was little more than a gesture towards Egypt's interest in following any potential negotiations. Since the talks in August, the government had anyway gone ahead with what was officially its own alternative programme for peace talks, the centrepiece of which was the 'National Dialogue Conference on Peace', which it convened in Khartoum in September. The conference had been supposed to come up with recommendations for solving Sudan's political problems, including the war, but had excluded the SPLM/A and the main opposition parties (many of whose leaders had been imprisoned after the coup) from participating. By November, therefore, the SPLM/A had been waiting three months for a response from the government to its own four-point peace proposal, or for the government to offer its own proposals. When the SPLM/A then agreed to the talks proposed by Carter, the government also claimed wrongly that the SPLM/A had agreed to 'dialogue without preconditions'.[2]

It was therefore little surprise that when the two sides met in Nairobi in December 1989 the talks were largely unsuccessful. Carter had wanted to get a ceasefire, but the parties failed to agree even a temporary one.[3] As Steven Wondu and Ann Mosely Lesch write, 'Both sides arrived in Nairobi more geared for confrontation than for dialogue and reconciliation.'[4] The government rejected the SPLM/A's call for it to abrogate two military pacts between Sudan and Egypt and Sudan and Libya; the parties disagreed about the inclusion of democracy in the political process; and they deferred the questions of *sharia* and a ceasefire for discussion on an unspecified future occasion. Carter showed his disappointment in the statement that he delivered to the press at the end of the talks:

> In my opinion neither side came to Nairobi prepared to take the difficult steps necessary for peace. The Sudan government team was eager for me to help with mediation, but did not have full authority to make decisions on the key issue, the Sharia laws. The SPLM/SPLA

delegation had authority, but were not willing to accept necessary mediation services. Both sides, at the end, seemed ready to emphasize their differences, postpone further action, and let the war continue.[5]

Nevertheless, Carter still believed that the results of the talks might still 'provide some constructive starting point for future peace talks if and when they occur'.[6] Moreover, he was able to announce one tangible agreement, which was for the resumption of relief operations in Southern Sudan and for relief flights to begin following a conference of the government and donors in Khartoum.[7]

Opinions among the parties about the usefulness of the talks confirm the impression that the negotiations were largely destined to fail. The head of the government delegation, Mohammed el-Amin Khalifa, claimed that the talks were a success from the government's point of view; but Khalifa had also claimed that the August talks had been 'positive' for the government.[8] In Khalifa's view, Carter 'played a negligible role' and the parties therefore 'agreed to do without his mediation'.[9] In the opinion of one of the SPLM delegates at the Carter talks (and subsequent negotiations in the 1990s), the government 'didn't take the peace talks seriously', not least because the talks came so soon after they came to power and they were still 'developing ideas and surveying the field'.[10] This opinion is echoed by Hussein Abu Saleh, who served as Foreign Minister in 1988 and again between 1993 and 1995: in his view, 'the Carter meeting in Nairobi was a futile exercise'.[11]

The Cohen initiative

Despite the failure of the talks organised by Carter in December 1989, in March 1990 Bashir invited the USA to take on the role of mediator. Carter's belief that the talks in Nairobi had yielded some progress encouraged the US authorities to respond favourably. The US assistant secretary of state for African affairs, Herman Cohen, prepared a proposal which was then delivered to Khartoum by a former Sudanese ambassador, Francis Deng, and the former Nigerian head of government (and future president), Olusegun Obasanjo. Bashir promptly rejected the proposal, which was premised on the assumption that the government was seeking a way out of the war. The proposal advocated the complete evacuation of government forces from Southern Sudan and the holding of a constitutional convention, both of which the government had so far shown itself unwilling to do.[12] Cohen therefore personally delivered a modified proposal to Bashir and Garang. The proposal still assumed that the SPLA was approaching military victory, but proposed a more balanced withdrawal of government and SPLA forces from areas of fighting, to be accompanied by the establishment of an internationally supervised ceasefire, and the designation of civilian safe havens to which relief could be delivered without obstruction.[13]

The government responded by accepting a ceasefire but refusing to withdraw its forces from the south. Meanwhile the SPLA refused to impose a ceasefire and rejected the new proposal, on the grounds that it favoured the government. Any prospect for revising and developing the proposal further was then blocked by the Gulf crisis that began in August 1990, in which the Sudanese government chose to support Iraq against the wishes of the USA and the coalition that ousted it from Kuwait. Following this, the USA shelved the Cohen initiative.

However, even without the intrusion of the 1990–1 Gulf crisis, it is unlikely that the Cohen initiative would have developed fruitfully. In truth, neither the government nor the SPLA were looking for a peaceful solution to the war. As Wondu and Lesch indicate, the USA was mistaken in its assessment that the government was looking for a way out of the war. Instead, what appeared to be the case was simply that fighting had intensified and the government was wanting a ceasefire for tactical reasons, not because it had abandoned its goal of military victory. Indeed, the government's real intentions were soon illustrated by the renewed offensives which it launched in the south, and the ensuing sudden shift in the balance in the war towards the government's favour in early 1991. In retrospect, therefore, the government's approach to the USA in 1990 appears to have been little more than an attempt to appear ready to negotiate and perhaps to gain some tactical benefits from talks.

Assessing 'good offices' initiatives in Sudan

The Carter and Cohen initiatives were the most prominent attempts at external mediation by individuals. Between 1989 and 1992 the Ugandan government organised a number of meetings between the government and the SPLM/A at Jinja in Uganda. The meetings reportedly never went beyond the stage of arguing about the agenda, and as a result were fruitless.[14] In 1993–4, Norway sponsored four 'back-channel' meetings in Oslo between the two sides, but these too were fruitless.[15] Besides these initiatives, over the course of the war a number of other persons and states offered to mediate on their own, including France and South Africa. But, as with many offers of good offices, these all came to nothing.

The failure of the various initiatives of 'good offices' and eminent persons was overwhelmingly due to the fact that the warring parties – and in particular the government – were unwilling to pursue the initiatives seriously. In short, domestic factors, in particular the political programme of the Sudanese government under Bashir, were sufficient to ensure the failure of any peace initiative, even when, as with the Cohen initiative, it had potential superpower backing. At the same time, international factors – i.e. factors among the backers of the various initiatives – were insufficient to ensure the success of any of the initiatives.

REGIONAL INITIATIVES

Attempts by regional states and organisations to mediate in Sudan's civil war came as something of a logical development, following the failure of the parties to solve the conflict either without mediation or with only the mediation of individuals such as Carter. The regional initiatives were more substantial in all respects (in particular the extent and duration of talks, and progress on agendas). However, like previous attempts to mediate in the conflict, they also sooner or later failed to produce the results they aimed at.

Abuja I

In mid-1991, the Nigerian president and head of the OAU, Ibrahim Babangida, contacted Omar al-Bashir and John Garang to offer to host a peace conference for Sudan, under the auspices of the OAU and with Nigerian mediation. Both accepted, and talks were slated to be held that October in Abuja, Nigeria. However, as a result of fighting between SPLM/A factions, following the SPLM/A split earlier that year, which the government had sought to widen, the conference did not convene until May 1992.

Once again, the circumstances for the talks were not auspicious. The split in the SPLM/A had greatly strengthened the government's position in the war, giving it little incentive to negotiate in earnest, as Lesch notes.[16] Moreover, the government was persisting with its efforts to widen the divisions in the SPLM/A, by means of such tactics as pursuing separate negotiations – outside the framework of the proposed Abuja talks – with the SPLM/A faction led by Lam Akol and Riek Machar, known as SPLM/A-Nasir. This culminated in the government and the SPLM/A-Nasir reaching an agreement in Frankfurt on 25 January 1992: the agreement, which was only one and a half pages long, provided loosely for a 'transitional period' after which Southern Sudan could freely decide its 'political and constitutional status'. This was far from a commitment to self-determination, although the Nasir faction nonetheless presented the agreement as amounting to this. However, when delegations from the government and the two SPLM/A factions eventually gathered at Abuja, the inadequacy of the Frankfurt Agreement became apparent. The Sudanese government and the negotiator who had signed the Frankfurt Agreement on its behalf, Ali al-Hag, argued that the agreement provided only for a referendum on the extent of decentralisation in the south and did not include the option of secession.[17]

The Frankfurt Agreement aside, the government position at the talks was as uncompromising as in 1989–90, if not more so. Its delegation refused to discuss security issues, such as a ceasefire and confidence-building measures, and offered no concessions on the issues of religion and national identity. Faced with this, on the sixth day of talks the SPLM/A-Nasir and the SPLM/A mainstream (known as SPLM/A-Torit) delegations merged, despite their differences, and took a common position demanding self-determination for Southern Sudan.[18] The talks continued, but after another four days without progress, they closed, once more without any concrete agreements on the core issues.[19] The parties could not even agree on a ceasefire, in the absence of agreement on what would follow.

Abuja II

Nearly a year later, in April 1993, Nigeria convened a second conference at Abuja, once again bringing together the government and an SPLM/A delegation which represented a merger of the SPLM/A factions. The prospects for the talks, however, were not good. Shortly before the conference convened, the government tried again, as it had the year before, to negotiate separately with the SPLM/A factions. And soon after the talks began, it became clear that the parties could not agree on the status of religion in the state, and that the failure to do so would frustrate the entire talks. Nigeria once again tried to get the parties to agree to an internationally monitored ceasefire, but with no success. As Wondu and Lesch argue, both the government and the SPLM/A realised that a ceasefire could not be implemented if they could not agree on political principles.[20] Moreover, after recent successes on the battlefield and in fostering the factionalisation of the SPLM/A, at the time of the talks the government was preparing to launch a major offensive against the SPLM/A and therefore wanted to stall on the issue of a ceasefire. For its part, the SPLM/A feared that the government would use a ceasefire to legitimise the redeployment of government forces in the south.[21]

The difference between the two parties on the issue of a ceasefire was clear in the wording of the final press statement issued by the Nigerian chair of the conference, Tunji Olagunju, concerning the composition of a ceasefire commission:

> The Government of Sudan wants only the Sudanese, SPLM (Mainstream), and other factions as members, while Nigeria is to be

the sole observer. The SPLM/A wants other observers from Kenya, Uganda, EEC, and USA.[22]

With the parties unwilling to renegotiate their positions even on this, the conference broke up without any tangible result.

At root, it is not surprising that Nigeria was unable to prevent the failure of the conferences. Quite apart from the gulf between the parties and the difficulty of formulating an agreement that was attractive to both sides, Nigeria had little economic or political capacity to make 'side-payments' to incentivise co-operation from each party. Even so, to some extent Nigeria did well in just bringing the parties together and establishing an agenda. However, as Wondu and Lesch observe, Nigeria's involvement was 'a mixture of mediation and arbitration', and this was not necessarily helpful:

> At Abuja, Nigeria was a mediator on the question of the relationship between religion and the state, although it did betray its preference for secularism in public law. On the subject of the territorial unity of the Sudan, Nigeria played judge and ruled in favor of the Sudan Government. The dual face of Nigeria contributed to the demise of the peace process in the sense that both parties had reason to suspect it of bias. [23]

Reflecting this problem, some SPLM members felt that Babangida was unduly sympathetic to the government.[24]

On the other hand, no-one from the parties appears to have believed that Nigeria's mediation caused the failure of the talks. In the view of one SPLM delegate at the talks, Babangida had 'really tried', and the failure was not due to a lack of serious mediation. Instead, it was because the government 'still believed that the SPLA could be defeated', and because the SPLA had its own problems and was trying to regroup its army.[25] In short, the basic reasons for the failure of the Abuja talks were little different from the failure of the first talks between Bashir's government and the SPLM/A in 1989. The fundamental reasons were contextual: the government was still largely uninterested in a negotiated settlement to the war and was trying to encourage splits in the SPLM/A, so that it could negotiate from a position of greater strength. In the blunt view of the man who in 1994 took over as the government's chief negotiator, Ghazi Salah al-Din Atabani, 1992 was a missed opportunity to make peace, but not through lengthy negotiations. In his opinion, the SPLM/A 'had suffered a crushing military setback and split', and the government 'squandered a chance to dictate terms for a peace'.[26] Likewise in the opinion of Aldo Ajo Deng, who at the time of the Abuja talks was an adviser to President Bashir on dialogue on the south (and who subsequently quit his position and left Sudan), 'There was a lack of good faith from the SPLM/A and from the government too.' For the government at least, if not for the SPLM/A too, 'The idea was to seem to be talking peace, while the real intention was war.'[27]

Failure aside, the Abuja conferences marked a significant development in the international response to Sudan's war. This point is noted by Wondu and Lesch:

> Although Abuja did not resolve the conflict or even halt the fighting in Sudan, it resulted in several significant achievements. First, it brought the conflict to international attention. For the first time since the insurrection flared up in 1983, a third party offered a forum and assistance to the warring parties to negotiate a peace settlement. Abuja introduced Sudan to the international agenda of conflict resolution.[28]

Indeed, despite the failure of the talks, as Johnson suggests, 'they demonstrated that the main parties to the conflict were willing to engage in mediated talks'.[29] Reflecting this, Sudan stayed on the agenda for international action to support the resolution of conflict, and it was not long before another forum for peace talks was arranged, this time through regional mediation in the Horn of Africa.

IGAD I

The failure of the two Abuja conferences led to disappointment internationally and calls for something to be done. Bashir responded by requesting mediation by Sudan's neighbours in the regional Intergovernmental Authority on Development (IGAD), on the grounds that they knew the problem of Sudan's war well. IGAD's members had become more concerned about the destabilising effects of Sudan's war, and they therefore decided to try to start talks under the auspices of IGAD.[30] A ministerial committee, chaired by the Kenyan president Daniel Arap Moi, then convened four rounds of talks in Nairobi in close succession, on 17–23 March, 17–22 May, 18–29 July and 5–7 September 1994. At the third session, the IGAD mediators issued a Declaration of Principles (DOP). Unlike at the Abuja conferences, where the Nigerian mediators had always given priority to the unity of Sudan, the DOP endorsed the right of self-determination for Southern Sudan and set the establishment of a secular state as a precondition for unity. The SPLM/A welcomed and accepted the DOP, while the government flatly rejected it.[31] After the fourth round of talks, the government refused to continue with the process.

As Johnson, Lesch and others relate, there is no doubt that it was the government's refusal to accept the DOP which led to the suspension of the IGAD talks for Sudan after September 1994.[32] The government's displeasure at the DOP also led it to reshuffle its negotiating team, with Mohammed el-Amin Khalifa and Ali al-Hag (the government's lead negotiators since 1989) being shunted to new jobs. According to Ghazi Salah al-Din Atabani, who at the time was a minister of state to the Sudanese president and succeeded Khalifa as lead negotiator:

> When Ali al-Hag and Mohammed el-Amin Khalifa came back from Nairobi where they had accepted the DOP they were reprimanded by the leadership office. ... I had the job [of doing that]. The objective was to [terminate] the IGAD initiative.[33]

Furthermore the Sudanese government did nothing to conceal its displeasure with the DOP. Although the government had invited IGAD's mediation, influential government figures strongly disliked IGAD and what it proposed. In Atabani's opinion:

> For the IGAD countries [the DOP] was a way of embarrassing Sudan. The IGAD countries had nothing in common except that they viewed Sudan unfavourably. And they came up with the DOP which was the most unfair document presented to the government. ... It gave the government the choice of accepting a definition of religion and state which was impossible for us [or the secession of the south].[34]

Having rejected the DOP, the government evidently felt that in terms of political and military consequences it could afford to leave the IGAD talks. Politically, the IGAD member states had little leverage with Khartoum, and relations with Eritrea and Ethiopia had soured since the brief improvement in relations after the overthrow of Mengistu in 1991. And as SPLM/A delegates at the talks in 1994 sensed, the government appeared to feel that the battlefield situation at the time was in its favour, following its military gains since 1991.[35]

Although the tabling of the DOP culminated in the suspension of talks after September 1994, the DOP was nonetheless an important new development. As Lesch writes:

> At Abuja, the Nigerian mediators prioritized the unity of the Sudan and rejected self-determination if that meant secession of the south. In contrast, the IGADD mediators emphasized that unity was

conditional on the establishment of a secular state and that, in the absence of such a state, the south had the right to vote for separation.[36]

Self-determination in the form of secession, subject to conditions, subsequently became a basis of negotiations when, from 1997, the government returned to talks under IGAD. Furthermore, as Johnson comments, 'the very existence of a widely agreed set of principles on which peace could be based was to have a significant impact on the international community and, ultimately, on the Sudanese opposition'.[37] It was not apparent at the time, but the DOP therefore constituted the most significant outcome from mediation to date, although ironically it was also linked with the temporary abandonment of mediated talks.

As an alternative to further talks mediated by IGAD or any other outside party, from 1994 until 1997 the government turned to a policy which it called 'Peace from within'. In reality, the name masked a strategy of continuing with existing attempts to foment factionalism in the SPLM and make unmediated agreements with fragmented, rival groupings rather than with a united opposition.

The policy gained little credibility at home or abroad, but it nonetheless yielded some dividends for the government, in particular a series of agreements with groups that had split from the SPLM/A. In April 1996, Riek Machar and Kerubino Kuanyin Bol, leaders respectively of the South Sudan Independence Movement/Army (SSIM/A) and the SPLM Bahr el-Ghazal, signed a 'political charter' with the government in Khartoum.[38] The charter provided for the peaceful resolution of Sudan's war and an interim period of unspecified duration at the end of which a referendum of the people of Southern Sudan would be held to determine their 'political aspirations'. The charter did not offer the possibility of secession, but explicitly provided for '[t]he unity of Sudan with its known boundaries [to] be preserved'.[39] In June 1996 Theophilus Ochang Lotti, leader of the Equatoria Defence Force (EDF) – a southern armed group which was not an SPLM/A faction – and a number of other southern figures added their names to the charter. Separately from this, in July an SPLM/A splinter group in the Nuba Mountains led by Mohammed Haroun el-Din agreed 'principles' with the government for solving the conflict in the Nuba Mountains. Then, in April 1997, the charter was consolidated as the Khartoum Peace Agreement between the government and the SSIM, the SPLM Bahr el-Ghazal, the EDF, the Union of Sudan African Parties (USAP), and a number of individuals (under the name the South Sudan Independents Group).[40] In September the government and Lam Akol, the leader of another SPLM/A faction (who had been part of the split in the SPLM/A in 1991), concluded the Fashoda Agreement, which came under the umbrella of the Khartoum Peace Agreement.

As these agreements were reached only with factions and not with the SPLM/A led by Garang, and were besides not honoured by the government, they achieved nothing positive for peacemaking in Sudan. Indeed, through the bargaining and negotiations under the auspices of the 'Peace from within' strategy, and the awarding of powers and privileges to rival leaders, the government aimed to foster divisions in the opposition that it faced in the south. In particular, it tried to take advantage of the local conflict between Nuer groups, which Johnson aptly calls the Nuer civil war:

> It was, in fact, the 'peace from within' which added fuel to that civil war. ... The fostering of the civil war among the Western Nuer, while intensifying insecurity in what was supposed to be a government-held area, served the government's purpose in neutralizing the Southern guerrilla factions best positioned to interfere with the exploitation of the Bentiu oilfields.[41]

Although these tactics served the government well over the coming years, during which commercial development of the oilfields took off, at the same time it was apparent that the 'Peace from within' strategy was not going to enable the government to win the war. Meanwhile, by 1997 the government was instead facing new threats on two fronts. On the battlefield, the SPLM/A had won a string of military victories and, in partnership with the NDA, it had opened a front in eastern Sudan. Internationally, hostility to the government was bringing new pressures, including threatened or actual support for armed opposition groups operating out of neighbouring countries, and UN sanctions imposed in 1996. Together, these factors prompted the government to accept a return to talks through IGAD, which offered the possibility of deflecting some of the international and domestic pressure it was under, but with no immediate likelihood that the negotiations would be any more effective than before.

Resuming talks under IGAD required the Sudanese government to accept the DOP. It did so, but with sufficient qualifications to ensure that when talks resumed in July 1997 in Nairobi they quickly ran into difficulties. The government indicated that it accepted the DOP only as one of a number of potential bases for resolving Sudan's war, which included its programme of 'Peace from within' and the Khartoum Peace Agreement. Moreover, other differences about self-determination soon arose, in particular when the SPLM/A proposed that Abyei, the Nuba Mountains and Southern Blue Nile be considered part of Southern Sudan and should therefore be subject to the self-determination provided for by the DOP. The government rejected the proposal, and the talks shortly ground to a halt.[42]

Subsequent rounds of IGAD talks similarly struggled to produce substantive progress. This was not for a lack of meetings. Talks were held again in Nairobi in October–November 1997 and May 1998, and in Addis Ababa in August 1998. Meanwhile, IGAD and its member states remained unable or unwilling to exert more pressure on the parties. Thus, for example, at the IGAD summit in March 1998, the IGAD heads of state merely reiterated their support for the talks, and discussed the matter only briefly, pending the next round of talks.[43] But at the next round, the gaps between the parties remained large. The government wanted a ceasefire to facilitate the delivery of relief, but the SPLM/A objected on the grounds that relief should not be linked to a ceasefire, and that a ceasefire should be negotiated separately, in line with the DOP; both parties agreed again on the right of self-determination through an internationally supervised referendum, at the end of an interim period, in accordance with the DOP; but they disagreed on the boundaries of the south and on the perennial question of the relationship between religion and state[44]. Furthermore, the government made clear that it still considered self-determination secondary to unity, contrary to the spirit of the DOP.[45] The next round of talks, in August 1998, similarly failed to resolve these differences, despite producing a temporary ceasefire (partly coinciding with the wet season, when there was normally a lull in fighting).[46]

During this period, a number of European countries supporting IGAD were also unable or unwilling to exert pressure on the parties at the talks. In 1994 an informal grouping of 'Friends of IGAD' had been established, and in 1996 IGAD approved the proposal of several donor countries to formalise the group as the IGAD Partners Forum (IPF). Prior to the establishment of the IPF, donor countries and organisations held only the position of 'Partners in Development' for IGAD.[47] However the first ministerial-level meeting of the IPF was not held until January 1998, and this produced little besides assurances of continued 'political and financial support' for IGAD's efforts on Sudan.[48] But over the next four years, the IPF would come to play a significant role in the eventual internationalisation of the IGAD Sudan talks, partly in reaction to the parallel Egyptian–Libyan initiative launched in 1999.

The Egyptian–Libyan initiative

The joint Egyptian–Libyan initiative was launched without fanfare in February 1999, but gradually gained attention during the course of that year. Both Egypt and Libya opposed self-determination for Southern

Sudan, and therefore premised their initiative on maintaining the unity of Sudan. The initiative had no fixed forum for meetings or for observers, but was loosely supported by the Arab League.[49] At root, it was therefore seen by many parties, including IGAD partners, as being intended to offer an Arab solution to the conflict and to eclipse IGAD.

The Sudanese government welcomed the initiative, and in May 1999 it also accepted an attempt by Libya to get an agreement between Sudan and Eritrea to stop supporting rebel movements in each other's country. Encouraged by the inclusivity of the Egyptian–Libyan initiative, the NDA too gave its support to the initiative, endorsing it in Tripoli in July 1999.[50] The DUP and the Umma Party also endorsed the initiative, partly because of their long-established links with Egypt and Libya, and partly because of their ambivalence towards self-determination for Southern Sudan. Indeed, the DUP – or at least a faction within the DUP led by Sharif Zain al-Abdin al-Hindi – claimed to have written the initiative.[51] The SPLM/A also nominally welcomed the initiative.

Despite the general welcome for the initiative, a proposal from Egypt and Libya to organise a 'reconciliation' conference in September 1999 came to nothing. Although the latest round of IGAD talks in July had broken down without agreement, and although it had officially welcomed the Egyptian–Libyan initiative, the SPLM/A said that it preferred to continue with talks under IGAD.[52] In keeping with this position, at a meeting of the NDA in October 1999, the SPLM/A opposed a proposal to merge the Egyptian–Libyan initiative with the IGAD initiative. The same month, Sadiq al-Mahdi wrote to the IPF to counter criticisms of the Egyptian–Libyan initiative and to appeal for it to be included in a revised framework for talks on Sudan. There had, he wrote, been much 'unwarranted disinformation' about the initiative, and Egypt and Libya had assured the Umma Party that the initiative was not 'an attempt to side track the IGAD initiative' or to help the government or northern opposition parties 'renege on self-determination'.[53] The IPF ignored the appeal, as did the IGAD ministerial sub-committee which was managing the IGAD process.

However, the Egyptian–Libyan initiative continued, sustained by intermittent statements of support from Egyptian, Libyan and Sudanese officials, including statements from the government, the NDA and opposition parties. At a summit of IGAD heads of state and government in November 2000, held in Khartoum, Libya's minister for African unity, Ali Teriki, made a statement in which he appealed for IGAD to see the Egyptian–Libyan initiative as complementing the IGAD initiative.[54] Again, the appeal had no impact. Although the summit passed a resolution on the conflict (the first ever IGAD resolution on Sudan), it did not mention the

Egyptian–Libyan initiative. Furthermore, the resolution merely called for the warring parties to be 'flexible in their position' so that negotiations could make progress, and encouraged perseverance with the IGAD Sudan talks and continued support from the IPF.[55]

Further calls to merge the two initiatives were periodically made, but a merger was never attempted, and nor was anything done to resolve the tension between the two initiatives. Mediators in the IGAD process did not show any real interest in engaging with the Egyptian–Libyan initiative, or in allaying Egyptian and Libyan apprehensions about IGAD. For their part, the Egyptian and Libyan foreign ministries did little to develop their initiative.[56] As a result, although both the government and the SPLM/A had met independently with Egyptian and Libyan officials, by the end of 2001 the Egyptian–Libyan initiative had still not led to a single round of talks between the warring parties.

Johnson suggests that the 'intrusion' of the Egyptian–Libyan initiative in 1999 'helped not only to halt the IGAD process, but to split the NDA's temporary unity'.[57] But this is only partly true. As of early 1999, the IGAD process was still struggling to make any headway, and the apparent involvement of NDA members in the initiative indicates that a large part (if not all) of the impetus for splitting the NDA's unity came from within the NDA itself.[58] Moreover, the IGAD process did not stop but in fact continued and, as was to emerge in the next two years, it did so to the exclusion of the Egyptian–Libyan initiative, thereby contributing to the demise of the initiative.

Assessing regional initiatives in Sudan

While the Abuja conferences, the IGAD process and the Egyptian–Libyan initiative were all more systematic and more concerted attempts to mediate in Sudan's war than the initiatives of good offices and eminent persons that had preceded them, none was able to end the war. In varying degrees, the regional initiatives did not aim merely to initiate talks or to establish an agenda or agree a ceasefire. Essentially, they aimed at reaching a full settlement of the war, although the proponents of the initiatives appear to have had little idea of how this could be done. In addition, the Egyptian–Libyan initiative aimed in part to thwart the IGAD process, if it could not be merged with it.

As with previous initiatives, the failure of these regional initiatives to bring peace was again overwhelmingly due to domestic political factors. Other factors played some role in their failure, in particular the weakness of the mediators and shortcomings in the processes used. But leaving aside the overall failure of the initiatives, two significant developments occurred during this period. These were firstly the consolidation of self-determination through a referendum as an essential part of any potential settlement to the war; and secondly the establishment of a basis for wider international involvement and mediation in peace talks for Sudan.

AN INTERNATIONAL INITIATIVE

The third type and phase of external mediation in Sudan's war – international mediation involving non-regional and regional actors – evolved out of the preceding regional mediation initiatives. In short, the basis for wider, more international mediation was provided by IGAD and the IPF. Nonetheless, the peace talks that ensued were substantially different from what had gone before, both technically and in terms of their outputs, as was manifested by the agreements culminating in the CPA.

IGAD internationalised

The internationalisation of the IGAD talks for Sudan occurred despite previous insistence within IGAD that the IGAD initiative was 'an African initiative and should remain so'.[59] But the end result was a process which, although still African-led, involved Britain, Norway and (most significantly) the USA, and which effectively excluded Egypt and the Egyptian–Libyan initiative. The internationalised IGAD talks were not separate from what had gone before, but they had closer participation from significant international actors, with greater international attention to what occurred, and different individual mediators and modalities from the previous rounds of IGAD talks.

In the internationalisation of the talks, several developments were of particular note. In early September 2001 the US president appointed John Danforth as his special envoy to Sudan. Relations between the USA and Sudan then assumed new importance after the attack on the World Trade Center on 11 September 2001, due to Sudan having been home to the leader of al-Qaeda, Osama bin Laden, between 1991 and 1996. This added to the vigour with which Danforth set about his mission, culminating in the Nuba Mountains ceasefire agreement brokered by Danforth in January 2002. This small but significant breakthrough agreement coincided with increasing calls from the IPF for the peace talks being convened by IGAD to make progress.[60] Reflecting this, in January 2002 the IPF co-chair, the Norwegian Development Minister Hilde Johnson, addressed the IGAD summit in Khartoum, and called for the 'opportunity' to make peace in Sudan not to be missed:

There is now ... a 'Window of opportunity' to make peace, with renewed engagement by IGAD and supported by the international community. The war must stop! Peace must come! I urge you – and all of us – to use this opportunity to make peace in Sudan, as well as within the region, within the year 2002![61]

More generally, Hilde Johnson's call reflected a view that had been growing since the late 1990s, internationally and in Sudan, that it was high time for Sudan's war to end. Exemplifying this was a report on Sudan published by the Brussels-based NGO, the International Crisis Group, in January 2002, which argued that 'a comprehensive peace may be possible if the international community for the first time makes its achievement a significant objective, and commits the necessary political and diplomatic resources'.[62]

Despite these developments, the IGAD summit in January 2002 produced few if any specific recommendations for action. The summit noted the 'increase in numbers of parallel initiatives' and mandated President Moi to try to harmonise them with the IGAD talks.[63] But its only other comments on the process concerned the role of the IPF: IGAD's main expectation of the IPF was that it should provide more aid money for IGAD projects and help to mitigate recurring funding shortfalls within the IGAD secretariat. Thus at the 2002 summit, IGAD noted of its relationship with the IPF 'that this relationship that had grown from friendship to partnership had not lived up to the expectation [viz. of aid money]'.[64] In fact, problems with IGAD funding expectations and donor satisfaction with IGAD performance were not new: according to the US ambassador to Sudan in 1994, Don Petterson, it was because of poor Kenyan management of the IGAD peace talks in 1994 that the USA did not provide financial support for them, even when Kenya asked for it.[65]

In the years between 1994 and 2002, the relationship between the IPF and IGAD had improved, partly because major problems in the Horn of Africa had persisted, and both IGAD and the IPF retained an interest in resolving these problems. But there was good reason still to be cautious about the commitment of the Sudanese government and the SPLM/A to making peace. John Danforth therefore tried to make US participation in the peace process contingent on the parties' commitment to peace. As he wrote in his report to President Bush in April 2002:

> The history of Sudan is littered with dozens of proposals and agreements to end the fighting. These agreements all have one thing in common: none was implemented, and none brought Sudan closer to peace. ... Therefore, instead of drafting yet more new comprehensive

peace agreements, I decided to test the parties' commitment by submitting to them a series of concrete proposals that would challenge them politically while at the same time reduce the suffering of the Sudanese.[66]

But as Danforth noted then, 'progress even on the four test points has been exceedingly difficult, and such agreement as has been reached has been grudging. Both sides want the conflict resolved, but on their own terms.'[67]

Nonetheless, gradually the USA and the IPF increased their involvement in and support for the IGAD process, encouraged along the way by other concerned parties. A group of six INGOs, for example, published a joint report in April 2002 urging progress in the peace talks.[68] The same month the International Crisis Group published another report calling for the intensification of efforts 'to construct a meaningful [peace] process and achieve a comprehensive agreement'.[69] In these circumstances, and also thanks to his own efforts, the new chairman of the IGAD Sudan talks, General Lazaro Sumbeiywo (whom President Moi had appointed in October 2001), gained support from both the USA and the IPF. That support, both political and financial, helped Sumbeiywo to establish a secretariat and initiate a new programme of talks, facilitated by several staff and involving the IPF and in particular the troika of Britain, Norway and the USA.

Collectively, these developments meant substantial changes for the peace talks, both in the management of the talks themselves and in the regional and international environment within which they were held. These changes were felt by the parties. Thus, according to one of the government negotiators between 2002 and 2004, when the government came to the first meeting convened by Sumbeiywo in May 2002, in Nairobi, 'there was a realisation that what was abhorred – the internationalisation of the conflict – had already happened'.[70] That meeting, which was to agree the work programme and modalities of the talks, ended abruptly with the government objecting to the proposed use of the words 'transitional' and 'interim' and accusing Sumbeiywo of bias.[71] Shortly afterwards, however, the government dropped its objection and agreed to attend the first full round of talks convened by Sumbeiywo, in Machakos, Kenya. The talks, which began on 18 June, culminated in the agreement of the Machakos Protocol, which was signed on 20 July 2002 and constituted a major breakthrough in negotiations between the government and the SPLM/A. It was the start of a series of agreements resulting from mediated talks for Sudan; but those agreements were also accompanied by significant failings.

Agreements

The principal success of the peace talks between 2002 and 2004 was the series of agreements that the parties negotiated and signed, culminating in the CPA. Together, the agreements surpassed any other agreement reached since 1972, in detail and in promise, and in the mere fact that they were made between the government and the whole of the SPLM/A.

The first of the agreements, the Nuba Mountains ceasefire agreement, was signed on 19 January 2002 at Bürgenstock in Switzerland, six days after the parties gathered there at the invitation of the US and Swiss governments. The agreement itself was signed by the SPLA commander for the Nuba Mountains, Abd al-Aziz el-Hilu, and a government minister, Mutrif Siddig Ali, and was witnessed by US and Swiss officials. Although the agreement related only to a ceasefire in the Nuba Mountains, and was nominally reached outside the IGAD framework, it was explicitly intended to support progress towards a wider peace. In the agreement, the parties agreed to:

> an internationally monitored cease-fire among all their forces in the Nuba Mountains for a renewable six (6) months with the broader objectives of promoting a just, peaceful and comprehensive settlement of the conflict.[72]

The agreement to and introduction of foreign observers was a minor but significant milestone.[73] Coupled with the support that Danforth voiced for the IGAD process in his report to President Bush in April 2002, the experience of the Nuba Mountains agreement encouraged the USA to join the IPF as observers at the IGAD talks at Machakos and subsequently.

The next agreement, the Machakos Protocol, was signed in the presence of observers from the troika and Italy. The protocol contained the parties' agreement on the issue of – most importantly – self-determination for Southern Sudan, as well as other issues, such as state and religion, the transition process and government structure. On most issues, however, the protocol represented only an agreement on 'principles', the expectation being that details would be worked out in subsequent talks and eventually set down in an overall or final agreement.[74] The next round of talks at Machakos was at first threatened by outbreaks of fighting between the government and the SPLM/A, which in September 2002 prompted the government to withdraw from the talks. But in early October the parties signed a renewable temporary ceasefire (technically a cessation of hostilities), paving the way for the resumption of talks that month. This was the first ceasefire between the government and the SPLM/A for political rather than humanitarian purposes, although it was followed by agreements on 28

October to allow unimpeded humanitarian access, and on 19 November to extend the ceasefire until the end of March 2003.[75]

Together, the Nuba Mountains Agreement, the Machakos Protocol and the ceasefire agreement strengthened the grounds for further talks and renewals of the ceasefire over the next two years. During that time, the government and the SPLM/A reached five further agreements which, like the Machakos Protocol, were intended to be incorporated eventually into an overall agreement. These were an agreement on security arrangements, two protocols on wealth sharing and power sharing, and two protocols on governance arrangements for disputed areas – namely Southern Kordofan and Blue Nile States (also known as the Nuba Mountains and Southern Blue Nile) and Abyei. The latter were signed in May 2004. Just over six months later, after negotiating various implementation modalities for the preceding agreements, the government and the SPLM/A agreed a permanent ceasefire and finalised and signed the CPA.

During this process, opinions about the reasons for the success of the talks varied. Overall, no one factor was seen to be pre-eminent, and few participants in the talks considered their own involvement to be of particular importance. Instead, the reasons that participants in and observers of the talks generally cited for the relative success of the talks fell into three categories. These were (i) changes in the international environment; (ii) changes in the regional context; and (iii) changes in the domestic scene. In each case, the common view was that various factors had come together to make peace a greater priority and more possible; in short, there was a 'desire for peace inside Sudan, in the region and internationally'.[76] The engagement of the USA in the peace process for Sudan, alongside Britain, Norway and other members of the IPF, was widely seen as being the most important international factor. Thus, in the opinion of one former Foreign Minister of Sudan, what had changed at Machakos was that 'the USA at last thought that the war should be stopped and that they should make an effort'.[77] Regional factors consisted principally in the perceived will of IGAD and its member states to see an end to Sudan's war; in the opinion of the Ugandan envoy to the talks in Kenya, even the mere establishment of an IGAD secretariat dedicated to the talks was a particularly important factor.[78] Meanwhile, the domestic changes that favoured progress in the peace process were changes in the government and the SPLM/A, and to some extent influences from the Sudanese public. In the words of one SPLM/A delegate at the talks in Kenya, 'The big pressure on us is from our people. If we are trying to please anyone at all, it is our people. So if there is an opportunity we must go for it.'[79]

Failings

To talk of failings at the same time as acknowledging successes may seem begrudging. But the peace process between 2002 and 2005 showed a number of significant limitations, which had the potential to contribute to the eventual unravelling and failure of the agreements. Three deficiencies stand out.

The worst failing of the peace process and agreements between 2002 and 2005 was that they did not prevent the persistence of conflict during this period, and in particular the escalation of the Darfur conflict. Overall, the scale and frequency of armed clashes between the government and the SPLA fell. But in their place, clashes between the government, other armed groups, militias and proxies became more prominent. To some extent, there was also a connection between these conflicts and the on-going government–SPLM/A peace process. This was first illustrated when the Nuba Mountains ceasefire was signed in January 2002. The ceasefire was monitored by the Joint Military Commission (JMC), which found over the next two years that the parties largely complied with the ceasefire.[80] However, the ceasefire also contributed to an escalation of fighting in the oil-producing region of Western Upper Nile. This was principally because the ceasefire freed up troops and resources that could be redeployed to the area to counter the SPLM/A, which had been strengthened in the area by a merger in early 2002 with a splinter group based in the region.[81]

Similar problems were visible after the government and the SPLM/A agreed the ceasefire in October 2002 for Southern Sudan. An internationally staffed Civilian Protection Monitoring Team (CPMT) was set up, on the model of the JMC, to monitor compliance with the ceasefire and to investigate alleged breaches. The CPMT had meagre resources: for most of 2002–4 it had a handful of staff, led by a retired US army brigadier, and it used just one light aircraft to fly around Southern Sudan investigating allegations. Nonetheless, it did an efficient job of investigating and documenting allegations. It found many allegations to be substantiated, others not. Overall, however, its investigations confirmed that persistent and significant ceasefire violations were occurring. A CPMT report on fighting in the Western Upper Nile region in January 2003 provides an example:

CPMT Verification investigations found:
(1) In the Mayom–Mankien–Lara–Tam–Leel area: Military attacks against villages and non-combatant civilians have been conducted by GoS-allied militia, supported directly by GoS military forces.
(2) Non-combatants have been abducted, including men/boys (for military service), while women and children, have been taken to GoS

controlled towns (probably Mankien, Mayom, and Bentiu) where the children are held captive and women forced to provide manual labor and sexual services (based on multiple interviews with escaped abductees, both male and female).
(3) Cattle and crops were reportedly looted from villagers and moved to the GoS-controlled towns noted above. It was confirmed that food stocks and personal possessions were looted from Lara.
(4) GoS direct support to attacks included artillery, and helicopter gunships in Lingara and villages north of Tam.[82]

In this case, the CPMT concluded that many thousands of civilians had been forcibly displaced from their homes by direct military attacks, a conclusion which was shared by many UN organisations and INGOs.[83]

Still more substantial and serious than these examples of on-going fighting was the escalation of conflict in Darfur from February 2003. Although the fighting in Darfur was at first small-scale, before long it escalated to levels far in excess of any of the fighting seen in Western Upper Nile or elsewhere in Southern Sudan since the start of 2002 and the process leading to the CPA. As recounted earlier, by the end of 2004 (a little over two years since the SPLM and government signed a ceasefire) many thousands of people – perhaps around 50,000 – had been killed in fighting and a further two million displaced. Increased mortality rates as a result of displacement had caused the premature death of tens of thousands more people by the end of 2004.[84]

Whatever the exact death toll, the dimensions of the conflict were clearly similar to some of the worst periods of Sudan's civil war in the preceding twenty years. In these circumstances, the conclusion of the peace process in Kenya and the signing of the CPA in January 2005 were a paradoxical victory: they brought a much-anticipated peace, but were accompanied by a more destructive level of conflict in Darfur than had been seen in the civil war since before 2002.

A second and less dramatic failing of the peace process in Kenya was its slow pace. In the view of Sumbeiywo, the chairman of the talks, the process was sometimes one of 'two steps forward, three steps back', although overall there was progress.[85] However the faltering progress and protraction of the talks did have its own consequences. During the two-and-a-half years that the process took, a view grew among members of the SPLM/A and the public at large that the protraction of the talks principally served the interest of the government: as the talks went on, the situation came to be criticised as one of 'no peace, no war'. This was bad for building trust between the parties and for building public confidence in the process. The following opinion, voiced by one SPLM/A commander, was typical of what many people thought:

> The delay has given the government time. The government is enjoying [the situation of] no peace, no war. ... Six fronts have been frozen and the government has shifted forces to Darfur. ... The oil is flowing and the government is buying arms in Eastern Europe and arming the militia and building up its businesses. [86]

Even a member of the government delegation at Naivasha was also ready to admit that the protraction of the talks was 'to the advantage' of the government.[87] Publicly, therefore, a common opinion was that the parties – and in particular the government – were not 'serious' about peace. This opinion was as prevalent among northern Sudanese as among southern Sudanese, even though the hope of peace was widely shared.

Curiously, though, the protraction of the talks appeared to surprise the people who were involved in them (as well as many other people, in Sudan and around the world). To begin with, when the Machakos Protocol was signed, the common expectation was that the talks 'would all be finished in three months'.[88] However schedules and deadlines quickly began to slip. As mentioned above, following a series of military victories and reversals for both the government and the SPLM/A, the government walked out of the next round of talks after just two weeks, on 2 September 2002. Eventually, the second round of talks resumed in Machakos in October. It was then followed by a third round in Karen, Nairobi, beginning on 22 January 2003, and then by more rounds during the first half of 2003. In May 2003, Sumbeiywo talked of having a 'completed draft agreement' by mid-August, though not necessarily a signed one.[89] But when the government rejected the 'Nakuru document' tabled at talks in Nakuru, Kenya, in May–July 2003, the peace process was set back again. More rounds of talks ensued and the USA attempted to set the end of 2003 as a deadline for reaching a final agreement.[90] But even when that deadline was missed, and the talks continued into 2004, mediators and observers were still prone to over-optimism, often expecting that the next breakthrough would be the decisive one, and that a final agreement was much nearer than in reality it turned out to be.[91] Thus, the round of talks that began in February 2004 was widely expected to be the final one: in March 2004, Bashir, Garang and the US Secretary of State Colin Powell all indicated that they expected a final agreement within a month.[92] Instead, that round of talks continued until May, when three new agreements were signed; and those agreements in turn led to further rounds of talks that ran through much of the rest of 2004.

Eventually, it took the end-of-year deadline set by the UN Security Council at its session in Nairobi in November 2004 for the parties at the talks to reach a final agreement, finalised at Naivasha on 31 December 2004 and then formally signed in Nairobi on 9 January 2005.

The third failing of the process between 2002 and 2004 was that it did not prevent the proliferation of other talks between the Sudanese government and armed or unarmed opposition groups. All of these took place in forums outside the IGAD talks in Kenya; some of them were externally mediated.

The most prominent of these talks involved the government and the SLM/A, later joined by JEM, on Darfur. The first such round was convened in N'djamena, Chad, in September 2003, at which the government and the SLM/A agreed a one-month ceasefire, which was largely ineffective.[93] At a second round of talks in Abéché, Chad, in October 2003, the parties failed to agree an extension to the ceasefire, and the SLM/A criticised Chad's mediation as being too friendly to the government, and called instead for 'neutral observers from different countries'.[94] In December 2003, Darfurian members of Sudan's National Assembly described the talks as a 'waste of time' and called for a 'quick international intervention to protect civilians', and for the issue to be discussed at the talks in Kenya.[95] Instead, talks on Darfur continued to be held separately from the talks in Kenya, during the course of 2004 being hosted by Chad, Ethiopia, Libya and Nigeria. In April 2004 the parties agreed to a 'humanitarian ceasefire' in Darfur, to be monitored by an international ceasefire commission, and in November the parties agreed the 'Abuja protocols' on security and humanitarian matters.[96] But the ceasefire and protocols were repeatedly violated and proved largely ineffective, and as of the end of 2004, fighting in Darfur and sporadic talks for Darfur were continuing.[97]

Less conspicuously, throughout this period the government also continued to hold talks with the NDA, usually in Cairo but also in Saudi Arabia. Unlike the Darfur talks, there was no foreign participation in these talks. However the talks were similar in that they failed to produce an effective agreement. In December 2003 the government signed a 'framework agreement' with the NDA in Jeddah, Saudi Arabia, which led only to more talks. At the same time it refused to allow the Beja Congress and the Rashaida Free Lions – both members of the NDA – to participate in the talks, which meant that the talks were essentially between the government and the mainstream DUP, led by Mohammed Othman al-Mirghani. Meanwhile the government continued to hold occasional talks in Khartoum with the Umma Party, a DUP faction and other factions. These yielded modest results for the government, such as the defection of individuals or small groups of opposition politicians to join the government. However, as with the Darfur and NDA talks, no overall agreement was reached, nor was any attempt made to harmonise the talks with those going on in Kenya.[98]

Collectively, these talks raised questions about the validity of the process in Kenya or the agreements arising from it. In particular, they highlighted the exclusivity of the process in Kenya, which was restricted to the government and the SPLM/A, and which excluded Egypt.[99] By extension, they illustrated that it was wrong to claim that the government–SPLM/A talks were providing a 'comprehensive' solution to Sudan's civil war. Ultimately, the CPA was comprehensive only in the sense that it covered all issues between the government and the SPLM/A; it was not comprehensive in the sense of providing a comprehensive peace – as was illustrated by the continuing conflicts in Darfur and the east, and the continuing negotiations between the government and various armed and unarmed groups and opposition parties.

Responses to the peace process and developments between 2002 and 2004

The combination of positive and negative developments between 2002 and 2004 – the agreements and the failings outlined above – presented the mediators at the IGAD talks with questions about how to proceed with their mediation, and what to do about Darfur.

After the Machakos Protocol was signed in July 2002, some Sudanese and foreign observers warned against the exclusivity of the peace process in Kenya. Opposition parties and leaders lobbied to be included in the process, especially if they were not engaged in separate talks with the government.[100] Some also warned that the restriction of the talks in Kenya to the government and the SPLM/A, on the grounds that they were the two main arms-bearing parties, was an invitation to other groups to take up arms (if they had not already done so) and to resort to violence to make themselves heard. The warnings were frank and pessimistic, and sometimes threatening, and the escalation of the Darfur conflict during 2003 seemed to vindicate them. In the words of Sadiq al-Mahdi, for example, in December 2003:

> If the peace process is a bilateral process, it will be a very temporary peace that will unravel very soon. … There is a cocktail of ethnic based political dissent, armed and supported from outside. [Darfur] is going to be copied by others unless problems are universally addressed.[101]

Meanwhile, external observers and INGOs such as the UK-based Justice Africa and the International Crisis Group made similar warnings. Thus, for example, in March 2004 Crisis Group warned that 'Sudan, where prospects for peace had looked so promising for much of 2003, has become a potential horror story in 2004'.[102] But with the apparent progress in Kenya, few people except some Sudanese opposition figures opposed the continuation of the talks in Kenya. Instead, observers and INGOs tended to call for stronger international mediation in the Darfur talks and for the process in Kenya to be concluded, so that it might provide a model for resolving the conflict in Darfur and allow international attention to focus on that problem.[103] In effect, the presumption was that it was too late to change the framework of the IGAD talks.

As for the troika and other IPF members, they did not ignore the problems. Even before the escalation of the Darfur conflict, the US government had warned about violations of the government–SPLM/A ceasefire. In a statement in late January 2003, for example, it said that any offensives in Western Upper Nile or troop build-ups at garrison towns in Southern Sudan constituted 'a flagrant violation' of the ceasefire. It further warned that if the reports of attacks were true, the Sudanese government risked 'losing its credibility as a serious partner for peace with both the United Sates and the international community'.[104] To some extent this was what some INGOs warned. In April 2003, for example, the UK-based NGO Christian Aid wrote:

> The international community should not undermine Machakos process [sic] by overlooking, for reasons of political expediency, serious violations of the cessation of hostilities and monitoring. It is vital that the international community holds the parties to the peace publicly accountable for violations.[105]

But as violations of the government–SPLM/A ceasefire became less frequent, and the IGAD process in Kenya moved slowly forward, it was the escalation of the Darfur conflict that raised questions about the Sudanese government's commitment to peace.

The response of the troika and IPF members to the Darfur conflict was at first slight, but slowly became more substantial. In 2003 the USA and the IPF took no public action, despite the growing scale of the conflict in Darfur and warnings and advice from some Sudanese and NGOs such as Justice Africa and the International Crisis Group. One recommendation that seemed to be ignored was Crisis Group's recommendation in December 2003 that the troika and the IPF '[b]egin consultations on a possible joint mediation mechanism that could help the Sudan government and rebels in the west address more comprehensively the resolution of the Darfur conflict'.[106] During 2004, however, the scale of the conflict in Darfur and its human costs – and the accompanying international outcry – propelled the troika and IPF members to respond more actively to the situation. Their response, however, did little about the nascent peace process for Darfur, for although the troika and the EU made some effort to involve themselves in the Darfur talks, this was largely ineffective. Instead, their response was manifested principally in four UN Security Council resolutions on Sudan during 2004, a vast increase in funding for relief operations in Darfur, and support for an increased AU ceasefire-monitoring mission in Darfur.[107] Meanwhile the US Congress kept in place a bill designed to exert pressure on Sudan, the Sudan Peace Act, but on the basis that the parties had not abandoned the talks in Kenya the US government did not implement the punitive measures that the act threatened. The US Congress also drafted a 'Darfur Accountability Act'.

These responses were largely ineffective, as the continuation of the Darfur conflict and the failure of the Darfur talks showed at the time. That the troika and the IPF did not take stronger action is indicative of the dilemma in which they found themselves, and the choice that they consciously or unconsciously made, namely to prioritise getting an overall peace agreement out of the peace talks in Kenya over resolution of the conflict in Darfur.

Assessing the internationalised IGAD initiative

Certainly, the positive outcome of the internationalised IGAD process was that it produced the CPA, which was the first overall agreement between the government and the SPLM/A to end their two-decade old war. The process also produced a ceasefire that by the time the CPA was signed had already lasted for more than two years. But on the negative side, the process failed to prevent the escalation of the Darfur conflict and possibly contributed, indirectly, to that conflict and potentially to others. Events will be the final judge of the process between 2002 and 2004 – in particular whether the CPA holds and, to a lesser extent, how long it takes for the Darfur conflict to be resolved, or end, and at what cost.

In the meantime, however, some observations about mediation in this period can be made. Firstly, in so far as the troika and the IPF wanted to advance the peace process and see an end to the war, the basic aim of international mediation in Sudan between 2002 and 2004 was achieved. Secondly, as already indicated, the main determinants of the positive outcome of the peace talks in Kenya – namely the CPA and the ceasefire – were contextual: they were the changes in the domestic, regional and international contexts, which entailed stronger external mediation and greater tractability from the parties. It is true that some people saw the conflict as ripe for resolution. But it is another question whether this perception was necessary for the talks to produce a peace agreement, and we will consider this more closely in Chapter 5. Process-related factors – such as the progression through sequential rounds of talks, with the participation of influential mediators and a dedicated secretariat – were evidently also important in bringing about the outcome. These factors were also partly a manifestation of the commitment of some international actors to resolving Sudan's war. The troika and the IPF, their participation in and funding of the talks, the UN Security Council resolutions, and the mechanisms that they established and supported (such as the JMC and the CPMT): these reflected a more credible international commitment to resolving the war than ever before. However these commitments were not accompanied by an equal commitment from the parties to resolving the war peacefully.

As a result, the prospects of the peace settlement reached during 2002–4 were mixed: in the short term they were good, because international interest in and commitment to the settlement were relatively strong. That commitment was manifested in the actions taken by the UN Security Council, culminating in the authorisation in mid-2004 of an advance mission to prepare for an eventual UN peacekeeping mission in Sudan (UNMIS) that would support the CPA.[108] But the longer-term prospects of the peace settlement were less certain, because potential spoilers (domestic and external) of the agreement had not been dealt with, and the commitment of the parties to the agreement appeared to be weak.

DARFUR MEDIATION AND FRAGMENTATION

When the CPA was signed in early January 2005, peacemaking efforts for Darfur remained slight in comparison with the strident international outcries about the conflict. Nonetheless, efforts were being made and appeared to be becoming more systematic, though ultimately the outcomes were poor.

AU-led Abuja talks

After the unsuccessful start to Darfur talks in September and October 2003, and the humanitarian ceasefire agreement signed in Ndjamena in April 2004, a peace process for Darfur had begun to take shape, with the AU leading the mediation and Addis Ababa and Abuja hosting talks. In April 2004 the AU appointed Hamid Elgabid, a former Nigerien prime minister, as head of the AU mediation team for the talks, but after a disappointing performance as mediator he was replaced in September by Sam Ibok, a Nigerian diplomat and AU official.[109] In February 2005 a new round of talks loosely began, and in May the AU appointed Salim Ahmed Salim, the former OAU secretary-general, as special envoy for Darfur, supported by Ibok's mediation team. In April the government, JEM and the SLM/A signed a 'framework protocol' for the resolution of the Darfur conflict. This essentially was an agreement to negotiate, and was followed up by a 'Declaration of Principles' in July 2005, copying the example of the 1993 DOP in the SPLM–GOS talks. A sixth round of talks in Abuja ran from mid-September to 20 October, and was meant to make progress on power sharing, wealth sharing and security arrangements.

In November a seventh round of talks began in Abuja. Successive deadlines of the end of December 2005 and then the end of February 2006, set by the UN Security Council and UN and AU officials, were missed, as the talks made little progress.[110] On 12 March 2006 Sam Ibok issued a press statement saying that the mediation team's experience over the previous 16 months had led it 'to conclude that there is neither good faith nor commitment on the part of any of the parties'[111] All the same, the AU Peace and Security Council set a deadline of the end of April 2006 for a peace agreement for Darfur, and the UN Security Council endorsed this deadline. In mid-April, JEM and the SLM/A warned that the lack of concessions being made by the government meant that the peace process was at imminent risk of collapse.[112] Five days before the end-of-April deadline, the mediators presented the parties with the draft DPA. When the parties stalled on accepting the text and agreement, the AU conceded an extension, and in a flurry of international diplomacy senior officials from the USA and UK (respectively the US Secretary of State for Africa, Robert Zoellick, and the British Secretary of State for Development, Hilary Benn) flew in to Abuja to urge the parties to reach an agreement. Eventually, the diplomatic pressure produced a limited agreement: on 5 May 2006 the government and one SLM faction, led by Minni Minnawi, signed the DPA.

However, the agreement was still-born, as the culminating stages of the talks were fatally flawed by a combination of factors. The DPA text was drafted too quickly and dominated by the AU mediation team and its advisers, rather than being developed more slowly through negotiations between the parties themselves. JEM did not participate fully in the talks, and the mediators underestimated the importance of JEM being part of a peace agreement for Darfur, if the agreement was to be effective and worthwhile. Collectively, the mediation was well intentioned, but hubristic in its self-belief and ability to produce a technically adequate peace agreement.[113]

Subsequently, the SLM/A of Abdul Wahid said that it had rejected the DPA on procedural, legal and technical grounds. Explaining this, Abaker

Mohamed Abuelbashar, who was the SLM/A head of the wealth-sharing 'commission' (committee) at the talks, argued:

> The AU Mediation concluded in February 2006 that there is no need for more plenary; accordingly they decided to produce one compiled document for the Parties to sign. Since then there were no formal negotiations, particularly in the Wealth Sharing and Power Sharing Commissions. As a result there were many issues in all Commissions left out. The legitimate question is on what basis the Movement has to sign an agreement which it did not participate in discussing?
>
> ... The compiled document was prepared 6 weeks before it was presented to the Movements on 25th April 2006, but it was kept in AU drawers, and then presented to the Movements when they were given just 5 days to respond and sign it. Bear in mind that there were issues that had not previously been discussed at all.[114]

Such criticisms glossed over the failure of the parties themselves to negotiate in earnest during the preceding months, and the failure of the rebels not to factionalise. But the criticisms also echoed the criticisms of some of the more experienced advisers in the AU mediation team. Reflecting on the DPA talks, Jeremy Brickhill, a security adviser seconded to the AU mediation team who had also been an adviser during parts of the IGAD CPA talks, wrote of 'the disastrous international and AU strategy for the Abuja peace talks'.[115] Laurie Nathan, a conflict-resolution specialist who was present as a resource person in the final Abuja talks, wrote in September 2006 that the talks had three primary dynamics:

> the negotiating parties were unwilling to engage in negotiations and failed to forge agreements; the AU and its international partners, desperate for a quick accord, pursued a counter-productive strategy of deadline diplomacy that inhibited progress; and the mediators were consequently unable to undertake effective mediation. As a result of these dynamics, the DPA was not a negotiated settlement and its fulfilment was bound to experience severe difficulties.[116]

As Nathan noted, 'the manner in which peace agreements are prepared and concluded is as important as their contents'.[117]

Post-DPA disarray

The inadequacy of the DPA was immediately apparent, but the international community backed it nonetheless. In the weeks after the agreement was signed, additional mediation efforts were made to persuade 'non-signatories' to sign up, but although well intentioned, these efforts were also doomed. On 8 June 2006 some members of the SLM-Abdul Wahid and JEM signed a 'declaration of commitment' to the DPA, but at the same time the rest of JEM and other non-signatories (though not SLM-Abdul Wahid) announced in Asmara the formation of the National Redemption Front. Meanwhile in Darfur fighting had broken out between rebel factions, and public protests in some of the displaced persons' camps – though not representative of all views – showed widespread rejection of the DPA. Nonetheless, the government and Minni Minnawi took advantage of the notional peace agreement, and simultaneously continued trying to win over or eliminate factions of rebels, exploiting the rebels' susceptibility to factionalism, much as the government had done with the SPLM/A in the civil war. In August Minni Minnawi was sworn in as a senior assistant to President Bashir, which officially made him the fourth most senior figure in government (after the president and two vice-presidents), and head of the Transitional Darfur Regional Authority, which in theory was to be set up under the DPA, but which did not materialise. In November 2006 the government signed an agreement in Tripoli with Abul Gassim Imam, a former SLA commander, although that month some members of Minni Minnawi's faction defected away from the government and joined the nascent National Redemption Front.[118]

Subsequent developments in 2007–9 continued the pattern seen in the last round of Abuja talks and in the months immediately after the DPA was signed. Beyond the appointment of Minnawi, the agreement was essentially not implemented, and there was no sustained ceasefire or disarmament. All the same, international mediation efforts adhered to the implicit goal of consolidating or enlarging the DPA. The mediation was led jointly by Salim Ahmed Salim, for the AU, and Jan Eliasson, who was appointed UN Special Envoy for Darfur at the end of 2006. But their effectiveness was handicapped by a combination of factors, in particular their failure to accord a greater role for JEM and SLM-Abdul Wahid in any eventual peace talks, and their apparent belief that the onus of responsibility lay mainly on the rebels and that the government did not need to negotiate much more than an addendum to the DPA. In August 2007 the mediators convened a pre-talks meeting at Arusha, Tanzania, at which a number of minor rebel factions (but not JEM or SLM-Abdul Wahid) agreed a common negotiating platform for direct talks with the government and recommended that final talks be held within two to three months.[119] Sporadic talks between rebel factions were also held in Juba, at the SPLM's invitation. In October 2007 all-party talks began in Sirte, Libya, but were almost immediately abandoned because JEM, SLM-Abdul Wahid and the SLM Unity faction were not attending. Symptomatic of the government's confidence that it did not need to negotiate in earnest, the 'Darfur portfolio' at this time was handled not by a noted peace negotiator but by Nafi Ali Nafi, an assistant to the president with strong connections to the national security organisation, the National Security and Intelligence Service (NSIS), and Salah Abdallah Gosh, the head of the NSIS. With no prospect of being held to account, the Sirte talks presented the government with an easy opportunity to announce a unilateral ceasefire in Darfur, which it then did not observe.[120]

Given its problematic basis, the mediator's approach to peace talks made no progress, and mediation efforts gradually fell into disarray. After some months of internal wrangling, in mid-2008 a new joint AU–UN chief mediator for Darfur, Djibril Bassolé, was appointed. In his contacts with JEM and the SLM/A, Bassolé had the advantage of not being closely associated with the DPA, but efforts to organise new peace talks were complicated by a profusion of offers from Egypt, Libya and Qatar, often motivated more by regional political rivalry than by concern to resolve the conflict. Amid these efforts, Bassolé struggled to generate a concerted approach to resolving the conflict. Moreover, other developments during this period overshadowed and in some ways complicated efforts to convene talks.[121]

Internationally, much attention was given to efforts to arrange a transition from AMIS to UNAMID, which eventually happened at the start of 2008. In May 2008 a column of JEM forces crossed North Darfur and North Kordofan and made a surprise attack on Khartoum, although they were repelled in Omdurman. Much attention also focused on the question of justice: in June 2008 the chief prosecutor of the International Criminal Court (ICC), Luis Moreno Ocampo, announced his charges against President Bashir and stated that he was seeking an arrest warrant, which the ICC judges subsequently issued in March 2009. In October 2008 the government launched a short-lived and ineffective internal peace initiative, known as the 'People of Sudan' initiative. Lastly, fluctuating relations between Sudan and Chad also diverted attention, and between 2006 and 2009 the two countries signed a number of agreements which were meant to end hostilities between them, but which were not implemented effectively.[122] Amid these developments, during the rest of 2008 and 2009 the totality of talks assisted by the AU–UN mediation and Egypt, Libya and Qatar amounted only to various preparatory talks between some of the rebel factions, and initial talks between JEM and the government, held in Doha, Qatar. The latter, in February 2009, constituted the first direct talks between the government and JEM since the abortive DPA talks in Abuja in 2006, and produced only an agreement to continue talks.

The failure to reach a peace agreement or political settlement to the Darfur conflict between 2005 and 2009 was only leavened by the parallel implementation of the CPA and separate progress on reaching a political settlement for the low-level conflict in Eastern Sudan. The fact that the CPA did not cover Eastern Sudan, and that it demanded the withdrawal of SPLA troops from the region, left the SPLM/A's former partners in the east, the Beja Congress and the Rashaida Free Lions, unable to pose a significant threat to the government. Needing to reach an agreement which gave some rewards, the Beja Congress and the Rashaida Free Lions therefore announced the formation of the Eastern Front in February 2005. For its part, the government also needed to reach an agreement, as the vital economic importance of the east meant that it could not afford an escalation in conflict in the region (in contrast with Darfur). In low-profile talks hosted and mediated by Eritrea, and helped by some Track 3 initiatives to prepare the Eastern Front, on 19 June 2006 the government and the Eastern Front agreed a 'Declaration of principles for the resolution of the conflict in Eastern Sudan'. Following further talks on security arrangements and power sharing, on 14 October 2006 the government and the Eastern Front signed an Eastern Sudan Peace Agreement (ESPA).[123] This agreement brought an end to the Eastern Front's very weak armed challenge to the government, in return for a small share of positions in central government and various undertakings to support development in the east.

Assessing the Darfur mediation

In terms of resolving conflict and making peace, the overall results of mediation efforts for Darfur between 2005 and 2009 were very poor. It was not the first time that deadlines had been set and missed, or that an agreement had been signed between the government and only one or several rebel factions. Nor was it the first time that peace talks had been divisive and had caused or exacerbated splits among rebels, in some cases with the government's encouragement.[124] But it was the first time that the international community had thrown its weight behind a partial agreement, the DPA, that did not have the backing of the main rebel groups or their supporters. The negotiated settlement of the very low-level conflict in Eastern Sudan (by then little more than a weak threat of conflict) did not make up for the failure to resolve the conflict in Darfur. Nor did the existence of the CPA diminish the need for efforts to find a negotiated settlement in Darfur.

Certainly contextual factors, such as the attitudes of the parties, were not conducive to an easily reached and successful outcome to talks for Darfur. But process factors – in particular the poor handling of what talks there were, and the poor approach to mediation both before and after the DPA

– clearly played a significant role in the failure to generate a peace process with traction and to reach an effective agreement. At the same time, the commitment of the international community to supporting peace talks and the search for a negotiated settlement to the conflict was uneven, especially in contrast with the more sustained commitment in the CPA talks. This was evident in the sudden surge in international pressure at the Abuja talks in 2006, and the subsequent ebbing and disarray in international mediation efforts. It is not surprising that in these circumstances credible commitments to a negotiated settlement were not forthcoming from the Sudanese government and the Darfur rebel groups.

Conclusion

Taken together, what do the various attempts to resolve the civil war and the Darfur conflict tell us? Firstly, and most basically, in the absence of reaching a final agreement, the most important criterion for measuring the success of peace efforts was or should have been progress on an agenda agreed to by the parties. Secondly, there was no single key determinant of the positive mediation outcome embodied by the CPA, but international context and process seem to have been important factors and, at a glance, more important than perceptions of a mutually hurting stalemate and a situation of 'ripeness for resolution'. Conversely, domestic factors were surely the most important determinant of failure. And thirdly, by extension, credible international commitment mattered both in helping to achieve a settlement through talks and in giving positive prospects to that settlement. Nonetheless, the capacity of external commitments to produce and sustain effective peace agreements remained less than the capacity of domestic parties to spoil an agreement or obstruct, as was manifested by the shortcomings in the CPA peace process between 2002 and 2004, and the DPA and subsequent efforts.

These are answers that invite more questions. In particular, what could mediators have done to have achieved a better outcome, such as the earlier settlement of the civil war? Or a peace agreement with wider participation or without the accompanying escalation of the conflict in Darfur? Or a swift settlement of the Darfur conflict after the CPA was signed in 2005? These questions will be considered in Chapter 5. Before then, however, it will be useful to consider the other dimension of constructive international engagement in Sudan's conflicts, namely humanitarian relief, and the foreign policies and strategies used by states that contributed to conflict resolution and relief efforts in Sudan.

3
RELIEF

Humanitarian relief has been the most consistent response of the international community to Sudan's conflicts. Over the course of the civil war after 1983 and the Darfur conflict after 2003, four roughly distinct periods in relief can be discerned. These are (i) 1983–9, when relief was mostly *ad hoc* and the foundations of longer-lasting structures began to be laid; (ii) 1989–2001, when relief was systematised, and the patterns of relief delivery were maintained year after year and were embodied by OLS and non-OLS relief; (iii) 2001–4, when the context for relief changed significantly and efforts were made to shift to peace-related activities and to terminate OLS; and (iv) 2004–5 and after, when a new humanitarian operation developed for Darfur. There are important questions to ask about the political effects of this aid, as well as the humanitarian effects. Did relief prolong the conflicts? Did it depoliticise the war-time humanitarian crises and have anti-democratic effects? This chapter explores what the aims of relief were and how it affected prospects for resolving conflict.

RELIEF BEFORE OPERATION LIFELINE SUDAN, 1983–9

Between 1983 and 1989 international relief in Sudan increased rapidly in response to humanitarian crises inside and outside the war zone. In the provision of relief, relatively little attention was paid to the role of the war. However, temporary frameworks for relief were set up, and the foundations were laid for the longer-term, more systematic provision of relief in the war.

Humanitarian crises and the response of relief agencies

During the early years of the war, a series of humanitarian crises occurred, establishing a pattern that was to continue throughout the war. Fighting in the war caused the internal displacement of large numbers of people, some of whom remained in the south, while others moved to the north, out of the war zone. Meanwhile, droughts in 1983 and 1984 and low rainfalls in other years caused harvest yields to fluctuate dramatically. The combination of these factors caused localised famines and widespread suffering, characterised by increased mortality rates and impoverishment.

In response, international governmental and non-governmental organisations organised large relief programmes, focused on delivering food aid to affected populations. At first these programmes were concentrated in the north, serving Darfur, Kordofan and the Red Sea Hills. But as relief organisations increasingly identified food shortages in the south, they began to launch relief programmes to serve these areas. Famine conditions had developed in some government-controlled garrison towns in the south as early as 1984. More generally, raiding on a large and prolonged scale by militias armed by the government led to the destruction of livestock and villages in the south, and the displacement of rural populations. Famine situations became more common in the south, and severe famine occurred in Bahr el-Ghazal in 1988.

The size of the early relief programmes grew rapidly, as did expenditure and the number of international organisations and NGOs dealing with relief. In 1985 the UN set up an Office for Emergency Operations in Sudan, a sub-office of its temporary Office for Emergency Operations in Africa. By then there were already some 57 NGOs in Sudan working with refugees, up from 23 in 1981 and seven in 1978;[1] in 1985 more than 400,000 tons of food aid was delivered to Sudan, and total foreign aid expenditure was around US$1bn, of which US aid accounted for some US$350m.[2] However, information about the impact of relief between 1983 and 1989 (and subsequently) was patchy.[3] Worst-case predictions that millions would die from famine were not fulfilled. On the other hand, even a relatively cautious estimate based on sample studies suggests that in 1984–5, which was possibly the period of highest mortality, as many as 250,000 may have died from famine.[4] These deaths should probably be understood to be the result of a 'health crisis' caused by mass displacement and changes to the health environment which raised mortality rates, rather than the result only of basic food shortages.[5]

The responses of the warring parties

The government and the SPLM/A were initially slow to respond to the humanitarian crises within the territory that they controlled. Indeed, it seems clear that in Northern Sudan public dismay at the government's slow and inadequate response to the 1984–5 famine was one of the motivating factors behind the uprising that overthrew Nimeiri in April 1985.[6] However, in May 1985 both the new government (the TMC) and the SPLM/A established their own formal relief organisations. The TMC established the Relief and Rehabilitation Commission (RRC), within what was then called the Ministry of Social Welfare, Zakat and the Displaced, while the SPLM/A established the Sudan Relief and Rehabilitation Association (SRRA).

The RRC and the SRRA were a significant step in the institutionalisation of relief systems in Sudan: in one form or another they remained in place for the rest of the war, through to 2004. At root they were intended to help co-operation with relief agencies and the delivery of relief. However they also constituted a means for regulating relief. Sadiq's government, for example, officially welcomed the work of international organisations and NGOs, but it also expected such organisations to be obedient to the government, as a policy statement by Sadiq in 1988 made clear:

> In order to achieve the utmost from this co-operation between the above organisations and the Government, it is necessary to unify communication channels and co-ordinate closely and constantly. All concerned Ministries are to monitor closely the work of these organisations and approve their programmes, activities and travel plans, in accordance with the Government's relevant policies, regulations and by-laws.[7]

The SPLM/A held similar expectations of the relationship between the SRRA and relief agencies. As Alex de Waal argues, at least in its early years the SRRA generally lacked a 'strong mandate or a genuine humanitarian strategy', and most if not all of its officials were soldiers drawn from the SPLA.[8]

More significantly, however, the existence of the RRC and the SRRA did not mean that the government and the SPLM/A were committed to minimising humanitarian crises and maximising the correct use of relief. From the beginning of the war, military methods and actions by both the government and the SPLM/A had – as David Keen, Alex de Waal and others have argued – been fundamental to the creation of the famines and humanitarian crises in Sudan.[9] In short, each side was willing to exploit famine as a tool for control in the war and more widely in Sudan. This did not change with the establishment of the RRC and the SRRA, nor on the part of the government did it change with the election of Sadiq in 1986. Keen, for example, argues that '[t]he democratic government of Sadiq el Mahdi was among those that promoted famine most vigorously'.[10] The SPLM/A also continued to pursue an opportunistic approach to relief, exemplified by a statement by John Garang on Radio SPLA in May 1985, in which he said:

'[The government's] garrison towns in the South are famine-stricken and are real disaster areas, and this is good; our military strategy is working.'[11] Similarly, in an interview in November 1988 Garang admitted that the SPLM/A had been blocking food supplies. He justified the obstruction with the claim that the government had been manipulating relief agencies in the north and allowing food intended for displaced southerners to be stolen by traders and the army.[12]

Temporary frameworks for relief

With the government and the SPLM/A pursuing their own official and unofficial relief strategies, and relief agencies aiming to improve their response to the successive crises in Sudan (and in particular to reach populations in Southern Sudan that were otherwise inaccessible because of the war), a number of initiatives and frameworks for relief in Sudan were attempted between 1985 and 1989. In March 1986 a basic framework for the provision of relief in the south was established when the Combined Agencies Relief Team was set up in Juba.[13] At around the same time, 18 NGOs and INGOs, including Oxfam, Sudanaid, the Sudan Council of Churches (SCC) and World Vision, formed a group called the Agencies Involved in Southern Sudan and, in July 1986, called for an immediate 'food truce in South Sudan'.[14] In the same year, it is alleged that a group of INGOs gave US$150,000 to the SRRA in secret, intended mainly for relief in Bahr el-Ghazal, but that little of the relief was delivered.[15]

Also during 1986, the UN made an abortive attempt to start an airlift to the south, called Operation Rainbow. However the government took exception to the operation (and how it was announced), and responded by expelling the UN Resident Co-ordinator in Sudan, Winston Prattley, and forcing the operation to stop after only eleven flights.[16] International donors subsequently ruled out providing relief to SPLM/A-held areas in the south during 1987 and most of 1988. But at the end of 1988 the UN Children's Fund (UNICEF) opened a 'co-ordinating office' in Nairobi to assist NGOs that were starting small-scale operations in SPLM/A-held areas.[17] At the time, the UN described its relief activities in Sudan as an 'interim programme', the strategy of which was framed around two overall objectives:

(a) to reduce incidence of famine, starvation and disease throughout the south;

(b) to increase the support available to persons in situ so that they are not forced to migrate or undertake hazardous forays in search of food.[18]

However, the UN also recognised, at least officially, that its programme could not solve Sudan's problems. Rather, the 'ultimate solution' was 'to remove the causes of displacement by establishing a lasting peace, thereby prompting development in the areas most affected by war, drought and extreme poverty'.[19]

Despite these words, UN and non-governmental relief agencies still tended to understate the political dimensions of the humanitarian crises in Sudan. This was partly because of the recurrence of droughts and severe dry seasons, and the persistent tendency in the 1970s and 1980s to assume that famines were natural phenomena. That assumption was widespread among Westerners and was often reinforced by the way in which international media covered the humanitarian crises in Sudan (which echoed the coverage of famine crises in Ethiopia and the Sahel), and sometimes by the way in which development and relief agencies themselves represented the crises, stripped of their political contexts. It was also true that Sudan was faced with other challenges, in particular a refugee population of around one million for much of the second half of the 1980s.[20] In this context, it was perhaps difficult to be certain about the severity and role of the civil war itself, and it was sometimes easier to talk instead of 'civil strife', even though the government itself estimated that by 1988 two million people had been internally displaced.[21]

Assessing relief before OLS

Relief in Sudan before OLS, between 1983 and the start of 1989, was largely *ad hoc* and aimed straightforwardly at saving lives and reducing suffering. However, to a small degree, relief was sometimes intended to benefit one side rather than the other. This was true of US relief while Nimeiri was in power, when the USA wanted Nimeiri to survive but did not want to provide support for the SPLM/A. However, after the fall of Nimeiri and the arrival of a Sudanese government over which the USA found it had little influence, US support for the Sudanese government began to decline.

Unsurprisingly, there is no evidence during this period to suggest that relief prolonged the war or significantly contributed to its duration: these were only the first six years of the war. However, this period does offer evidence of relief contributing to the depoliticisation of humanitarian crises. Externally, that depoliticisation was exemplified by the way in which the crises in Sudan were represented and seen internationally. Domestically, the depoliticisation was manifested by the gradual institutionalisation of relief systems that did not involve domestic political accountability. It is debatable just how much the 1985 uprising was motivated by the famine (some participants in the uprising say that famine was not a significant factor).[22]

However, it seems clear that the great expansion of relief in the first half of the 1980s meant that by 1985 the foundations had already been laid for what de Waal accurately calls 'a loss of domestic political accountability for humanitarian action', and that this trend continued through to 1989.[23]

Overall, therefore, it is fair to say that relief during this period was of some help in responding to humanitarian needs. It did not help to resolve the conflict, but nor did it hinder doing so, except to the degree that it sometimes obscured the political causes of the humanitarian crises. In late 1988 and early 1989, however, the possibility of linking relief with peace was briefly raised during the formation of OLS, the relief framework that succeeded the preceding temporary frameworks and which would last through to 2001 and beyond.

OPERATION LIFELINE SUDAN AND RELIEF, 1989–2001

After 1989 the provision of relief in Sudan became systematised in the form of OLS, a framework agreed with the warring parties that was briefly associated with resolving the war. However, OLS became detached from the question of peace as it developed into a longer-term operation, contending with the responses and tactics of the government and the SPLM/A, and other war-related difficulties in the field. In turn, OLS and relief organisations tried to respond to the problems they encountered, but with limited success.

The origins of OLS

The possibility of linking relief with peace – or, more accurately, with a peace process – arose during the negotiations between the government and the SPLM/A that led up to and followed the DUP–SPLM/A accord signed in November 1988. The SPLM/A had tabled relief for discussion in its talks with the DUP in the months leading up to the accord. At first, however, the DUP was reluctant to give the issue prominence, possibly because, as de Waal suggests, 'it feared that a re-run of Operation Rainbow would lead to an abrogation of Sudanese sovereignty'.[24] However, at the press conference at the signing of the accord, the DUP joined with the SPLM/A in calling for emergency relief to be extended to the whole of Sudan, north and south. It was in the context of this call, and the government's faltering uptake of the accord over the first quarter of 1989, that a new framework for relief began to be made, culminating in OLS.

By late 1988 the severity of the humanitarian crises in Sudan had already convinced the UN that it should expand its operations in Southern Sudan.

This view did not change when, after lengthy negotiations, the International Committee of the Red Cross (ICRC) began relief and rehabilitation work in government- and SPLM/A-held areas in December 1988.[25] Shortly afterwards, the SPLM/A launched its largest offensive to date, capturing a number of towns and entering the Nuba Mountains. On the back of this, Garang publicised the idea that the SPLM/A was aiming to create a 'New Sudan' and invited the UN to meet with him outside Sudan, indicating however that he was opposed to a ceasefire. The UN Secretary-General's Special Representative for Sudan, James Grant (the head of UNICEF), accepted and on 9 March 1989 he met with Lam Akol, Garang's representative, in Addis Ababa. Grant proposed a six-month ceasefire; Akol rejected this and instead agreed to 'corridors of tranquillity' through which relief could be delivered. Grant accepted. Based on this and subsequent verbal commitments (including assurances from the government), and a UN 'plan of action', OLS thus came into existence on 1 April 1989.[26]

At the time, the creation of OLS was a new and significant step, both for the UN and for the SPLM/A. The UN had never before dealt directly with what would previously have been considered only a rebel movement, fighting against a sovereign African state. It was therefore, as de Waal comments, a political coup for the SPLM/A to receive *de facto* recognition from the UN. Furthermore the SPLM/A had more to gain than the government from the establishment of a major relief programme covering Southern Sudan and the areas under its control, since up until then relief had mainly been going only to Northern Sudan and government-held areas in the south. In short, like the government, the SPLM/A had 'its own clear political and material interests in a UN-led relief operation', and Garang consequently declared (unilaterally) a one-month ceasefire in May as a gesture of co-operation.[27]

However, OLS was soon interrupted by the change of government in Khartoum. Four months after the coup, Bashir issued a decree terminating OLS, and in November the new government closed its airspace to relief flights. As Millard Burr and Robert Collins describe, the government appeared to want to pursue a new approach to foreign aid, and it indicated its dissatisfaction with existing practices when the new UN Resident Representative, Michael Priestley, was granted an interview with the Sudanese President on 16 November 1989. Bashir claimed that OLS had been used to provide the SPLA with material assistance, and that this had contributed to the SPLA gains in Bahr el-Ghazal. He therefore warned that if OLS was to resume, it would depend on much greater co-ordination with the government.[28]

Faced with this attitude and the difficulty of raising funding while fighting was continuing in Southern Sudan, efforts to re-launch OLS at first stalled.

But in the absence of alternative mechanisms for getting relief to Southern Sudan, relief officials were reluctant to give up on the idea of OLS. The idea that OLS could contribute to peace also remained: as of September 1989, the UN felt able to say that OLS showed that humanitarian programmes undertaken by neutral and impartial parties could be 'catalysts for peace'.[29] Shortly afterwards, efforts to re-launch OLS were boosted by the talks between the government and the SPLM/A mediated by Jimmy Carter and held in Nairobi. Although the talks were unsuccessful on political matters, on relief they produced the basis of an agreement. Following this, on 26 December the government announced that OLS would resume. In accordance again with a UN-drafted 'plan of action', and after talks with donors in late March 1990, the government agreed to the resumption of operations under the principle of neutrality.[30] The SPLM/A disputed the shares of relief proposed under OLS, but gave its agreement again to the principle of OLS, thereby allowing operations to resume.[31]

The framework and operation of OLS

The framework and *modus operandi* established for OLS in 1989–90 would remain largely unchanged for the next decade. OLS was organised in two geographic sectors, the northern and southern sectors. Heading it was the most senior UN official in Sudan, the UN Co-ordinator for Emergency and Relief Operations, later known as the Humanitarian Co-ordinator, who was based in Khartoum and also held the title of UN Resident Co-ordinator. The World Food Programme (WFP) was the lead agency for OLS in the northern sector, and UNICEF the lead agency for OLS in the southern sector. Under the auspices of OLS, a consortium of other UN agencies and local and international NGOs also worked in relief in the two sectors. Relief in the northern sector was delivered through Port Sudan and by air, land, rail and river routes through the north; relief for the southern sector was delivered by air and land from Lokichokio, a small settlement in the north-west of Kenya, close to the border with Sudan, which OLS used as a forward staging and logistics base.

The volume and nature of relief delivered through OLS, and the geographical distribution and means, varied over the years according to assessed needs, available resources and logistical constraints. Estimated relief needs fluctuated widely, as did levels of assistance provided. Thus, for example, the total value of estimated needs in 1991 was US$717m – which was higher than for several years, because of a famine crisis in 1990–1 – whereas in 1993 and 1994 it was US$195m and US$186m respectively. The total value of assistance actually provided was sometimes close to the assessed needs, and at other times much less, as in 1997, when it was around only 40 per cent of assessed needs.³² Meanwhile, the number of NGOs and INGOs operating within OLS also varied, rising from around six or seven in 1992 to nearly 40 in 1996 and some 58 in 1999 (18 in the northern sector, 40 in the southern sector). As of August 1999, about 10 INGOs were operating outside OLS.³³

In 1998 OLS reached a peak in terms of scale and complexity. Faced with a severe food crisis in Bahr el-Ghazal in 1998, OLS raised additional funds and increased deliveries. Finding that Lokichokio was too small to support the heavy cargo aircraft needed for flying relief into Southern Sudan, OLS sought and gained permission from the government to use El Obeid, a town in the northern sector, as a second logistics base for the south.³⁴ At the height of the crisis, WFP was delivering 15,000 tons of food per month to an estimated one million people, using a combination of air, river and road corridors (road accounting for about 40 per cent of deliveries). As a whole, in the year 1998–9 60 per cent of deliveries were by air, 33 per cent by road, and 7 per cent by barge.³⁵

The government response

From the beginning the Sudanese government responded to OLS with a mixture of support, suspicion and hostility. Despite the continuation and gradual consolidation of OLS, these attitudes persisted throughout the 1990s.

After initially stopping OLS, in December 1989 Bashir said that the continuation of OLS would depend on security considerations and on donors guaranteeing that relief would 'actually be delivered to the afflicted'. The government, he said, had ignored 'some malpractices'. Mohammed el-Amin Khalifa, a member of the governing RCC, alleged that when government troops occupied an area in need of relief, relief did not arrive, but when the SPLA did, relief arrived in large quantities, and arms came with it.³⁶ However, the government did not substantiate its claim. As Burr and Collins note:

> When the United Nations urged the junta to produce what Khalifa called 'irrefutable evidence that arms were being smuggled to the rebels through Operation Lifeline,' Bashir responded by reiterating that 'weapons were reaching rebels in Southern Sudan through a famine relief operation led by the United Nations.'³⁷

Regardless of its failure to substantiate its allegations, the government maintained a ban on relief flights from December 1989 to April 1990, when it allowed OLS to resume. The famine crisis of 1990–1 then contributed to the government's decision to accept the continuation of OLS, albeit with much bluster and denial about the severity of the crisis. This was epitomised by a government official in October 1990, who declared 'We will never accept any food aid, even if famine is declared.'[38]

During 1992–3 the government continued to reluctantly accept the continuation of OLS. In 1994 it signed the first written agreements with the UN and the SPLM/A governing OLS.[39] However, these tripartite agreements did not herald a change in the government's attitude towards OLS. As Ataul Karim et al. point out, the agreements ostensibly endorsed the principle of international access to war-affected populations, but they were also ambiguous about what constituted 'war-affected areas'.[40] The government exploited this ambiguity to try to limit the geographical scope of OLS. In November 1995 it went a step further, unilaterally abrogating the 1994 OLS agreement and in its place negotiating a new access agreement with the UN. Through this, the government sought to impose 'no-fly' zones, in addition to the flight bans that it had hitherto imposed.

The SPLM/A response

The SPLM/A responded to OLS partly as the government did, with a mixture of support, suspicion and criticism, but rarely with outright hostility. Although the SPLM/A was not a sovereign power, it had an interest in maximising control over relief and, if possible, in benefiting from it or minimising the benefit to the government. Occasionally the SPLM/A accused OLS or member agencies of meddling, as in September 1991, when the SPLM/A mainstream (SPLM/A-Torit) accused relief agencies of involvement in the SPLM/A split, which was also known as the 'Nasir coup':

> There is sufficient documented evidence that individuals within the NGO relief community were deeply and actively involved in the recent Nasir theoretical abortive coup by Commander Riek and Commander Lam. Relief planes and foreign relief personnel were the main agents used in the abortive coup. The movement strongly condemns the use of relief as a political weapon. [41]

The claim was unsubstantiated and was almost certainly false (the split in the SPLM/A was overwhelmingly the result of internal political dynamics). More commonly, though, the SPLM/A's criticisms of OLS were confined to technical matters and complaints. Over time, some SPLM/A officials felt – understandably, perhaps – that the UN agencies working in OLS tended to respect the government more than the SPLM/A, and that UN agencies were guilty of treating Southern Sudan as if it were a territory mandated to the UN for administration. As a result, according to one head of the Sudan Relief and Rehabilitation Commission (SRRC) – as the SRRA became known after 2003 – in its meetings with the UN, the SRRC/SRRA sometimes tried 'to make [the UN] realise that it should be them co-operating with us, not us with them'.[42]

Until the OLS agreements signed in 1994, the SPLM/A's acceptance of OLS was (like the government's) based on verbal rather than signed agreements. Following the killing of four aid workers by the SPLM/A in September 1992, near Nimule in Eastern Equatoria, UNICEF began to develop a set of 'ground rules' for the southern sector, which initially covered mainly security issues and to which the SPLM/A, but not the government, was party. This culminated in 1994 in the main SPLM/A factions signing an 'Agreement on Ground Rules', which covered pragmatic regulations for relief as well as principles and support for the 1989 Convention on the Rights of the Child, the 1949 Geneva Conventions, and the 1977 additional Protocols to the Geneva Conventions. But beyond these contents, the Ground Rules also represented an effort to improve the terms of access under which OLS operated. As Karim et al. have noted, at the start OLS had depended on 'corridors of tranquillity' linked to temporary ceasefires, but by mid-1991 it was depending more on ad hoc requests for access. The Ground Rules partly reflected relief agencies' wish to have a less contingent means of access, closer to an 'open corridors' approach.[43] As such, the Ground Rules helped OLS to expand its activities in the southern sector, while in the north OLS remained more constrained by the government.

Following the signing of the tripartite agreements in 1994, OLS continued to develop the Ground Rules in the southern sector, leading to the signing of a new agreement by the SPLM/A mainstream and the SSIM/A (the renamed SPLM/A faction led by Machar) in July and August 1995. To some extent this co-operation over the Ground Rules contributed to improvements in the civil administrative structures and practices of the two movements, in particular in the SPLM/A, as Karim *et al.* argue:

> The mutual obligations established within the Ground Rules ... played an important role in shaping the development of social welfare structures in opposition movement areas. In this regard, there is a symbiotic relation between the two processes. This can be seen most readily in relation to the programme of capacity building and institutional support that OLS ... developed for the humanitarian wings of the opposition movements.[44]

True though this was, up to a point, it did not ensure that the SPLM/A was henceforth always compliant with OLS and ready to allow unfettered humanitarian access. For example, in response to the government's flight bans, from 1996 the SPLM/A began to impose its own flight bans on a small number of locations.[45] Moreover, in SPLM/A-controlled areas as in government-controlled areas, problems of relief diversion, obstruction and insecurity persisted through the second half of the 1990s and beyond.

Problems in the field

In its operations, OLS encountered many of the problems that confront relief operations in any setting, such as bottlenecks in funding, difficult terrain, and logistical and communications constraints. But three kinds of problem – insecurity, obstruction and diversion of relief – are particularly relevant to assessing the humanitarian and political impact of the operation.

Despite the various OLS agreements, insecurity was a persistent problem for relief delivery. UN agencies, INGOs and local NGOs faced risks ranging from land-based fighting and aerial bombings, to shootings, hostage taking and mine explosions. Incidents – especially fighting and bombings – often necessitated the evacuation of staff and the suspension of activities; sometimes they merely delayed work. Table 3 gives some examples.

Table 3: **Examples of security-related incidents**

Date	Details
October 1992	4 international OLS relief workers killed by SPLM/A in Eastern Equatoria.[46]
1994–5	More than 50 evacuations or relocations of relief workers from locations in Southern Sudan.[47]
February 1995	11 international relief workers from UNICEF and INGOs taken hostage by militia in Waat for four days.[48]
May 1995	22 staff from UNICEF, WFP and barge crews taken hostage at Tonga, Upper Nile, and detained for several days.[49]
November 1996	3 international ICRC staff and 5 war-wounded discharged from ICRC hospital held hostage by militia for five weeks at Wunrok, Bahr el-Ghazal.[50]
1997–8	More than 200 relief staff evacuated from 37 locations.[51]
June 1998	2 WFP staff and 1 Sudanese Red Crescent Society worker shot and killed during ambush in government-held area of Nuba Mountains.[52]
May 1999	1 person killed and 3 injured (including 2 WFP staff) in attack on OLS barge convoy at Adok, Western Upper Nile.
December 1999	2 staff of NGO CARE International killed, and two taken hostage on road between Bentiu and Mayom, Upper Nile;

	8 church aid workers killed by Lord's Resistance Army in Eastern Equatoria.[53]
August 2000	Aerial bombardment of UN aircraft and facilities on ground at Mapel, Lakes Region, prompts UN to suspend operations.[54]
December 2000	2 NGO relief workers ambushed and killed in Eastern Equatoria.[55]
May 2001	ICRC pilot on scheduled flight killed by ground-fire in Eastern Equatoria.[56]

The OLS agreements did not prevent the warring parties from directly or indirectly obstructing relief agencies and their work. Indeed, as Table 4 shows, obstruction was common, occurring particularly in the form of delays or refusals to issue visas, import permits and travel permits.[57] More severely, obstruction often came in the form of refusal of access to specific areas. On air access, the government had more control than the SPLM/A, by virtue of having an air force and being more willing to threaten military action against any aircraft breaking a flight ban on a specific landing site or region. Nonetheless, as indicated, the SPLM/A also attempted to impose flight bans, and was able to threaten action against any aircraft breaking a ban.

Table 4: **Examples of obstruction of relief agencies**

Date	Details
September 1996– July 1997	Government refuses to issue permits for relief barge convoys, therefore no convoys travel.[58]
September 1997	SPLM/A expels Action Contre la Faim (ACF), an NGO-member of OLS.[59]
1997–8	Confiscation of communications equipment and looting of relief-agency compounds, including those in Bor, Juba, Malakal and Wau.[60]
January– March 1998	Government imposes a two-month ban on all flights to Bahr el-Ghazal.
April 2001	Government imposes requirement for OLS relief workers in SPLM/A-held areas to have entry visas, breaking with prior practice.[61]
April– August 1999	Bureaucratic delays to release of WFP shipments at Port Sudan, combined with insecurity in the area, contribute to temporary shortages of food stuffs.[62]
2000–1	Government and SPLM/A disagreement over air access routes delay efforts to launch an integrated relief programme for Nuba Mountains.[63]

Like insecurity and obstruction, the exploitation and diversion of relief materials are common problems for relief agencies in almost any situation. Relief materials are often diverted from their intended recipients by warring parties, private traders or civilians, who may gain control of the materials during their transportation or distribution. In Sudan, diversion of all kinds, but notably by the warring parties, occurred during the 1980s and persisted throughout the 1990s, despite the mechanisms of OLS and the related agreements. Such diversion occurred by a variety of means, some more blatant than others, as indicated by the examples of diversion before and during OLS in Table 5.

Table 5: **Examples of exploitation and diversion of relief**

Date	Details
February–September 1987	Relief convoys from Raga to Wau looted by government soldiers and subject to extortion; about 9,000 tons of relief food stored at Raga looted by government soldiers and local traders.[64]
June 1989	16 out of 50 wagons on a relief train from Muglad to Aweil looted en route through government and SPLM/A-held territory by villagers and armed men.[65]
January 1990	Government troops commandeer relief food in Juba after evacuation of relief workers (who subsequently returned).[66]
1991	Both SPLM/A factions loot UN camps at Bor and Kongor, and accuse each other of responsibility.[67]
January–March 1993	SPLM/A Nasir faction instigates establishment of relief centre at Yuai, near Waat, to its benefit in conflict with SPLM/A Mainstream.[68]
1994	At Jebel Lafon in Eastern Equatoria, SPLM/A faction led by William Nyuon uses starving children to attract relief which is diverted to soldiers.[69]
May 1994	954 tons out of total 1,439 tons looted from UN relief train by soldiers and civilians in government- and SPLM/A-held areas between Meiram and Aweil.[70]
June 1994	UN barge convoy forcibly stopped by SPLM/A in Jonglei and nearly 2,000 tons of food and non-food relief items looted over eight days.[71]
March 1996	UN barge and crew held for two days near Doleib Hill and 50 tons of food materials looted by unidentified militia.
April 1999	WFP-contracted food trucks looted in Eastern Equatoria, contributing to suspension of road deliveries in May.[72]

Diversion was sometimes the result of advance planning, rather than unpremeditated looting. As de Waal notes:

There were many incidents of relief food being taken to military stores to which relief staff were denied access, foreign NGO evacuations being required shortly after distributions, 'taxes' being levied on recipients of food relief, and other subterfuges.[73]

Both the government and the SRRA made use of fixed exchange rates to profit from relief agencies.[74] Government and rebel attacks sometimes targeted relief centres or areas that had just received food drops, and SPLM/A factions sometimes looted UN or OLS bases under the cover of rival attacks. Such attacks could be carefully timed, as Karim *et al.* noted in 1996:

> OLS-issued two-way radios are particularly prized objects in factional fighting, and there is evidence that they have been used (for example, by Kerubino) to listen to OLS networks in order to time attacks to coincide with relief deliveries.[75]

Military commanders also sometimes took advantage of official roles and responsibilities for relief to facilitate its diversion. Burr and Collins describe one example from 1989:

> In Malakal ... the sequestering of donor food by the government became a very real problem that was blamed on the military governor, Lieutenant Colonel Gatluak Deng, who took control of the distribution of food aid in September and appointed his personal representative as chair of the Malakal Relief Committee.[76]

The potential for diversion was increased by the close relationship between the government and the SPLM/A's relief organisations and their soldiers in the field. As Michael Medley notes, in the field the secretaries of the SRRA 'were usually soldiers assigned to it by the local commander'.[77] Therefore it is unsurprising that, as Medley claims, when abuses of relief or human rights were substantiated, the SPLM/A authorities usually insisted that it was the responsibility of the individuals involved, and not the SPLM/A itself.[78]

The tendency of the SPLM/A to try to 'capture' material and political benefits from OLS should be seen partly in the light of the movement's organisation and policies. The SPLM/A was weak at mobilising the populations under its control. In this it contrasted significantly with other insurgent movements, such as the Eritrean People's Liberation Front (EPLF) and the Eritrean People's Revolutionary Democratic Front (EPRDF), both of which were more effective at mobilising popular support. This weakness was recognised by some members of the SPLM/A, and was sometimes highlighted by disaffected former members or otherwise. For example, in his book *The Politics of Liberation in South Sudan: An Insider's View*, Peter Nyaba, a former SPLA captain, compares the SPLM/A's lack of a clear and simple position on the question of unity with the approach of the EPRDF, which used the slogan 'Peace is better than unity' to mobilise support.[79]

In Nyaba's view, the dependence of the SPLM/A on external resources – military and humanitarian – contributed to its failure to mobilise people under its control, and its lack of respect for human rights (at least in earlier periods). This was 'completely different from the Anyanya':

> With the Anyanya there wasn't relief. [But] with the SPLA it was systematic use of relief. [The SPLA] engineered displacements, for example moving people to Ethiopia. It used the humanitarian situation to feed the army.[80]

Such criticisms came not only from outside the SPLM/A. As one SPLM adviser at the peace talks in 2004 put it to the author, the movement was 'very strong as a military body, but not as a party'.[81] This was despite efforts by the SPLM/A during the 1990s to improve its human-rights record and its governance practices.

Detailed records or estimates of the overall level of relief diversion do not exist (the compilation of such data not being a priority for any of the parties involved). Evidently, though, the level of diversion on a single consignment of relief could range from nothing (for example on small consignments over whose delivery and distribution relief agencies could be confident of maintaining full control), to at least 60–70 per cent (taking the example of the looting of a relief train in May 1994). The estimate of one OLS logistician who worked on large-scale relief delivery for more than five years, including on WFP barges, was that on average around 30–40 per cent of all relief was diverted: diversion was 'inevitable', he felt, but ultimately did not matter, provided that 'the rest was going to people who needed it'.[82] Although that estimate is little more than an informed guess, it is plausible and resembles other estimates that have also pointed to a high overall level of diversion.

Reflecting the problems with insecurity, obstruction and diversion of relief, in 1994 the UN special rapporteur on human rights in Sudan concluded that looting of relief convoys or stores had 'become the order of the day'. As the rapporteur noted:

> While the different factions of SPLA must bear responsibility for the lootings committed by local commanders, the Government of

the Sudan is responsible for an arbitrary policy of denying access, including flight clearance, to areas that have a clear and incontestable need for humanitarian assistance.[83]

All the same, despite such condemnations, looting and access denials continued. The warring parties also continued sometimes to deny access even during ceasefires, as for example in 1995 when the government and the SPLM/A agreed in March a two-month ceasefire (negotiated by Jimmy Carter), which they then extended for two more months before letting it lapse in July.[84] Indeed, according to UN records, during the first half of 1995 the number of flight clearances denied by the government increased, and by June OLS was regularly being denied flight access to a monthly average of 12 locations. To add to this, in the second half of 1995, the SPLM/A 'prevented the delivery of food and non-food relief to populations along the river corridors', and the government blocked the departure of a relief train to northern Bahr el-Ghazal.[85]

The responses of OLS and relief agencies

Prompted by difficulties over access and fundraising – and also by donor concerns and calls from the Sudanese government and the SPLM/A for structural reforms – in the second half of 1995 the UN Department of Humanitarian Affairs commissioned a major review of OLS.[86] The review culminated in a long report, published in 1996, covering the mandate, structure, co-ordination and *modus operandi* of OLS.[87] The overall conclusion was that 'OLS should continue', but in a revised form, as 'a more unified humanitarian programme' which removed the divisions and differences in approach between the northern and southern sectors.[88] In favouring this option for the future of OLS, the review rejected three other options that it had considered, namely: (i) the transfer of all OLS co-ordination to government-held areas (an option favoured by the government); (ii) the replacement of OLS with a donor–INGO consortium', entailing a purely cross-border operation (an option favoured by the SPLM/A); and (iii) the formal splitting of the northern and southern OLS sectors.

The review contained much of merit, in particular its analysis of the problems of OLS's management and structure,[89] and its highlighting of instances where implementing a 'relief–development continuum' policy in government-held areas had benefited government war tactics of resettlement and land control.[90] The review was critical of OLS programming, saying:

> There is a lack of coherence and depth to much of OLS programming. ... A particular weakness is the failure to adequately monitor programme

delivery and implementation, as well as impact. As a consequence, little is known about the effectiveness of OLS programmes.[91]

The review also called for 'greater care' in the calculation of population and beneficiary figures, and for relief agencies to use 'more restraint' in their claims for the number of people assisted.[92]

However, one overall shortcoming in the review was that it did not address the lack of a coherent political component in OLS, even though it ostensibly concluded that humanitarian action could not be an effective substitute for political action.[93] That is to say, as Minear pointed out, the review did not address why the UN was 'still devoting abundant resources to relief but few to diplomacy', nor what the impact of relief was on the conflict.[94] The review did examine lower-level political weaknesses in OLS, in particular the degree to which it was more subject to government control and aims in the northern sector than it was to SPLM/A control and aims in the southern sector. But it did not address higher-level questions about the impact of OLS on the conflict and efforts to resolve it. Similarly, the review did not directly address the issue of relief diversion and abuse.[95]

Notwithstanding these shortcomings, the UN judged that the review 'unequivocally reaffirmed' the 'continued relevance of [OLS] for war-affected and other displaced persons in the Sudan'.[96] The UN Country Team and system in Sudan then proceeded to try to act on the review, and by April 1998 it had ostensibly implemented almost all of its 41 recommendations.[97] During this time, and subsequently, some improvements were realised in the operating conditions and effectiveness of OLS, but failings remained. Notably the problems of insecurity, obstruction and diversion persisted, as did the pattern of intermittently recurring humanitarian crises and famines, the worst of them in Bahr el-Ghazal in 1998. For humanitarian, political and religious reasons, some agencies continued to work outside OLS; some (inside and outside OLS) also began to try to promote peacebuilding.

One aspect in which OLS sought improvements in the situation was access. In November 1995 and March 1996 the special envoy of the UN Secretary-General, Vieiri Traxler, visited Sudan to try to persuade the parties to improve implementation of the existing access agreements and gain access to SPLM/A-held areas in the Nuba Mountains that the government had persistently cut off from relief programmes.[98] In 1997, after another visit by the Secretary-General's special envoy (then Robert van Schaik), the government reduced the number of flight bans from an average of 17 per month to seven, and approved all requests for barge transport. However, in January 1998 the improvement was reversed, after the southern faction leader Kerubino Kuanyin Bol defected from the government to the SPLM/A, and the SPLM/A launched new attacks against the government-held towns of Aweil, Gogrial and Wau. In response the government imposed a total ban on flights over Bahr el-Ghazal, which was gradually lifted after high-level calls from the UN and another visit by van Schaik in February 1998.

The gradual lifting of the ban was too late to prevent a humanitarian crisis in Bahr el-Ghazal in 1998. According to the UN, the ban 'paralysed [OLS's] operations in the area and caused a massive deterioration in humanitarian conditions'.[99] In response, relief agencies appealed for and received greatly increased funding to support additional emergency operations. Levels of suffering and loss of life in the famine were still high. But in hindsight, the UN considered the response to the crisis to have been largely successful in saving lives:

> By late September, due to the massive efforts of United Nations agencies and partner non-governmental organizations in the consortium, the humanitarian situation in the southern sector had eased considerably. Daily mortality rates declined from 63 per 10,000 in July to 3 per 10,000 in September, for a total of 48,000 beneficiaries.[100]

Following the crisis, in July 1998 the government and the SPLM/A announced unilateral temporary humanitarian ceasefires. Both sides subsequently renewed the ceasefires every three months, after consultations through the UN, until July 2000, when they allowed the ceasefires to lapse.[101] However, the ceasefires were not comprehensive and were far from fully observed. Indeed between 1998 and 2000, fighting intensified in Western Upper Nile, where oil exploration and production were increasing, and in Eastern Sudan, where the SPLM/A had opened a front with the NDA.

Meanwhile efforts were also made to improve the distribution of relief and to tackle the problem of diversion, albeit with modest success. At the IGAD-led peace talks in August 1998, the government and the SPLM/A agreed to reactivate a Technical Committee on Humanitarian Assistance to Sudan, comprising representatives from the government, the SPLM/A, the UN and OLS. Tasked with investigating allegations of diversion, the committee concluded 'that some food and other relief items were being redistributed by powerful local figures and some were being taxed'.[102] The government and the SPLM/A thereupon gave their agreement 'not to divert relief supplies and, further, not to use these supplies for military and/or political purposes'.[103] But despite reported improvements in relief distribution by the end of the year, the issue continued to need attention in 1999 and subsequently. Thus, although reports of large and unconcealed diversion of relief were less common in the late 1990s than in the first half of the 1990s, it is apparent that diversion continued to occur on a significant scale.[104]

In truth, it was not surprising that it remained difficult for relief agencies to overcome the problems of insecurity, obstruction and diversion, and to secure the full co-operation of the warring parties. Despite the written agreements signed in 1994 and the OLS southern-sector Ground Rules, the legal basis of OLS was still weak. The principles of the 1994 agreements and the Ground Rules were frequently violated, not just by the warring parties but also, as Michael Medley observes, 'by members of humanitarian agencies as well as other parties'.[105] Agencies therefore sometimes resorted to suspending activities and threatening withdrawal.[106] In 1998, for example, a group of INGOs operating in Southern Sudan successfully opposed a draft memorandum of understanding put forward by the SPLM/A, which would have imposed new restrictions on their work.[107] A similar incident occurred in March 2000, when 11 INGOs (including Care International, Oxfam and Save the Children) refused to sign an operating agreement drafted by the SRRA which would have strengthened the SPLM/A's controls over relief. The agencies instead suspended their operations in Southern Sudan until the SPLM/A compromised over the terms of the agreement.[108]

The boundaries of OLS, and definitions of what did and did not constitute OLS relief, were subject to interpretation and change over time. Technically OLS was intended to serve only war-affected areas or war-affected populations (who could be present outside the war zone, as with displaced populations in the north). But in practice, it was difficult always to maintain a distinction, especially since the lead OLS agencies, UNICEF and WFP, and a number of INGOs, also carried out relief operations in parts of the north, serving populations that were not affected by the war. Whether relief outside the war zones was labelled OLS or not, in so far as it still had economic and political consequences (albeit not in the context of fighting and displacement), it is relevant to the questions being explored in this chapter.[109]

In a slightly different category was non-OLS relief to war-affected areas, principally in the south but also in the Nuba Mountains and Southern Blue Nile. As mentioned above, a number of INGOs and Sudanese NGOs operated outside OLS to deliver relief materials and aid to these areas. The best-known example was Norwegian People's Aid (NPA), which operated only in the south and supported and co-operated closely with the SPLM/A. Other examples included World Vision (a US-headquartered INGO) and various small Christian missionary organisations or charities, such as Frontline Fellowship and Samaritan's Purse. Where the agencies co-operated closely with the SPLM/A, they also became a target for government suspicion and charges of involvement in supplying arms to the SPLM/A (although the same charge was also made against OLS agencies).

In comparison with OLS, non-OLS relief to war-affected areas was small in volume. But where agencies provided relief to areas which otherwise were not served by OLS (such as the Nuba Mountains and Southern Blue Nile, during most of the 1990s), the relief could be locally significant, in either humanitarian or political terms. Some relief organisations were willing to support the SPLM/A more directly than others did. The NPA, for example, initially worked directly with the SPLM/A, rather than the SRRA. This was largely due to one member of staff, Egil Hagen, a former soldier who had worked for NPA in Lebanon. After subsequent staff changes, in 1996 the NPA reduced its proximity to the SPLM/A, but continued its operations outside OLS.[110]

In response to the continuation of the war and the failure of peace talks, UN agencies such as UNICEF moved towards introducing (or 'mainstreaming') peacebuilding as a priority in their programmes in Sudan.[111] Thus, as of 2001 the overall UN strategy in Sudan was shaped around three themes:

(i) Emergency preparedness and emergency response, involving preparation and response to acute emergencies and support for community preparedness;
(ii) Internal displacement, focusing on the needs of displaced and host populations, including the long-term displaced;
(iii) Peace-building, aiming at the facilitation of community-based rehabilitation of services and peace-building efforts.[112]

Around the same time, UN agencies collectively became more insistent about the need for a political solution to the war. In the annual or bi-annual reports of the UN Secretary-General on humanitarian assistance in Sudan, mention of the need for a political solution had in the past been rare. But in 2001, for example, it was explicit:

Humanitarian assistance is at best slowing the overall deterioration of the situation. In this context, only a negotiated and lasting peace settlement between the parties, supported by local and regional actors and the international community as a whole, can provide the fundamental solution. All peace efforts, local and international, must be actively pursued and encouraged by all relevant parties.[113]

Short of a peace settlement, for the sake of the civilian population the UN called for the resumption of humanitarian ceasefires, considering that the ceasefires from 1998 to 2000 had 'contributed, however little, to containing armed confrontation'.[114] Although the call was not immediately answered, political developments and the mission to Sudan in late 2001 of John Danforth, the special envoy of the US President, soon provided a long-sought for humanitarian ceasefire in the Nuba Mountains.

Assessing OLS and relief from 1989 to 2001

Between 1989 and 2001, relief in Sudan became systematised, principally through OLS, but also through repetitive patterns of humanitarian crisis and response. As before, the levels of relief fluctuated considerably, according to perceived needs. But even though all parties concerned – donors, the UN, relief agencies, and the Sudanese government and the SPLM/A – experienced frustrations and dissatisfactions with the system of relief, and sought its reform, ultimately the system continued year after year, with minor changes and reforms but no fundamental ones.

Throughout this period, insecurity, obstruction, denial of access, and diversion of relief were persistent problems, which arose from the military tactics of the warring parties. In short, the government and the SPLM/A tried to take advantage of relief when and where they could. Up to a point, therefore, OLS and relief did become 'integrated with the political dynamics of the war',[115] and relief food was sometimes used as a 'weapon'. Plainly, looting and obstruction sometimes had consequences for civilians. Although it is difficult to quantify the overall consequences, at a localised level agencies often saw situations where shortages of food or other basic items led to suffering and death. By extension, in the longer run, obstruction and diversion entailed more suffering and loss of life than would otherwise have been the case.

In these circumstances, it is understandable that some people working in relief in Sudan – and some outside observers and scholars – began to argue that relief was prolonging the war. Even the UN head in Sudan from September 1994 to March 1998, Christoph Jaeger, became 'convinced that OLS was prolonging the war'.[116] The UN annual report for Sudan for 2000 also repeated the claim, reflecting the views of at least two senior UN officials in Sudan at the time.[117] However, two general observations argue against concluding that the UN and donors were perpetuating the war by allowing the parties to dedicate more resources to it. Firstly, the will to fight was high: there is nothing to suggest that if relief supplies had been withdrawn, the warring parties would have quickly settled the conflict peacefully. Secondly, the share of relief accruing to the warring parties was not critical to their survival: the nominal value of relief in Sudan tended to be far greater than its real value. Even though relief was being provided in a situation of war and poverty, it was only one part of an economy and certainly not the largest. For comparison it is worth recalling that in the first civil war, from 1955 to 1972, the rebel Anyanya and the governments of the day were able to prosecute the war for many years while little relief went into the country.

However, there is good reason to judge that relief between 1989 and 2001 did contribute to the depoliticisation of the humanitarian crises in Sudan and that it had some anti-democratic effects. In general, OLS bypassed or undermined previously existing systems of authority, responsibility and accountability. While those systems were not entirely replaced, they were partially superseded by a composite structure of externally accountable relief organisations, whose principal partners in Sudan were the humanitarian wings of the warring parties. This reduced the burden of responsibility on the warring parties for the humanitarian situation, while at the same time offering some of the benefits of involvement in or control over the delivery and distribution of relief. This much is evident and significant. But it is unlikely that relief contributed decisively to the survival of undemocratic regimes. In 1984–5, a particularly severe famine in the north added to the pressures which led to the overthrow of Nimeiri; but there is no evidence that relief was a decisive factor in the ability of the government of Bashir to weather the famines of 1990–1 and 1998 (which were a smaller threat than other pressures on his government).

These questions aside, it seems evident that relief between 1989 and 2001 was of some overall help in meeting humanitarian needs. However it is fair to conclude too that it was of no particular help for conflict resolution. In a minor way, relief was even unintentionally a hindrance: relief arrangements were often the default outcome from talks between the warring parties, and the focus on humanitarian action tended to obscure the need for political action. This was not so much a mistake of *commission* as one of *omission*, and it was always a less significant obstruction to peace than the actions of the warring parties. Nonetheless, as doubts grew about the role played by relief in the war, relief organisations and donors tried to draw more attention to the need for a political solution and to connect relief with peace. These efforts – and the limits to them – could be seen in the last years of the civil war, from 2001 to 2004.

RELIEF, 2001–2004

Between 2001 and 2004 some efforts were made to change OLS and the main approaches used for relief in Sudan. These efforts coincided with changes in the context, in particular the Nuba Mountains ceasefire and the progress in the IGAD-led peace process, but also the escalation of the Darfur conflict. These changes brought a new opportunity for relief as well as new demands.

Attempts to change OLS and the approach to relief

In the years after the 1996 OLS review, a number of senior UN officials in Sudan tried to resolve the problems caused by the separation of OLS into northern and southern sectors. However, from around 2000, some senior officials sought to move away from representing relief operations in Sudan as 'OLS'. The rationale for this move was that in strict terms OLS did not constitute the totality of relief in Sudan or the relief provided by agencies participating in OLS. In the words of one agency head at the time, 'OLS had lost meaning – because what was and wasn't OLS?'[118] Some officials therefore tried to present relief in Sudan as consisting of a more general humanitarian operation, rather than just OLS with its accompanying northern/southern sector divisions in outlook and approach. At the same time, a new effort was made to reform the UN command structure in Sudan and to resolve the conflicts between UN staff in Khartoum and Nairobi.

However, organisational pressures and changes in UN leadership in Sudan meant that the momentum for reforming OLS and the UN system in Sudan was not steady. Some further progress was made during 2003–4, at the instigation of the then UN Resident and Humanitarian Co-ordinator, Mukesh Kapila. But as of late 2004, OLS remained the prevailing framework through which relief was seen and delivered: relief continued to be delivered out of twin *de facto* headquarters (Khartoum and Nairobi), and senior UN officials were still calling for improvements in co-ordination between northern and southern operations. Thus even in late 2004, when asked what the UN and INGOs could do better for peacebuilding in Sudan, one UN field co-ordinator replied instantly: 'Easy: they could stop operating out of separate offices or operations in Sudan and Nairobi.'[119]

Meanwhile, during the same period, two new developments occurred which presented relief agencies with a new opportunity to link relief with peace, but also with new demands for relief. These were firstly the 2002 Nuba Mountains ceasefire, and the ensuing progress in the government–SPLM/A peace talks, and secondly the escalation of the Darfur conflict and the ensuing humanitarian crisis.

The Nuba Mountains were not covered by OLS when it started, even though from 1989 onwards they were part of the war zone in which the government and the SPLM/A fought. In response to evidence of widespread suffering in the region, for much of the 1990s relief agencies sought to gain humanitarian access but were denied it by the government and the SPLM/A. Thus, for example, it was not until 1999 that, after much negotiation, a UN humanitarian assessment mission to SPLM/A-controlled areas of the Nuba Mountains was conducted.[120] Even after this, it was not until the signing of the Nuba Mountains ceasefire in 2002 that a full relief programme to both government- and SPLM/A-controlled areas could be launched.

The new programme, known as the Nuba Mountains Programme for Advancing Conflict Transformation (NMPACT), was an inter-agency relief and rehabilitation programme and was not part of OLS. More significantly, unlike OLS relief it contained measures to build co-operation between the government and the SPLM/A across the lines of territorial control. These measures reflected the circumstances and expectations surrounding the Nuba Mountains ceasefire agreement, namely that the agreement was a step towards negotiating a wider ceasefire and eventually a peace agreement between the government and the SPLM/A. In this respect, the ceasefire was different from the humanitarian ceasefires that the warring parties had declared unilaterally or jointly over the preceding years, covering areas in the south.

To be implemented, NMPACT depended on the parties renewing the Nuba Mountains ceasefire. This happened – with the ceasefire being renewed for six months at a time –and the programme therefore continued throughout the next two years. However, no linkage otherwise existed between the programme and the political process of the peace talks in Kenya, although UN agencies and INGOs in Sudan did try to encourage the apparent progress in the peace talks. Thus, for example, after the breakthrough of the Machakos protocol, at the end of 2002 UN agencies in Sudan called for a 'unified strategy' from the international community, which would include 'the necessary political and diplomatic commitment … required to re-engage the parties in peace and cease-fire negotiations and address secondary conflicts'.[121] The International Crisis Group also argued that the peace process offered an opportunity to end the use of food as a weapon:

> Warring parties and international aid providers in Sudan have an historic opportunity to bring to an end what is perhaps the most extreme and long-running example in the world of using access to humanitarian aid as an instrument of war[122]

In practice, however, these hopes were only partly fulfilled. On the positive side, international mediation of the talks between the government and the SPLM/A continued through 2003 and 2004, and humanitarian access improved as the parties approached a final agreement. But on the negative side, the conflict in Darfur escalated, and humanitarian access to Darfur began to be used as a weapon of war.

The escalation of the Darfur conflict brought new demands for relief. Darfur was largely outside the areas covered by OLS, but many UN agencies and INGOs had nonetheless been working in the region since the early 1980s, providing relief and some development assistance. However, faced with a very rapid increase in the number of people displaced by fighting in Darfur, relief agencies struggled to meet the associated demands for humanitarian assistance. Agencies made emergency appeals ('flash appeals') for funding for operations in Darfur, and tried to construct programmes that were coherent and effective. At the same time they continued with their programmes in other parts of the country, some of which they were trying to re-orient away from relief and towards 'recovery' and development, in the light of the ceasefires covering the Nuba Mountains and the south.

To some extent, the UN and partner INGOs in Sudan were unprepared for the Darfur conflict, and their response to it was slower than they themselves would have liked. In general, though, they were alert to the escalation of the conflict, and they were alert to the other areas in Sudan where fighting was occurring outside the international spotlight.[123] Thus, following the signing of the first ceasefire for Darfur in September 2003, the UN Country Team in Sudan launched a 'Greater Darfur Initiative', a relief programme which was intended to 'help consolidate fragile peace on the ground.'[124] The programme was initially expected to cost some US$22m, but as the fighting and insecurity in Darfur worsened, the estimated humanitarian needs grew. By the end of 2003 the UN estimated that a total of nearly 600,000 people had been displaced in Darfur, and it had increased its estimate of the total cost of assistance required for Darfur to around US$171m.[125] In 2004 the situation deteriorated even more rapidly than expected, with the number of IDPs reaching around 1.8 million by the end of the year.[126] As a consequence, as of the end of 2004, relief agencies were aiming to provide assistance to some 2.5 million 'conflict-affected' people in Darfur, at a projected total cost of US$621m, which represented 42 per cent of the projected total cost of US$1,483m for relief, recovery and development work in Sudan in 2005.[127]

Overall, therefore, the relief response to the Darfur conflict was very conventional: agencies appealed for funding; relief consisted of food and non-food items (the latter including shelter, water, sanitation and health assistance); and agencies contended with the logistical, political and security obstacles to delivering relief to IDP camps and settlements across Darfur and in neighbouring Chad. International media widely reported the humanitarian crisis but also gave considerable attention to its political causes, namely the conflict itself and the policies of the warring parties – in particular the government, the Janjawid militia, and JEM and the SLM/A. However, despite the humanitarian ceasefires signed in November 2003 and March 2004, and despite the wishes or claims of relief agencies to be supporting a peace process for Darfur, no meaningful or effective linkage was made between relief and peace.

The responses of the warring parties

Between 2001 and 2004, the government and the SPLM/A responded to the humanitarian situation in the territories under their control much as they always had, namely by seeking to control humanitarian access to their advantage, while taking little or no direct responsibility for the situation. For example, in the same period that access to the Nuba Mountains improved as a result of the ceasefire there, the government tightened restrictions on access elsewhere. In April 2002 the government denied flights and general humanitarian access to around 40 locations, thereby cutting off access to large parts of Western Upper Nile, Eastern Equatoria and Bahr el-Ghazal; in September 2002 the level of access denial peaked when the government imposed a nine-day ban on all air access to Eastern and Western Equatoria, effectively causing the suspension of relief flights out of Lokichokio.[128] The government and the SPLM/A also continued to impose restrictive administrative requirements, as the UN Country Team in Sudan indicated at the end of 2002 in its review of the past year:

> Heavy administrative requirements imposed on humanitarian personnel by both the GoS and the SPLM/A for travel permits, work permits and similar documents also impact negatively on the ability of humanitarian staff to provide adequate and timely assistance.[129]

In Darfur it was a similar story. The government imposed flight denials while it used its own air force in the conflict (which it continued to do even after, under international pressure, it had undertaken to stop doing). The government also imposed obstructive visa and travel restrictions, and it eased these only in response to international and UN Security Council pressure in mid-2004.[130] Meanwhile JEM and the SLM/A broadly welcomed relief, in so far as relief benefited those inhabitants of Darfur whom they claimed to be fighting for. Where possible, they also tried to exercise some control over the delivery of relief to or through areas under their control, and incidents occurred of JEM or SLM/A soldiers attacking relief convoys. However, relief was targeted mainly on IDP camps, most of which lay in government-controlled areas, and as a result it brought few direct benefits to JEM and the SLM/A.

Assessing relief from 2001 to 2004

Between 2001 and 2004 there were few absolute changes to the means by which relief was delivered in Sudan, but there were significant changes in the context. As the peace process between the government and the SPLM/A progressed, and as cross-lines relief delivery began to be attempted (in particular in the Nuba Mountains), the rationale for OLS per se dwindled. However, the systems and assets of OLS and its bipartite structure persisted, despite efforts to reform the operation or subsume it under the name of a more general humanitarian operation covering all of Sudan.

The main aim of relief during this period continued to be saving lives. Relief agencies called for stronger involvement by donor or Western countries in the peace process. But only in the Nuba Mountains did relief itself make a contribution to conflict resolution, in so far as the Nuba Mountains ceasefire was bolstered by a cross-lines relief programme, and the ceasefire in turn helped the peace talks in Kenya between the government and the SPLM/A. In Darfur, however, relief agencies focused on responding to the escalating humanitarian needs, and relief itself did not have any bearing on the duration or resolution of the conflict. Furthermore, unlike in the past in the long-standing conflict between the government and the SPLM/A, the delivery of large-scale relief in Darfur did not prevent international attention focusing on the political causes of the humanitarian crisis. Domestically, however, relief continued to have the unintended effect of removing a humanitarian burden from the warring parties – and in the case of Darfur, the principal beneficiary of this was the government.

In short, between 2001 and 2004 relief did not affect the duration of conflict. In the case of Darfur, relief surely contributed to the domestic depoliticisation of a humanitarian crisis. Meanwhile, although relief contributed positively to conflict resolution in the Nuba Mountains, it did not do so in Darfur. Indeed, more generally, relief did not play a constructive role in either the IGAD or the Darfur talks.

THE DARFUR RELIEF OPERATION, 2004 ONWARDS

From 2004 onwards, a new and soon vast humanitarian operation began to be established for Darfur. At the same time, the CPA came into force and the patterns of humanitarian aid delivery in the south and other regions covered by the CPA began to change.

The surge in relief for Darfur

The relief operation for Darfur grew rapidly, responding to the rapid rise in the numbers of Darfurians displaced from their homes by the conflict. The operation had originated in September 2003, when the UN launched a US$23m 'Greater Darfur Initiative' which aimed to support the ceasefire signed that month by the government and the SLM/A, and to help people affected by the escalating conflict. In 2004 the Greater Darfur Initiative disappeared under an influx of relief, as flash appeals raised much larger levels of funding to support new and larger emergency operations. As a result, at the start of 2005 Darfur accounted for US$621m out of the US$1,483m total appealed for by the UN and partners in their primarily humanitarian 'work plan' for that year (humanitarian activities accounted for 82 per cent of the appeal, recovery activities 16 per cent, and development activities the remaining 2 per cent).[131] The basic aim of UN humanitarian aid in Darfur in 2005 was to save lives, though in theory it also aimed to strengthen human rights and humanitarian protection, ensure that any returns were voluntary, and improve the quality, targeting and cost-effectiveness of aid.[132]

Relief itself consisted of the usual spectrum of material goods and support, in particular the provision of food aid, shelter, water and sanitation, health-care, protection, and other services. Relief was delivered across the three Darfur states, with UN agencies responsible for the majority of relief, and INGOs and Sudanese NGOs working independently or being sub-contracted as implementing partners for UN agencies and their donors. Relief went to the camps for displaced persons around Nyala, El Fasher and El Gineina, the three state capitals in Darfur, and camps around some of the lesser towns, such as Kass, Kutum, Kebkabiya and Tawila. By January 2005, the UN estimated the total number of displaced in Darfur was 1.84m, and that it had humanitarian access to around 88 per cent of the 2.4m total of displaced persons and affected residents.[133] In parallel with this, a separate relief operation developed in Chad, serving the roughly 200,000 Darfurians who had fled across the border.

Inevitably, given the nature of relief and the on-going conflict, the delivery of relief was subject to problems of insecurity and obstruction similar to those that had been common in the civil war. The central government and local authorities in Darfur variously obstructed aid agencies seeking access to the region and to people affected by the conflict, as too did the rebel groups sometimes, though to a lesser degree. As the scale of humanitarian operations in Darfur grew, and as the lines between rebel groups, militias and bandits blurred, relief also became more vulnerable to looting, attacks and other hostile actions. The length of the main 'pipeline' for delivering or importing relief to Darfur was more than 1,500km overland, from Port

Sudan, by road and rail, a journey which typically took lorries around three weeks and provided ample opportunity for blocking or hijacking, especially in Darfur.¹³⁴ Two other land and air routes opened in mid-2004, from Benghazi, Libya across the Sahara to North Darfur, and from Douala, Cameroon, through Chad to West Darfur.

The Darfur relief operation was also subject to problems of targeting and waste similar to those encountered by relief agencies during the civil war. For example, pressed by signs at the outset of new operations in Darfur in 2004 that relief needed to be distributed urgently, WFP opted to risk 'inclusion errors' and begin distribution earlier, rather than conduct more rigorous registration and verification exercises and begin distribution later. A year later (and subsequently) registration and re-registration of prospective beneficiaries of relief remained fraught with problems, such as deliberate distortion by local populations (displaced and host), threats of violence, and actual violence.¹³⁵ As a result, according to an evaluation of WFP's operations in Darfur in 2004 and 2005, prior to some relief re-registration and head-counting exercises in 2005, 'inclusion errors in some of the camps near urban centres were over 40 per cent' – a strikingly high figure.¹³⁶

The funding for humanitarian aid in Darfur sought by the UN increased only slightly from 2005 to 2006, from US$621m to US$648m out of the US$1,731m total for which it appealed in its 2006 Work Plan.¹³⁷ When the DPA was signed in May 2006, preparations began for conducting a post-conflict needs assessment for Darfur, led by the UN and World Bank, copying the example of a separate post-conflict needs assessment conducted for the civil war in 2004–5, known as the Joint Assessment Mission (JAM). The assessment exercise for Darfur, labelled the Darfur Joint Assessment Mission, started in mid-2006; but, faced with the mounting evidence that the DPA was not succeeding, the exercise was suspended in October 2006 and the final report was not completed. For humanitarian aid and 'early recovery' assistance in Darfur in 2007 the UN sought US$651m, and in 2008 this increased to US$849m. In 2008 Darfur thus accounted for 45 per cent of the US$1,865m total sought for humanitarian and early recovery assistance across the whole of Sudan, and total planned aid for Darfur exceeded planned aid for Southern Sudan and accounted for 37 per cent of the US$2,271m total that the UN Work Plan sought for all aid across Sudan as a whole.¹³⁸ In 2009 the level of aid planned for Darfur went up again, to a total of US$1,053m for humanitarian and early recovery assistance for Darfur – which was almost half of the US$2,179m total for which the UN appealed in its 2009 work plan for Sudan.¹³⁹

As of 2008 and 2009, Sudan therefore remained one of WFP's largest operations in the world, and Darfur was still often described as 'the largest humanitarian emergency'.[140] In general, the UN and its partners received around 70 per cent of the total funding that they sought in their appeals. Meanwhile, relief operations continued to be subject to attacks and other difficulties. For example, in October and November 2008 alone, 28 vehicles belonging to humanitarian organisations were hijacked, 39 aid workers were kidnapped during those incidents (albeit briefly), 13 organisations' premises were attacked by armed men, and 10 relief convoys were looted.[141] In March 2009 the government expelled 13 NGOs in retaliation against the ICC arrest warrant for President Bashir (although the disruption caused by this was much less than many outsiders predicted).[142] Throughout, inefficient targeting of relief aid remained a problem, though one which received little attention. As one study published in April 2009 observed, as of late 2008 and early 2009 the entitlement to food aid in Darfur was still based firstly on registration that had been conducted in 2005 and secondly on status (as a displaced person or someone affected by displacement), rather than primarily on food need. As the study noted, this approach was initially the policy of aid organisations themselves, but was 'embraced by local government and especially by the recipient communities themselves'.[143]

Between 2005 and 2009, therefore, the Darfur relief operation essentially changed little. Efforts were made to increase the share of aid to Darfur that contributed to 'recovery' and development, but the large majority of aid for Darfur continued to consist of humanitarian assistance that aimed to respond to current or immediate needs. Food aid and related food security and livelihoods assistance accounted for the largest part of aid in Darfur. No attempts were made to link the delivery of aid to the negotiation of temporary ceasefires, as had been done in the 1990s during the civil war; nor was any attempt made to connect aid with wider political efforts to resolve the conflict.

Changes elsewhere

To a limited extent the extraordinary increase in relief funding for Darfur was matched by an increase in the level of relief provided for Southern Sudan and other parts of the country. By 2004 OLS had definitively ceased to exist. But between 2005 and 2009, Southern Sudan accounted for US$557m, US$571m, US$644m, US$778m and US$617m of the total funding appeals made by the UN and its partners in the respective annual work plans. These figures were substantially more than the annual totals of humanitarian assistance for the whole of Sudan in any year since 1991, as they included funding needs for early recovery and development projects.[144] But even excluding that, the level of humanitarian assistance sought for the south remained high – US$482m in 2006 and US$296m in 2007, against which funding or in-kind contributions were respectively US$307m and US$217m.

The increase in humanitarian, recovery and development assistance for Southern Sudan was due to a combination of factors. On the one hand, the CPA and the end of the civil war made it easier for assistance to be delivered to the south; on the other hand, the end of the civil war also meant that large numbers of southerners started returning to the south, leading to some demand for assistance with their return and new pressure on food supplies and agricultural resources in parts of the south. During the years of the CPA's implementation, new short-term humanitarian crises also sometimes occurred, for example as a result of clashes between the SAF and SPLA, intra-southern fighting, and upsurges in inter-tribal fighting. Meanwhile, international donors pledged larger sums than ever before in aid for Sudan. At a donor conference in Oslo in April 2005, leading donors pledged a total of US$4.5bn in response to the UN's 2005 Work Plan and the JAM, which set out Sudan's needs for the years following the CPA.

The high level of aid for Darfur came to be criticised by officials in the national and southern governments, especially when the level of aid for Darfur did not drop after 2005. With some justification, officials argued that donors were switching a large part of the pledges they had made at Oslo away from supporting the longer-term, developmental needs set out in the JAM, to fund short-term humanitarian assistance for Darfur instead. However, this criticism was muted by the awareness that, despite the high level of aid to Darfur, the south and Sudan as a whole were still receiving more aid than in many years. Furthermore, the treasuries of the national and southern governments were being swollen by an influx of oil revenues and by the strong growth of the economy. Net oil export revenues rose from around US$3.1bn in 2004 to US$4.2bn in 2005, US$5.1bn in 2006, US$8.4bn in 2007 and US$12.2bn in 2008. Between 2005 and 2009, the Government of Southern Sudan's annual share of oil revenues rose from around US$773m in 2005 to an average of around US$1.5bn per year, peaking at US$2.6bn in 2008. Over the same period (2005–9) GDP grew in real terms by an average of around 8 per cent per year (and growth in the previous five years, 2000–4, had averaged around 6 per cent per year).[145] Against such a background, humanitarian and development aid remained only a small part of the economy.

Assessing the Darfur relief operation

Between 2004 and 2009, the primary aim of international humanitarian aid in Sudan continued to be saving lives and reducing suffering. Success remained difficult to measure. The targeting of aid was still poor, as it had been in the civil war, and mortality and morbidity data were still sketchy. Still, it is surely true that relief did ease and limit the suffering of some people. Furthermore, there is no evidence to support a claim that relief prolonged conflict in Darfur (and, unlike in the civil war, this claim was not made). The conflict in Darfur was manifestly sustained and driven on by political factors and motivations, and the warring parties extracted no critical resources from it. Lastly, as noted before, relief in Darfur did not depoliticise the humanitarian crises internationally, in the sense of preventing the international community from being aware that an armed conflict was the cause of those crises.

However, critical observations also deserve to be made. It is true that the surge in humanitarian aid for Darfur was accompanied by an increase in humanitarian aid across Sudan, especially for the south. But the surge in relief for Darfur, and the fact that it was still poorly targeted in 2009, indicate that past lessons about relief, targeting and impact were not well heeded. Furthermore, the very high level of humanitarian aid for Darfur surely still had some depoliticising effects internally in Sudan. As in the civil war, relief in Darfur eased the humanitarian pressure on the national government and the local authorities; in effect, it continued the long-standing pattern in Sudan of absolving the governing authorities of responsibility for the well-being of civilians affected by conflict.

Conclusion

This chapter has looked to answer questions about the relationship between relief and conflict in Sudan, and in particular what the aims of relief were, whether it prolonged conflict, and whether it depoliticised conflict-related humanitarian crises and had anti-democratic effects. Taking together both the civil war and the Darfur conflict, the chapter suggests the following overall answers.

Firstly, the aims of relief in Sudan were generally the conventional humanitarian aims of saving lives and reducing suffering. At the outset of OLS, some senior UN officials and relief workers hoped that the programme might contribute to peace or at least a peace process, but the hope was soon forgotten amid the practicalities of maintaining the programme after a new government came to power. In 2002 the possibility of relief contributing to resolving a conflict was picked up again, in the Nuba Mountains, but almost as quickly it was forgotten amid the Darfur crisis. In the years after the CPA was signed, the enormous humanitarian operation that developed for Darfur was also entirely unconnected to efforts to resolve the conflict, with the exception of 'early recovery' aid that supported local, bottom–up conflict prevention and reconciliation initiatives. Thus, throughout the long span of war and conflict, relief agencies tended to use conventional humanitarian criteria and indicators to assess the success or impact of relief, such as basic health indicators (for example, mortality, disease and acute malnutrition rates) and data for the volume and cost of delivered relief – data which measured intentions rather than consequences.

Secondly, relief did not ultimately prolong conflict. In the short term, at the local level, relief certainly did sometimes benefit the warring parties, either tactically or materially, and the parties sometimes used their control over humanitarian access as a 'weapon'. But relief was otherwise a much less significant determinant of the continuation and duration of the war than other domestic political factors, above all the will and determination of the warring parties to fight on.

Finally, however, relief in Sudan sometimes did depoliticise in certain ways the humanitarian crises seen in the civil war and Darfur. In the 1980s and then under OLS in the 1990s relief did obscure the political causes of the humanitarian crises, at least from the international view. The same did not quite happen with relief in Darfur from 2003 onwards, when international coverage of the humanitarian crisis almost universally emphasised its political causes, although much coverage gave a simplified or slanted account of the causes. Meanwhile, domestically relief also had some anti-democratic consequences: on the one hand it gave power to local intermediaries who controlled the distribution of relief; on the other, more generally it reduced the responsibility of the government or SPLM/A or other rebel authorities for the humanitarian situation in the areas under their control.

As in the previous chapter, these answers beg further questions, above all about the policy choices of relief organisations in Sudan, and whether they could have done more to prevent the abuse of relief and to bring about a peaceful resolution of conflict in Sudan and associated humanitarian crises, for example by seeking more action from the warring parties, mediators and donors. These questions will be explored in Chapter 5. The next chapter, however, will examine a vital dimension for explaining and understanding the international community's response to Sudan's conflicts, namely the foreign policies of the donor and mediator countries.

4

FOREIGN POLICY

What foreign policies and strategies did the international community use in dealing with Sudan during the civil war and the Darfur conflict, and how did these affect prospects for ending conflict? This chapter aims to cast light on how foreign policy affected decisions about mediation and relief, and whether constructive policy linkages between mediation and relief were ever possible or made. As in Chapter 3, to make analysis easier the relevant history of foreign policy towards Sudan is here divided into four broadly distinct periods: firstly from 1983 to 1989, when Western policy towards Sudan was characterised by clientelism and aid, continuing the policies of the preceding Cold War years; secondly from 1989 to 2001, when Western policy was characterised by containment and aid that was largely restricted to relief; thirdly from 2001 to 2004, when Western policy was characterised by increased engagement and continued relief aid; and finally from 2005 onwards, when Western policy was characterised by a conflicting mix of increased engagement and containment.

CLIENTELISM AND AID, 1983–9

When the civil war began in 1983, Western foreign policy towards Sudan was overwhelmingly clientelist, reflecting the Cold War context and regional factors in the Horn of Africa and the Middle East. As the domestic policies of Nimeiri changed, and his government was succeeded by the governments of the TMC and Sadiq, this clientelism began to ebb. Meanwhile, as the humanitarian crises in Sudan escalated, humanitarian aid began to take a more prominent position in foreign policy towards Sudan. During this period, foreign perspectives on the war also evolved, with implications for policy towards Sudan after 1989.

The rise of clientelism

At the start of the 1980s, relations between the USA, Western Europe and Sudan were strong and followed a largely clientelist pattern, reflecting the strategic pressures and interests in the Horn of Africa that had evolved over the previous three decades of the Cold War. At the regional level, the USA and its Western allies were seeking to contain Libya and the Soviet-backed regime of Mengistu Haile Mariam in Ethiopia, while keeping Egypt, Sudan and Somalia as strategic allies. Soviet influence in Ethiopia had grown rapidly after the fall of Haile Selassie, and in 1981 Ethiopia, Libya and South Yemen had signed a tripartite pact which the USA saw as hostile to Sudan and Somalia and as part of an 'arc of crisis' reaching from Africa to Afghanistan.[1] A number of other factors specific to Sudan had further nurtured Sudanese–US relations and shaped the clientelist pattern of relations. In 1971 Nimeiri had broken with the Soviet Union, after a communist-backed attempted coup. Following this, in 1972 Sudan had become the first Arab state to resume relations with the USA following the break after the 1967 Arab–Israeli war, and Nimeiri had supported Egypt in its peace process with Israel. Nimeiri had also made peace in Southern Sudan in 1972 and in 1977 was reconciled with northern opposition parties. In 1978 the US oil company Chevron discovered oil in Sudan, and that year a Sudan–United States Business Council was established.[2] As a result, as Woodward notes, Sudan was seen as strategically important on three counts: 'with regard to Egypt and the peace with Israel; as a partner in the containment of Libya; and as a counter to the USSR in Ethiopia'. On top of this, the over-ambitious plans to develop Sudan into the 'breadbasket' of the Arab world embodied the hope that the country could become 'something of a show case for Western-backed modernisation', albeit with much funding from the Gulf States and Saudi Arabia.[3]

Sudan's clientelism had significant financial, military and security benefits. In 1983 alone, Sudan nominally received a total of US$970m in official development assistance, of which US$568m was in grants and US$158m from the USA.[4] Military aid was particularly substantial and supported close military relations between Sudan and Egypt and the USA, which after the overthrow of Haile Selassie had cultivated Sudan as a 'forward base' from which to pursue a policy of assertive containment of Ethiopia. US military aid itself increased from a total value of around US$30m between 1976 and 1981, to a total of US$201m in 1982 (in grants and sales credits), so that by 1983 Sudan was the largest recipient of US military aid in Africa (and the third largest recipient of US aid globally, after Israel and Egypt).[5] The USA gained naval access at Port Sudan and airport pre-positioning rights, and held joint military exercises with Sudan, notably Operation Bright Star in 1981 and 1983. In addition, Nimeiri co-operated with the covert US and Israeli operation to airlift Falasha Jews out of Ethiopia in 1984, Operation Moses. Under the auspices of the 1976 Egyptian–Sudanese Joint Defence Agreement, Egypt was also ready to provide direct military assistance, exemplified by its rapid deployment of 2,000 troops to Sudan after a Libyan air raid on Omdurman in March 1984.

The retreat from clientelism

Most of the external factors that had led the USA and Sudan's other major patrons to pursue a clientelist approach towards Sudan continued to apply after the civil war began in 1983. However, from the start of the 1980s a number of domestic developments in Sudan arising from the behaviour and decisions of Nimeiri began to weaken US satisfaction with its relations with Sudan. These developments included Nimeiri's re-division of Southern Sudan in July 1983, and especially his turn towards Islamisation, manifested by his introduction of *sharia* law in September 1983. Hopes that Nimeiri might retreat from these measures were disappointed, as Nimeiri went on to impose a state of emergency in April 1984 (lasting five months) and to order the execution of the Sudanese reformist Islamic thinker Mahmoud Mohammed Taha in January 1985.

By the time of Nimeiri's overthrow in April 1985 (itself the culmination of his domestic unpopularity), Western and Arab dissatisfaction with Nimeiri was such that his departure was quietly welcomed. However, hopes that the TMC government would enable previously good relations to be restored were disappointed. Although the TMC leader, General Sawar al-Dhahab, suspended the hudud punishments – which was welcomed by Sudan's Western and Arab allies – he also shifted Sudan away from Nimeiri's close relations with the USA and towards a more neutral foreign policy. As part of this he cancelled the Operation Bright Star[6] military exercises planned for 1985 and started a rapprochement with Libya which brought Libyan military aid to Sudan and made it easier for Libyan forces to operate in Darfur in the context of the Chadian–Libyan war.

In Sudan there was some public support for scaling down relations with the USA. Public revelations about Operation Moses had provoked much criticism, and in November 1985 anti-US protests in Khartoum prompted the USA to evacuate its embassy. Similarly, in April 1986 (just before the handover to civilian rule) protests against the US air raids on Libya were organised in Khartoum. Furthermore, the return of Sudan to civilian democratic rule in April 1986 did not reverse the shift in relations. Instead, Sadiq accelerated the realignment in Sudan's foreign relations, and his policies gradually pushed the USA, and to a lesser extent Sudan's main

European partners, as well as Egypt, Saudi Arabia and the Gulf States, to abandon their clientelist approach to Sudan.

The deterioration in relations between Sudan and its Western and Arab patrons and allies in the 1980s led to a reduction in the military and economic aid they provided, and its replacement with aid from new sources. From record levels in 1983 and 1984, the USA reduced its military aid to Sudan to US$20m during the term of the TMC, and only US$5m during the government of Sadiq, from 1986 to 1989.[7] To the annoyance of the US government, in January 1987 Sadiq cancelled an agreement for the pre-positioning of US military equipment at Port Sudan. In 1988 the USA therefore reduced its budgeted military assistance to Sudan to zero, although it continued to deliver logistics, transport, and training assistance which had been paid for in previous years.[8] This included the delivery in late 1988 of 41 'Hummer' vehicles, which were intended to be used for reconnaissance in Darfur, to counter Libyan activity.[9]

Egypt similarly reduced its military aid to Sudan. By the end of 1984 it had withdrawn its troops from Sudan, leaving only military and security advisers. After the fall of Nimeiri, it signed a new agreement to provide military aid to Sudan,[10] but implementation of the agreement was jeopardised by Egyptian concern about relations between the TMC and Libya.[11] The arrival of Sadiq in government further weakened Egypt's readiness to provide military support, and as a consequence in February 1987 the Joint Defence Agreement between Egypt and Sudan was replaced by a weaker agreement, the 'Brotherhood Treaty'.[12] Saudi Arabia and the Gulf States also reined in their economic assistance to Sudan. Already in 1984 some Arab investors had lobbied Nimeiri against economic policies, particularly Islamic policies, that might affect their investments,[13] and in August 1984 the Kuwait-based Arab Fund for Economic and Social Development suspended loans to Sudan.[14] After the overthrow of Nimeiri, Saudi Arabia lifted the restrictions that it had imposed on its financial aid to Sudan and allocated US$100m in aid for 1986, as well as agreeing to provide free oil. But when the TMC was succeeded by Sadiq, the Saudi government suspended much of its promised assistance.

For Sudan, the loss of military and economic aid from the USA and Western-allied Arab states was largely made up for by new sources, in particular Libya and Iran, and to a lesser extent Iraq. As well as the military protocol with Libya, the TMC signed agreements with Libya and Iran for the free supply of oil. These agreements continued under Sadiq, and although the supply of oil was sometimes erratic, the supply of arms was more reliable. This was exemplified when Sadiq appealed for Arab aid after the SPLM/A captured the town of Kurmuk in Blue Nile State in November

1987. In response, Libya provided eight MIG-23 fighter jets and Iraq reportedly provided 28 plane-loads of ammunition, mortars, rockets and trucks. In comparison, Egypt, Jordan and Saudi Arabia provided only a small quantity of light arms and ammunition.[15]

The rise of relief aid

The ebbing of the clientelist relationship between Sudan and its Western and Arab allies coincided with an increase in Western provision of relief in response to the famine crises in Sudan. In 1985 relief already accounted for around US$1bn of the estimated US$1.9bn total value of development and relief aid to Sudan that year.[16] Most of this was paid for or provided in kind by the USA and other Western donor countries, and was ostensibly provided regardless of political considerations. Thus, as of 1985, US policy on responding to famine in Sudan (and Ethiopia) had as its aims 'to avoid unnecessary human starvation, to mitigate the suffering, the pain and the dislocation and to minimize the disruption to national and human development'.[17] Notwithstanding the humanitarian basis, the US government did try to direct some of its relief provision for Ethiopian refugees in Eastern Sudan towards bolstering support against Mengistu.[18] However, it also tended to avoid drawing attention to political events in Sudan and their connection with the humanitarian crises across the country. As a consequence, in a US Congress hearing in September 1985, for example, on emergency famine-relief needs in Ethiopia and Sudan, the conflict in Sudan was not mentioned once, although the war and military expenditure in Ethiopia were discussed.[19]

Over the following three years, however, a combination of political changes in Sudan and media reports about the obstruction of relief by the Sudanese government made the US government readier to acknowledge the political dimensions of the humanitarian crises in Sudan. The US government therefore began to look more critically at the role of relief in the war, and in July 1988, for example, a Congressional hearing on war, politics and famine in Ethiopia and Sudan directly addressed the questions of whether the Sudanese government was using food as a weapon and whether the US strategic relationship with Sudan made it difficult for the US government to address such issues.[20] Despite the deterioration in relations with Sadiq, the latter question was still relevant because the USA – and other relief donors – remained reluctant to criticise the Sudanese government openly for its conduct of the war. By 1989, however, the evidence that the war and the policies of the government were having severe humanitarian consequences was unavoidable, and US officials were therefore ready to criticise recent US policy openly. That policy, as one Congressman described it in March 1989, had essentially been 'one of quiet diplomacy marked by an unquestioning faith in the integrity and motivations of the Sudanese Government'; It had, however, proved 'ineffectual and increasingly untenable on both political and moral grounds'.[21]

The rise of humanitarian aid in the place of Western economic and military aid reflected the lack of will or appetite among Sudan's former Western patrons for alternative approaches to the country. This quiescence was partly due to lingering hopes of maintaining Sudan as a client, and partly due to unwillingness to officially recognise the SPLM/A and either mediate in the war or support the SPLM/A in some way. The lack of sympathy for the SPLM/A was principally because in its early years the SPLM/A's most important backers were Ethiopia and Libya. After Libya switched its support to the Sudanese government in 1985, Ethiopia continued to give support and shelter to the SPLM/A. Through Ethiopia the SPLM/A also developed links with Cuba and East Germany which yielded modest amounts of support.[22] Even in Western countries which had little or no strategic interest in supporting the Sudanese government, views of the SPLM/A were tempered by concern about the SPLM/A's methods and its initially Marxist-influenced political programme. Indeed, some Western commentary on the SPLM/A was very critical. In August 1988, for example, *Africa Confidential* (which in the 1990s became more sympathetic to the SPLM/A) wrote: 'All the SPLA needs from a decimated population is acquiescence. ... This can be imposed by terrorism. The destruction of villages and villagers is by no means the prerogative of the armed forces or militias.'[23]

In the circumstances, therefore, between 1983 and 1989 the USA and other Western donors were content to avoid becoming involved in peace talks for Sudan (such as the Umma–DUP–SPLM/A dialogues).[24] Instead, they ostensibly tried to remain neutral and focused on relief and supporting the establishment of OLS. For the USA this meant officially supporting neither side in the war, but supporting 'the peace process and the efficient delivery of relief': according to the US Assistant Secretary of State for Africa, Herman Cohen, in May–June 1989, the USA did not want to 'take over the peace process' because '[t]he two sides were communicating and did not need a mediator'.[25] Underlying this approach, however, was the hope that Sadiq's government would be replaced by a more pliant government, which might allow a return to the clientelist pattern of relations seen under Nimeiri before 1983.

Assessing clientelism

Clientelism was the predominant foreign-policy approach to Sudan between 1983 and 1989, even after the US clientelist relationship with

Sudan began to decline. In essence, many countries sought to use Sudan as a platform for pursuing their own interests. For the USA and to a lesser extent Western Europe, those interests were primarily containing Soviet influence and Libya; for Arab and African states, the interests in Sudan were shaped by regional rivalries and conflicts, such as the Eritrean struggle for independence, the Chad–Libya war, and the Iran–Iraq war. But for all countries it was superficially easy to patronise Sudan: it was a poor country, with diverse foreign relations, and it was willing to accept aid from many different sources. But as was shown by the governments of Nimeiri, the TMC and Sadiq, giving aid did not make Sudan's government loyal clients. If anything, the multiple and varying sources of aid available to Sudan tended to exacerbate tensions and instability in Sudanese politics.

A consequence of the clientelist and Cold War politics of this period was that leading Western countries were not interested in mediating in the war. This remained the case even when clientelist policy began to be discredited. Relief was provided with little attention to the role of the war in causing humanitarian crises, and was in some respects an alternative to taking political action to deal with the war and the domestic policies of Sudan's governments. In the circumstances, therefore, no policy linkages between mediation and relief were made. Furthermore, the small possibility of linking relief with peace which emerged in 1988–9 (with the DUP–SPLM/A accord and the establishment of OLS) was quickly forestalled by the overthrow of Sadiq's government and the changes that this then brought to US and European relations with Sudan.

CONTAINMENT AND RELIEF, 1989–2001

The arrival of the government of President Bashir briefly led Sudan's erstwhile Western (and Arab) supporters to believe that Sudan might once more become a loyal client state. However, any prospect of a return to clientelist policies rapidly disappeared as the revolutionary and Islamist character of the government became apparent. Instead, the USA and (to a lesser extent) Europe turned increasingly towards ways of containing the Sudanese government. At the same time, they continued to fund relief for Sudan's recurring humanitarian crises. This combination of policy approaches – containment and relief aid – remained predominant until the late 1990s, when it began to be challenged by various developments, and new foreign-policy approaches to Sudan began to be explored.

The makings of a 'pariah' state

From its arrival in power in June 1989, through the first half of the 1990s, the government of Bashir steadily earned for Sudan a reputation as a 'pariah' state in Western eyes, and in the eyes of its regional Arab and African neighbours. The first element in the making of this reputation was the slow and unwelcome realisation internationally that Bashir's government was in reality the government of the NIF, headed by Hasan al-Turabi, and that it was espousing a revolutionary Sunni Islamist ideology. The Gulf crisis in 1990–1, precipitated by the Iraqi invasion of Kuwait, then brought about a sharp deterioration in Sudan's foreign relations, as a result of the Sudanese government's refusal to condemn the invasion. Although Sudan stated that Iraqi troops should leave Kuwait and the legitimate government be restored, it also denounced the build-up of US forces in the Gulf.

By itself, Sudan's position on the Gulf crisis might have prompted only a hardening of policies towards Sudan, similar to that incurred by the handful of other Arab governments that opposed the US-led campaign to liberate Kuwait. However Sudan's isolated position was compounded by growing Arab and Western concerns about the Sudanese government's political orientation and ambitions. Indeed, in the wake of the Gulf war, the two most important elements in making Sudan's reputation as a pariah state were the government's decision to allow visa-less entry to Sudan for all Arabs, and Turabi's establishment of the Popular Arab and Islamic Conference (PAIC), which embodied Turabi's Islamist views and his rejection of the post-Cold War 'new world order' and the Western presence in the Gulf.[26] Together, these two developments rapidly fed rumours and allegations of Sudanese support for and hosting of opposition groups from the Islamic world, fundamentalist, militant, or otherwise. In particular, it was increasingly alleged that Algerian and Egyptian Islamists, and Arab *mujahidin* returning from Afghanistan to the Middle East and North Africa after the Soviet withdrawal in 1989, were training in camps in Sudan, either by themselves or jointly with the PDF, the militia set up under Bashir for use in the war.[27]

The claims about dissident militants training in Sudan were generally unproven, but had some truth and were encouraged by the behaviour of the Sudanese government. To the alarm of Sudan's Arab neighbours – and the USA and Europe – the Sudanese government sought to develop its relations with Iran, and appeared to make progress in this. Thus, in March 1991 Iran reportedly agreed to finance a US$300m arms purchase by Sudan from China, and in December the Iranian president, Ali Akbar Rafsanjani, visited Khartoum accompanied by some 150 officials, following which Iran agreed to provide further economic assistance to Sudan, for example for road construction.[28] Prompted by these contacts, reports began to appear claiming that Iran had sent hundreds if not thousands of Iranian Revolutionary Guards to Sudan to help the regime in the war.

Other incidents and developments contributed to Sudan's worsening reputation. In 1991 the Tunisian government accused Sudan of allowing the Tunisian Islamist leader Rashid al-Ghannoushi to travel on a Sudanese diplomatic passport. Later that year Osama bin Laden settled in Sudan and began various business activities which at the time aroused little Western interest but which, from the late 1990s, retrospectively drew increasing Western attention, especially after the terrorist attacks on US targets on 11 September 2001. In 1993 Ilich Ramirez Sanchez – more commonly known as Carlos the Jackal, an internationally wanted terrorist – took up residence in Khartoum, after Iraq and Libya had refused to host him. But the critical factor in consolidating Sudan's reputation as a pariah state remained its hosting of members or offices of Arab and Islamic opposition groups, in particular Algerian, Egyptian, Lebanese and Palestinian groups, but also groups such as the Eritrean rebel movement Eritrean Islamic Jihad. Allegations about the presence and activities of these groups grew and seemed to be vindicated by the failed assassination attempt on the Egyptian president, Hosni Mubarak, in Addis Ababa in July 1995, in which the Sudanese authorities were widely believed to have been involved.

The shift to containment

Over the first half of the 1990s the USA and the major European states with relations with Sudan turned gradually towards a policy of containment, as too did regional Arab and African states. The shift, however, came with varying tactics, reflecting the varying interests of countries dealing with Sudan.

Prompted by its relief at the departure of Sadiq, and encouraged by Egypt, the USA at first welcomed Bashir's government and quickly recognised it. After officially condemning the coup, European governments followed suit. While some Western governments understood that the new Sudanese government might have connections with the NIF, most believed that they could still work with it. Thus, for example, Herman Cohen apparently believed that even if the new regime was fundamentalist, the US government could still work with it to achieve the 'main [US] objectives', namely implementation of OLS and the start of a peace process.[29] Despite Bashir's government banning all political parties and unions, and purging the army, the civil service and public institutions during the second half of 1989, the US position still did not visibly change. Indeed, as late as March 1990, Cohen was willing to say that the government was not an Islamic fundamentalist regime, that it was committed to a return to democracy through peace talks with the SPLM/A, and that it had been responsible for some human-rights improvements.³⁰ With that view Cohen explored developing a US peace initiative, following on from the Carter initiative in 1989.

The Gulf crisis was the first major challenge to US and European tolerance of Bashir's regime and effectively spelled an end to Cohen's initiative and any tentative US interest in mediating in the conflict. In mid-1992 US relations with Sudan were further jeopardised by the Sudanese government's execution of two Sudanese employees of USAID in Juba (on the purported grounds that they had been assisting the SPLM/A) and the disappearance of two other Sudanese USAID employees, whom the US government suspected had also been killed.³¹ The Sudanese government failed to give the USA satisfactory answers about these incidents. Meanwhile, US concern about Sudanese involvement in or support for international terrorism grew rapidly, leading the US State Department in August 1993 to add Sudan to the list of states that it accused of involvement in international terrorism, and to order a partial evacuation of the US embassy in Khartoum. The decisions were based on information about alleged new threats to US interests or personnel in Sudan, information which added to existing US concerns about the perceived presence in Sudan of members of Hizbullah, Hamas, the Abu Nidal Organisation, Palestinian Islamic Jihad and other groups.³²

The terrorism listing was not unanimously supported by US officials. Notably, the US ambassador to Sudan at the time, Don Petterson, later revealed that he did not believe that there were sufficient grounds for the terrorism listing or the embassy evacuation. Indeed, Petterson himself claims – almost certainly correctly – that during this period Egypt conducted a deliberate intelligence disinformation campaign which generated exaggerated stories in the media about the presence of Iranian Revolutionary Guards and the training of Algerian, Egyptian and Palestinian radicals in Sudan.³³ US officials did later conclude that the specific threat information on which they had based the evacuation decision was false, but the discovery was too late and too little to change US policy.³⁴ Instead, over the months and years after August 1993, the US belief that Sudan was involved in international terrorism continued to be fostered by subsequent intelligence reports and became firmly entrenched. The conviction in the USA of five Sudanese among a group of 12 men for the February 1993 World Trade Center bombing and the foiled plot to blow up tunnels, bridges and buildings in New York added to the apparent grounds for the terrorism listing.³⁵

According to Petterson, from as early as late 1993 a number of senior US officials at the State Department, the National Security Council and the

Department of Defense would have liked the USA to take stronger action against Sudan, but it was not politically practical:

> [O]nce faced with options that amounted to active US intervention, policy-makers backed off. They had no choice. They knew the administration was not in a position to advocate measures on Sudan that would be most unlikely to find favor with Congress or be understood by the American people.[36]

This lack of appetite for direct US intervention was understandable, given the lack of ideas about what it would aim to achieve, and the USA's embarrassing losses in Somalia in 1993. In the absence of more assertive measures, US Sudan policy therefore became one of defensive containment, and was stuck in a situation in which 'the US would stint on praise unless the Sudanese made major changes, and the Sudanese wanted more up-front praise from Washington before they would consider going in the direction Washington was stipulating'.[37] In December 1993 the State Department rejected calls from Congress for the President to appoint a special envoy for Sudan, saying that it would give an 'erroneous impression' at a time when Khartoum had 'made it clear that it rejects a role by the US in the peace process'.[38] But in response to continued pressure from Congress and the National Security Council, in May 1994 the US President appointed a special representative for Sudan, Melissa Wells, whose mandate was to help the IGAD peace effort and help the delivery of humanitarian assistance. Nonetheless, by 1995 Wells had concluded that both the Sudanese government and the SPLM/A were unresponsive to US concerns, and that both were obstructing or looting relief convoys.[39]

The Sudanese government rejected allegations about supporting terrorism and any alleged evidence, such as the USA presented in September 1994, which the USA believed was irrefutable proof of an armed training facility or camp north of Khartoum being used to train foreign militants. Publicly, President Bashir, Turabi, other officials, and sections of the Sudanese media openly accused the USA and the West of pursuing a 'crusade' against Sudan. Privately the government offered some co-operation on counter-terrorism measures, exemplified by its decision in response to French pressure to hand Carlos the Jackal over to French authorities in August 1994, for deportation to France. In 1995 the government reintroduced visa requirements for Arabs entering Sudan.[40] Eventually too, in response principally to Saudi pressure but also to US pressure, the Sudanese government prompted Osama bin Laden to leave Sudan in May 1996.

Despite the Sudanese government's protestations of innocence and its gestures of co-operation, the assassination attempt on Mubarak in 1995 seemed to confirm Western (and Arab and African) concerns about Sudan and reinforced the US view that Sudan posed a 'very real and imminent threat to US security interests and policy in the region'.[41] In 1996 Britain, France and the USA therefore voted for the imposition of limited UN sanctions on Sudan,[42] and the USA began to draft its own unilateral trade and economic sanctions against Sudan, which President Clinton signed into effect in November 1997. Faced with continuing concerns about the safety of US personnel in Sudan, in February 1996 the USA closed its embassy in Khartoum completely, while European countries maintained diplomatic relations with Sudan despite tensions.

During this period the USA also began to explore the possibility of more assertively containing the Sudanese government, by giving material support to neighbouring African states that were themselves trying to counter efforts by Sudan to destabilise them. The main element of this support was the decision in 1995 to supply nearly US$20m in 'nonlethal defensive military assistance' to Eritrea, Ethiopia and Uganda, countries which some US officials saw as members of an alliance of 'front-line states' that, along with Rwanda, was confronting hostile regimes in Sudan and Zaire (which at the time was sheltering the fugitive perpetrators of Rwanda's genocide). The first consignment of the aid (consisting of boots, rucksacks, rations and tents) arrived in Eritrea and Ethiopia in February 1997.[43] Coupled with a bill approved by the US Congress in 1997 authorising development assistance for the SPLM/A, the aid encouraged the expectation that the USA would yet give substantially more support for military action against the Sudanese government. But as a result of tensions within US policy on Sudan and the rapid unravelling of the 'front-line states' alliance, this was not to happen.

Meanwhile Arab and African states responded to Bashir's regime with their own methods of containment. Concern in Egypt, Saudi Arabia and the Gulf about the Islamist orientation of the regime, and the role of Turabi, grew more rapidly than in the USA or Europe, and there was widespread Arab condemnation in April 1990 when the government executed 28 army officers following an alleged coup plot.[44] Subsequently, relations deteriorated rapidly. In August 1990, in response to Sudan's abstention from the Arab League vote condemning the Iraqi invasion of Kuwait, Saudi Arabia suspended aid to Sudan, and the Gulf Co-operation Council (GCC) announced a boycott of Sudan.[45] In Khartoum demonstrations took place against Egypt and Saudi Arabia, and the largely government-controlled Sudanese press began a campaign supporting Iraq and criticising the countries that formed an alliance against it during 1990 and 1991, especially Saudi Arabia.[46] The war of words led to a proliferation of accusations. In January 1991, for example, it was alleged that Iraqi missiles had been stationed near Khartoum (at Jebel Awlia and Wadi Seidnaya) and on the Red Sea coast (at Aroussa), and that Iraqi fighter jets removed from Iraq at the start of the Gulf crisis had been flown to Sudan.⁴⁷ In August 1991 the Sudanese government accused the UAE and Saudi Arabia of funding an alleged coup attempt.⁴⁸

For its part, the Egyptian government intermittently alleged that Sudan was supporting militant opposition groups (an allegation that was repeated more widely in the West). Egyptian government ministers and President Mubarak made sometimes contradictory statements about the presence or absence of terrorist groups in Sudan, and Mubarak criticised Turabi and Sudanese fundamentalists but praised Bashir. After the Sudanese authorities confiscated Egyptian property in Khartoum, Egypt responded in September 1992 by annexing the Halaib triangle, a disputed border area historically administered by Sudan. Meanwhile, in a sign of Saudi displeasure with the regime, the Organisation of the Islamic Conference rescheduled its 1992 summit away from Khartoum.⁴⁹ From 1991 Egypt also allowed the leadership of a new but small Sudanese armed opposition group, the Legitimate Command, to be based in Egypt, but not (according to the Egyptian government) to carry out military operations from Egyptian territory.⁵⁰ Nonetheless, Sudan accused Egypt of providing direct military assistance to northern opposition groups, and in 1992 it even accused Saudi Arabia of sending two arms shipments to the SPLM/A, which it alleged were intercepted by Kenyan authorities.⁵¹

Arab pressure on Sudan reached its peak between 1995 and 1997. After the assassination attempt on Mubarak in 1995, Egypt offered to host meetings of the NDA and supported the passing of the three UN Security Council resolutions on Sudan. But it was careful to limit the pressure applied to Sudan. Chastened by the example of the economic and humanitarian consequences of the UN sanctions on Iraq – and not wanting to cause the collapse of Bashir's government – it in fact lobbied against the imposition of stronger UN sanctions. In this it was encouraged by the belated response of the Sudanese government to the pressures it had already been put under to abolish the PAIC, expel Osama bin Laden, and end its apparent support for Arab and Islamic opposition groups such as the Egyptian Gamaa Islamiyya.

During the same period, Sudan's African neighbours similarly used a range of political and practical measures to try to contain Bashir's regime and the threats that it posed them. In terms of consequences for the war in Sudan, the most important measure they took was to support Sudanese opposition groups, in particular the SPLM/A, thereby continuing the pattern of reciprocal destabilisation within the region. For example, after the overthrow of Mengistu in 1991, the shelter previously provided to the

SPLM/A by Ethiopia was to some extent replaced by support and shelter provided by Uganda. In providing this support, the Ugandan government was increasingly trying to respond to Sudanese antagonism. From the early 1990s the Sudanese government had tried to support the oppositionist Muslim Tabligh movement in Uganda and its offshoots, and in 1993–4 it began to support the rebel Ugandan movements the Lord's Resistance Army and the West Nile Bank Liberation Front, which were active along Sudan's borders with Uganda and Zaire.[52] By 1995, Uganda and Sudan were almost openly at war with each other, and diplomatic relations were cut. This situation continued through to 1997 and beyond. Meanwhile Ethiopia and Eritrea similarly responded to Sudanese support for Islamist opposition groups in their countries by offering shelter to Sudanese opposition groups and the SPLM/A. This led in 1995 to Eritrea allowing the NDA to take over the premises of the Sudanese embassy in Asmara, and to the encouragement of the short-lived idea of the 'front-line states' alliance. Officially, Eritrea, Ethiopia, Kenya and Uganda were all committed to the peaceful resolution of Sudan's war through talks convened by IGAD, but as these talks were frozen between 1994 and 1997, covert or overt support to the SPLM/A and the NDA was the only practical measure available.

Challenges to containment

Between 1997 and 2001, US policy on Sudan was increasingly called into question within the USA, and pressure rose for a change in policy. That change would eventually come in the form of the increased engagement of the USA with Sudan from 2001 onwards. During the same period, European policy on Sudan also converged towards more active engagement in resolving the civil war.

Three developments in 1997 and 1998 marked the start of the challenges to existing US policy on Sudan. The first was the revelation in 1997 that the US sanctions on Sudan did not apparently prevent a US oil company, Occidental, from pursuing business in Sudan's oil sector.[53] Following this, the outbreak of war between Eritrea and Ethiopia in May 1998 heralded the demise of the 'front-line states' alliance. Finally, the bombings of the US embassies in Nairobi and Dar es-Salaam in August 1998, and the US response of bombing the Al-Shifa factory in Khartoum – in the mistaken belief that it was being used to develop chemical weapons, for potential use in a terrorist attack in the USA – dealt a further embarrassing blow to the public credibility of US policy on Sudan. Although it is likely that Sudanese individuals had been involved in facilitating or carrying out the embassy bombings, which were (probably correctly) attributed to Osama bin Laden, when it emerged that Al-Shifa was a pharmaceuticals factory, and that the information on which the USA had based its decision was misconstrued or simply wrong, the Sudanese government was able to present itself as the righteous victim of US aggression.[54]

These developments coincided with the rise of Sudan as a popular issue within the USA, which made its impact on policy-making in Washington through voices in two main lobbying forces, the black American lobby and the Christian lobby. Allegations that the war and the Sudanese government were fuelling a slave trade, in which slaves could be 'redeemed' for money, received growing coverage in the US domestic media.[55] Behind much of the coverage were a few vociferous NGOs, notably Christian Solidarity International (CSI) and the American Anti-Slavery Group, whose head became the director of a 'Sudan Campaign' from 2000, representing a coalition of groups lobbying against alleged slavery in Sudan. The Sudanese government's persistent denial of humanitarian access to the Nuba Mountains, and crises such as the 1998 famine, added to the perception in the USA that the USA was not doing enough to prevent human rights abuses in Sudan.

Partly in response to this pressure, in 1998 the US Congress passed an 'International Religious Freedom Bill', which resulted in the establishment of a new office in the State Department and a US Commission on International Religious Freedom (CIRF). The US Congress then passed a resolution in May 1999 saying that 'genocide' was occurring in Sudan, and some members of Congress demanded that if the Clinton administration did not believe that genocide was occurring, 'it should clearly explain the basis for its belief'.[56] Shortly afterwards, the State Department designated Sudan 'a country of particular concern' on religion, and in May 2000 the CIRF published its first report on Sudan, describing the Sudanese government as 'the world's most violent abuser of the right to freedom of religion and belief'.[57] Most prominently, though, in 2000 the US Congress passed a bill on famine-relief efforts and support for a 'comprehensive solution to the war'.[58] The main effect of the bill – which became known as the Sudan Peace Act and would be maintained, with updates, over the following four years – was that it added to the pressure on the US government to do more about Sudan. It was also a sign that, contrary to the opinion of the US Secretary of State, Madeleine Albright, Sudan was (to some extent) 'marketable' in the USA as a popular foreign-policy issue.[59]

Overlapping with these pressures was the response of human-rights campaigners to the long-delayed expansion of Sudan's oil sector, which was marked by the start of oil exports in August 1999 following major investments in the oil sector, principally from the China National Petroleum Corporation (CNPC) and Petronas of Malaysia. While US companies were prevented by US sanctions from doing business in Sudan's nascent oil sector, Canadian and European companies at first faced no such constraint, and a few (notably Talisman of Canada and Lundin of Sweden) eagerly pursued opportunities in Sudan. By 1999, the activities of these companies in Sudan were attracting growing international criticism, and a stream of critical reports began to be published which aimed to bring about policy changes to stop such companies operating in Sudan.[60] Additionally, in May 2000 a coalition of European NGOs formed the European Coalition on Oil in Sudan (ECOS), to lobby European governments and companies, and in 2001 ECOS launched a public appeal aiming to establish minimum standards for doing business in Sudan's oil sector.[61]

During the same period, two significant developments in Sudan challenged existing US and European policy, by presenting an apparent opportunity for increased engagement, rather than adding to pressure against that. Firstly, from about 1997 the Sudanese government began to abandon the aggressive external aspects of its foreign policy and embarked on an international charm offensive which aimed to convince its opponents abroad that it had changed its policies.[62] Partly as a result, relations with Egypt began to improve and, following the Egyptian government's success in 1997 at neutralising the Gamaa Islamiyya, Egypt refocused its Sudan policy on the objective of isolating Turabi rather than Sudan as a whole. Egypt further rewarded Sudan for the improvement in relations by launching the Egyptian–Libyan peace initiative in February 1999, which the Sudanese government welcomed as an alternative to IGAD.

The second development which appeared to present the USA and Europe with a new opportunity in relations with Sudan was the expulsion of Turabi from government in December 1999. The expulsion was the result of pressure from Egypt and Saudi Arabia and from within the government, from President Bashir himself and two influential protégés of Turabi, Ali Uthman Mohammed Taha and Nafi Ali Nafi. The depth of distrust between Western governments and the Sudanese government, combined with doubts about the sincerity of the expulsion, meant that relations could not be transformed quickly. However, the expulsion added to the perception on both sides that the time was ripe for a change in relations.[63]

Amid the pressures and opportunities for US and European policy towards Sudan, actual policy remained a mixture of measures variously intended to contain the Sudanese government and to engage it in a limited fashion in dialogue about the normalisation of relations, the resolution of the war, and – principally for the USA – resolving concerns about Sudanese support for terrorism. Thus, for example, in September 1999 President Clinton appointed a new special envoy for Sudan, Harry Johnston; and following the visit of an EU mission to Khartoum, in November the EU formally opened 'political dialogue' with the Sudanese government, which was intended to be the start of a process of moving towards the normalisation of relations. In contrast, in the same year the US Congress passed an appropriations bill, allowing for food aid to be delivered directly to armed rebel groups in Sudan, at the discretion of the President. In response to pressure from international and US NGOs in Sudan against giving food aid directly to the SPLM/A (on grounds of SPLM/A abuses, NGO staff safety, and neutrality), in February 2000 President Clinton informed Congress that he would not allow aid to the SPLM/A at that time. However, by the end of 2000, the outgoing Clinton administration had approved US$10m in 'nonlethal nonfood' assistance to the NDA for the fiscal year 2001, as well as US$3m for a project to provide negotiation training and office support to the NDA, to build its capacity to participate in the peace process.[64]

The gradual movement of the USA during 1999 and 2000 towards engaging in the IGAD talks brought it onto common ground with European donor countries which were also trying to improve the effectiveness of the talks, through their participation in the IGAD Partners Forum (IPF). At the same time the USA continued to try to discuss terrorism issues with the Sudanese authorities; and partly as a result of dialogue opened through Johnston, in May 2000 a US counter-terrorism 'task force' arrived in Sudan with a list of six issues for Sudan to address in order to resolve US concerns about Sudanese support for terrorism.[65] Nonetheless, relations remained difficult. Johnston made no impact on the peace talks, and in July 2000 the USA successfully blocked Sudan's bid to become a temporary member of the UN Security Council, and blocked a proposal to lift the UN sanctions on Sudan.

Continuing with relief

While the USA and Europe (and Sudan's Arab and African neighbours too) wrestled with ways of politically containing the regime in Sudan, as the leading international humanitarian donors, the USA and Europe were also still faced with the need to respond to the continuing humanitarian crises in Sudan. Over the course of 1990 and 1991 leading donors suspended development aid to Sudan, in response to concerns about democracy, human rights and the war. Despite this, international donors continued to provide relief with some consistency, and from 1989 to 2001 (and beyond) they built on and continued with the systems of relief aid that had begun to be developed before Bashir came to power.

The provision of official US relief was overseen principally by USAID's Bureau for Humanitarian Response, working through its subsidiary offices, in particular the Office of Foreign Disaster Assistance.[66] Over the course of the 1990s, the total value of US relief ran into hundreds of millions of dollars, though much of it was food aid (which was a convenient way of using surplus grain production). Nonetheless, US officials were aware of and concerned by the looting and obstruction of relief supplies by the Sudanese government and the SPLM/A. Thus, for example, the US ambassador to Sudan between 1989 and 1992, James Cheek, believed that the SPLM/A's relief arm, the SRRA, 'could not be trusted to distribute food'.[67] Similarly his successor, Petterson, was sceptical about the implementation of the agreements between the Sudanese government and OLS, signed in 1994.[68]

European donors provided relief through their overseas development ministries or departments, and through the European Commission. The levels of relief that they provided were substantial, but were much less than the value of US relief. The largest donor was the European Community Humanitarian Aid Office (ECHO), which provided a total of US$159m in humanitarian assistance to Sudan between 1992 (when it was established) and 2000, making Sudan the third largest recipient of EC humanitarian aid in that period, after the Great Lakes region (US$423m), and the former Yugoslavia (US$2,121m).[69] In comparison, in the ten years following its suspension of development aid in 1991, Britain provided an average of only £7m per year for relief work in Sudan.[70] The other main European donors – France, Germany, Italy and the Netherlands – all provided similarly small amounts, while Norway provided much of its relief and development assistance to Sudan outside the OLS framework.

As discussed in the previous chapter, during the 1990s very little changed in the substance of relief and its actual delivery in the field. However, several significant changes occurred in donor policy on relief. The most important of these was that over the course of the decade, the USA and Europe in varying degrees shifted from distrusting the SPLM/A and being unwilling to engage with it, towards cautiously trusting it and co-operating with it. This shift did not entail the adoption of a firm policy of using relief to support a warring party, although some have argued that tacitly there was such a policy. For example, in the opinion of one former senior UN official who oversaw OLS in the late 1990s, 'certainly OLS in the south had a [US] political strategy attached to it, and that was [to support] the survival of the SPLA'.[71] But, as shown by the short-lived 'front-line states' strategy and the hesitant consideration in the late 1990s of whether to provide aid directly to the SPLM/A, the USA explored more direct ways of supporting the SPLM/A, although they ultimately had little effect.

By the end of the decade, however, several other factors were coming into place which reflected the desire of some donors to change what they did with relief in Sudan. Prompted by cases such as Sudan, USAID had established an 'Office of Transition Initiatives', which was intended to promote democracy and peacebuilding in transitional and post-war situations, and to fill the gap between relief and development assistance.[72] For Southern Sudan, USAID had also launched a 'Sudan Transitional Assistance for Rehabilitation' programme, and the share of US aid delivered to Sudan outside OLS had increased from 14 per cent in 1997 to 34 per cent in 2000. Meanwhile the EU's opening of 'political dialogue' with Khartoum in November 1999 was accompanied by the aim of launching a 'Humanitarian Plus' programme of €15m aid, which also aimed to start bridging the gap between relief and development assistance.[73] As it was, the combination of pressures from human-rights activists about Sudan, and the fact of the continuation of the war, meant that the Humanitarian Plus programme was not properly launched until 2002.

Assessing containment

Although it was not a uniform, consistent policy, containment was the predominant approach in US and European foreign policy towards Sudan between 1989 and 2001. In so far as external pressure on Sudan was responsible for the re-orientation of its foreign policy and outward behaviour after 1997, containment was broadly successful. But in terms of meeting specific objectives such as counter-terrorism co-operation and preventing the destabilisation of neighbouring states, containment had less success. Indeed, it was partly because of the shortcomings in US and European policy that by the end of the 1990s new policy approaches were being considered.

Given the course of Sudan's international relations over this period, it is understandable that the USA and Europe saw little to be gained from mediating in the war. After the rapid failure of the Carter and Cohen initiatives, African mediation efforts (the Abuja and IGAD talks) provided an apparent alternative to further Western mediation. When the IGAD talks resumed in 1997, and Sudanese foreign policy began to change, potentially the USA and Europe could have moved more quickly to support the IGAD talks. But uncertainty about the intentions of the Sudanese government, combined with pressures in the USA and Europe against engaging with Sudan, and some disarray in policy, meant that it was not until 2001 that the USA and Europe began to significantly increase their involvement in the IGAD peace talks.

Meanwhile, throughout the 1990s the most constant element in US and European policy towards Sudan was relief. In varying degrees, donors knew that relief benefited the SPLM/A, but (with some exception for Norway) there is no evidence that donors tried to use relief as 'a tool to influence the conflict'.[74] Instead, the provision of relief came in response to appeals from relief agencies and was overwhelmingly a humanitarian issue. Nonetheless, the focus on relief in response to the effects of the war also acted – albeit unintentionally – as a substitute for political action to try to resolve the war.

ENGAGEMENT AND RELIEF, 2001–4

In a continuation of the tentative changes begun in the preceding years, from 2001 US and European policy towards Sudan shifted significantly towards engagement. From late 2001 through to the end of 2004 and the signing of the CPA in January 2005, the USA, Britain and Norway, and to a lesser extent the EU, became increasingly involved in the IGAD peace talks for Sudan. This shift, however, was gradually challenged by the escalation of the Darfur conflict, and the Sudanese government's limited co-operation in dealing with the conflict and its humanitarian consequences.

The shift to engagement

The gradual shift in US policy towards Sudan accelerated with the arrival in office at the start of 2001 of President George W. Bush. In February 2001 a task force set up by a Washington-based think-tank, the Center for Strategic and International Studies (CSIS), published its recommendations on Sudan policy. The CIRF also published a report on Sudan, and in March 2001 a Congressional hearing on Sudan was held.[75] At the same time, the new Secretary of State, Colin Powell, announced that the administration was reviewing its Sudan policy.

The CSIS report argued that US policy in the 1990s had, ultimately, failed to significantly weaken the Sudanese government or strengthen the opposition, and had failed to moderate the conduct of the war, improve humanitarian access or promote productive peace negotiations. However, the report also argued that the USA had 'significant leverage' in Sudan, at a time when growing oil revenues had shifted the balance of military power in the government's favour, and 'significant internal rifts' had appeared in Khartoum (exemplified by the expulsion of Turabi from government). The report therefore made a number of recommendations for US policy, in particular that the USA concentrate its Sudan policy 'on the single over-riding objective of ending Sudan's war', and that it test the seriousness of other international partners to initiate a serious peace process; that it push for an expansion of humanitarian assistance in Northern and Southern Sudan and the addition of non-humanitarian assistance for the SPLM/A; that it increase the staffing of its embassy in Khartoum; and that it successfully conclude negotiations with Khartoum on terrorism.[76]

Some American officials remained sceptical about whether the strategy recommended by CSIS was appropriate and whether, for example, the USA should instead find ways to hurt the Sudanese government, rather than engage in dialogue.[77] However, what limited appetite there had been for increasing military pressure on Khartoum was already dwindling, with even the CIRF now shying away from advocating direct support to the SPLM/A, non-lethal or lethal.[78] Instead, cautious engagement – along the lines advocated by CSIS – appeared to offer the Bush administration a new way of managing the contradictory pressures on Sudan policy. These pressures included calls from Congress for capital markets sanctions to be added to the Sudan Peace Act (which the Bush administration opposed), on-going claims about slavery and slave redemption in Sudan,[79] and efforts to secure Sudan's co-operation on counter-terrorism. The Bush administration's refusal to involve itself in the Israeli–Palestinian peace process as the Clinton administration had done provided an added incentive to explore the idea of engaging with another peace process, such as Sudan's, even despite the minor embarrassment for the USA of being voted off the UN Human Rights Commission in May 2001 while Sudan was voted on to it.

The upshot of these pressures was the appointment on 6 September 2001 of John Danforth, a US senator, as the President's special envoy for Sudan. Given the commitment with which Danforth went about his task, and the increased international interest in resolving Sudan's war, by itself his appointment would have added to the momentum for engagement and dialogue. However, the 11 September 2001 terrorist attacks in the USA brought additional impetus to his mission, by helping to crystallise US Sudan policy around 'three very clear goals'.[80] As the administration made clear, these were firstly to prevent Sudan supporting or becoming a safe haven for terrorists, and secondly and thirdly to improve the humanitarian situation and to help to end the war. In varying degrees these goals were shared by Britain, Norway and the EU. Along with these partners, from late 2001 onwards the USA therefore began to increase its engagement with Sudan, most visibly through its mediation in the IGAD talks in Kenya. In doing so, the USA and its European partners tried to use a number of incentives and threats – or carrots and sticks – to encourage the Sudanese government and the SPLM/A to meet their various objectives. Some of these carrots and sticks were related to 9/11.

Like other countries which the USA had previously suspected of involvement in terrorism, Sudan tried and largely succeeded in getting on the right side of the USA and its 'war on terror' after 9/11. President Bashir quickly condemned the 9/11 attacks and within a few days the US Secretary of State Colin Powell telephoned the Sudanese Foreign Minister, Mustafa Othman Ismail, in the first such high-level contact since the early 1990s. The Sudanese government responded to the US government's intensified search for co-operation on counter-terrorism and intelligence, and reports soon began to circulate that it was offering to share with the USA intelligence which it had built up on Osama bin Laden and his supporters during their stay in Sudan.[81] Some reports also claimed that in the weeks after 9/11 the Sudanese authorities arrested several people accused of involvement in terrorism and handed them over to the USA, although Sudanese officials denied this.[82] Whatever the exact truth, the co-operation was enough for the USA to go along with a 14–0 UN Security Council vote on 28 September (with the USA abstaining) in favour of lifting the UN sanctions on Sudan.

However, the pressures and opportunities raised by 9/11 were not enough to transform Sudanese–US relations. In October 2001 Sudan's cabinet and national assembly criticised the US attack on Afghanistan, and demonstrations against the USA were mounted in Khartoum. In November the USA renewed its own unilateral sanctions on Sudan and kept Sudan's name on the list of states that it accused of involvement in terrorism.[83] All the same, in November Danforth visited Sudan, and, after some encouraging initial meetings in which he proposed four confidence-building measures or tests to the government and the SPLM/A, in December a State Department technical team went to Sudan to discuss details. From this process came the Nuba Mountains ceasefire in January 2002, followed by Danforth's report to President Bush in which he advocated US engagement with the IGAD peace process, subject to the compliance of the parties with the four confidence-building measures.

According to Sudan's chief negotiator at the IGAD talks in 2002–3, Ghazi Salah al-Din Atabani, Sudan's decision to accept a US role in the IGAD talks was 'based on a simple logic':

> This was that the United States was the principal backer of the war, regardless of what its official or semi-official or civilian institutions said, and its hostility reached the level of striking us with missiles, as everyone knows.[84]

This 'logic' did not mean, though, that the Sudanese government greatly feared that the USA might do for the SPLM/A what it did for the Northern Alliance in Afghanistan, although Sudanese officials may well have given the idea some thought in late 2001. For from early 2002 onwards it was increasingly apparent internationally that the next target for US military action was Iraq. In the meantime, the USA continued to seek Sudan's co-operation on counter-terrorism, and from the first round of the enlarged IGAD talks (with the participation of the 'troika') in mid-2002 and onwards, the Sudanese government showed that it was not afraid to drag its feet in the talks. Similarly, even after the US invasion of Iraq in 2003 it was still not afraid to be un-cooperative on peace talks or on Darfur.

The impact of 9/11 on Sudanese–US relations was therefore far from decisive. Its greatest impact was on US thinking, giving importance to the idea that the USA should prevent Sudan becoming a 'failed state' which could shelter terrorists in the way that Afghanistan had. [85] But other than the tenuous threat of stepping up support to the SPLM/A, the USA and Europe had only a modest range of carrots and sticks available to them with which to coax the Sudanese government into co-operating with their objectives. The carrots included the promise of debt relief and the normalisation of relations, if peace was achieved and the Sudanese government co-operated on terrorism matters and on improving humanitarian access. The sticks consisted principally of the threat of increased political isolation and the imposition of new sanctions. As would become apparent during 2002–4, these were far from enough to ensure the co-operation of the Sudanese government.

Challenges to engagement

The limitations to US and European leverage over the Sudanese government became apparent only gradually during 2002–4. On the counter-terrorism issues on which the USA sought Sudan's co-operation – which included the signature and ratification of some 12 international counter-terrorism agreements, co-operation about relations with Palestinian groups, and intelligence about al-Qaeda – the US government considered that it made good progress. According to the State Department, on the 'generic issue of terrorism' by March 2004 the Sudanese government was already 'about 90 per cent of the way there' (i.e. towards satisfying US concerns).[86] In May 2004 the State Department therefore removed Sudan from a list of countries which it deemed 'non-cooperative' in the US 'war on terror'. However, it kept Sudan on the list of countries that it accused of supporting terrorism, because of US concern about the representation of the Palestinian organisations Hamas and Islamic Jihad in Khartoum, and other matters.

Meanwhile, as described in Chapters 2 and 3, the USA and Europe met with a mixture of success and failure in their other main objectives, namely to bring about a resolution of the war (through their mediation in the IGAD peace talks) and an improvement in the humanitarian situation.

The achievement of the CPA was offset by the failure of the peace process to prevent the escalation of conflict in Darfur. Underlying this outcome were two connected problems: the dilemma that Darfur presented to the engagement of the USA and Europe with Sudan and the IGAD peace talks, and the weakness of the various carrots and sticks at their disposal.

In 2002 and 2003 there were warning signs that conflict in Darfur could escalate and was escalating, and warnings were voiced by Darfurian campaigners and human-rights advocates. But the warnings were not more widely heeded until well into 2003 and early 2004.[87] During 2003, the difficulties in the IGAD peace process, and the comparatively low scale of the conflict in Darfur, encouraged the USA, Britain and Norway (and their IGAD partners) to remain focused on the IGAD talks – in the hope of reaching a CPA between the Sudanese government and the SPLM/A – and to ignore Darfur. This approach became more difficult in early 2004, when the humanitarian consequences of the conflict began to worsen sharply, and the conflict began to receive more extensive international attention. Nonetheless, having committed so much to the IGAD framework and with a final agreement apparently in sight, the troika and IGAD remained reluctant to take strong action over Darfur, for fear of jeopardising the IGAD talks. The reluctance and uncertainty were noted by the International Crisis Group in a report in March 2004:

> As evidence of massive violence against civilians in Darfur mounted in the last quarter of 2003, Khartoum's international partners remained divided on how to react. While the diplomatic community in Khartoum explored possible vehicles for international action, such as a statement by a senior UN humanitarian official before the Security Council, some influential members, namely the UK and US, advocated a lower profile.[88]

Gradually, however, a tacit consensus evolved among the troika and IGAD partners to prioritise the aim of concluding the IGAD talks over the task of dealing with Darfur. The approach was aptly described by the UN head in Sudan between March 2003 and April 2004, Mukesh Kapila, as a '*de facto* policy of sequencing' on the part of the states pushing the IGAD peace process.[89] Furthermore, it seems clear that, as Kapila argues, the pressure to reach a final agreement between the government and the SPLM/A reduced the sense of political urgency to tackle Darfur.[90] In this regard, Kapila's words to a British parliamentary hearing in 2005 are instructive:

> There is no question in my mind and that of anyone who actually knows what is going on that there was a policy of sequencing. I do

not think it was an orchestrated policy, in other words I do not think people sat in the chanceries of the Security Council countries and said, 'We'll deliberately ignore Darfur and deliberately let the people of Darfur suffer and we will turn a blind eye to them until we have sorted out the Naivasha process.' It was the effect of a bandwagon which had not only rolled but had corralled a whole lot of other wagons around it, so they were all together.[91]

Significantly, too, Kapila has said that he himself received suggestions from the British government that he should ease up his comments and criticisms on Darfur until the peace process in Naivasha was concluded.[92] Kapila has also said that when he and the UN Under-Secretary-General for Humanitarian Affairs, Jan Egeland, asked Western capitals to refer the matter of Darfur to the UN Security Council, they repeatedly received the answer 'Not yet'. In the case of Britain, for example, Kapila says:

I remember saying to the Foreign Office, 'Please refer this matter. As a UN coordinator I am bringing to your attention that there are crimes against humanity being committed. This must be brought to the Security Council's attention', and I was told 'Not yet'.[93]

However, as the international outcry about the situation in Darfur increased during 2004, the troika and partners came under pressure to say and do more about the situation. This they did, principally by condemning the violence (in some cases eventually describing what was happening in Darfur as ethnic cleansing or genocide), and by passing UN Security Council resolutions, threatening sanctions, and providing funding for relief in Darfur. The troika and the EU also offered political, financial and technical support for the AU ceasefire-monitoring mission in Darfur and the subsequent AU peacekeeping mission in Darfur, AMIS. Thus, as of May 2004, the USA summed up its response to Darfur as follows:

We have taken a firm vocal stand in condemning the violence and atrocities in Darfur. We are intensively engaged in efforts to address this crisis as you know. US diplomacy was in fact instrumental in bringing the government into face-to-face talks with the rebels that have resulted in this April 8 cease-fire that was signed in N'djamena.[94]

In addition, the troika began to argue publicly that concluding the IGAD peace process would benefit Darfur by providing a 'template' agreement for resolving the Darfur conflict. This argument implicitly justified the level of prioritisation that the troika gave to the talks in Naivasha, over Darfur, and the troika were encouraged in this thinking by the signing of the Naivasha protocols in June 2004. Reflecting this, following the signing of the protocols, the US State Department special adviser on Sudan, Michael Ranneberger, said in an interview in June 2004:

> We [the USA] intend to continue to exert enormous pressure on the government to end the violence in Darfur. I think we have an opportunity now with the signing of the Naivasha accords to try to turn around the situation in Darfur. So I think those accords signed at Naivasha will have a very positive impact on Darfur.[95]

As events would show, this was not to be the case: essentially the Naivasha protocols and the CPA did not have the positive impact on Darfur that the troika hoped for – nor in truth did they have any significant positive impact on Darfur at all.

The dilemma that Darfur presented to Western engagement with Sudan and the IGAD peace process was exacerbated by the weakness of the 'carrots and sticks' at the disposal of the troika and the EU. At best, UN Security Council resolutions –instigated by Britain and the USA – prompted temporary co-operation from the Sudanese government with efforts to stem the fighting and insecurity in Darfur and to improve humanitarian access. The special session of the Security Council in Nairobi in November 2004 also helped to push the IGAD talks to their definitive conclusion. But otherwise the leverage of the troika and the EU was constrained by a number of factors, the most important of which were Chinese opposition to strong action against the Sudanese government, and their own unwillingness to attempt unilateral action – military or otherwise – without UN approval.

The constraint caused by Chinese opposition to sanctions was manifest. As the largest foreign investor in Sudan's growing oil sector, with substantial other business interests in Sudan and no commitment to resolving the civil war, China would not have accepted the imposition of substantial sanctions. In the words of John Danforth, who was US ambassador to the UN at the time (after his earlier service as the President's special envoy for Sudan), '[T]here was no doubt that we [the UN Security Council] were not going to impose sanctions because at least the Chinese would have vetoed the sanctions.'[96]

In contrast, the constraint caused by European and US unwillingness to attempt unilateral action on Darfur was less obvious, but was nonetheless significant. The constraint itself came from the combination of the fundamental reluctance of Western countries to commit troops to ventures in Africa (even after the pledges made after the genocide in Rwanda), and the pressures of the US 'war on terror' and the troubled outcome of the US-led invasion of Iraq in 2003. In the context of the 'war on terror' and counter-terrorism co-operation with the Sudanese government, the risks of a venture in Sudan were ones which Britain and the USA were even less willing to take than they would otherwise have been. Indeed, during Western countries' search in 2004 for ways to respond to the Darfur conflict, the Sudanese government even warned that bringing foreign troops into Darfur would risk creating a second Iraq. In short, military action against Sudan without Security Council approval but with 'at best a coalition of the willing', was not something Britain or the US favoured after Iraq.[97] Support for an AU mission in Darfur was therefore a convenient alternative.

These two major constraints largely explain why the various carrots and sticks which Europe and the USA attempted to use on Sudan were not more effective. As a consequence, although the decision by parts of the Bush administration to describe events in Darfur as 'genocide' was controversial and attracted much attention, it did not trigger any consequences for Sudan. (Even Danforth considered that it 'was something that was said for internal consumption within the United States', which would have little effect within Sudan.)[98] Sudan's rapidly growing oil revenues also meant, for example, that the British offer of debt relief, on the condition of concluding the CPA and making 'progress in dealing with the problems in Darfur', failed to influence the Sudanese government, even though Britain naively considered it 'a very powerful stick or carrot'.[99]

Attempting co-ordination with humanitarian policy

The shift in Western foreign policy towards Sudan to engagement after 2001 was accompanied by the continued provision of relief. As indicated in Chapter 3, the need for relief between 2002 and 2004 increased because of the escalation of the Darfur conflict, and despite the progress in the IGAD peace talks. However, partly as a consequence of the shift towards engagement and pressure from people who were responsible for relief and development policy, efforts were also made to bring together the political and humanitarian dimensions of policy. The US State Department, for example, and USAID's Bureau for Democracy, Conflict, and Humanitarian Assistance (DCHA) established a joint Sudan office. Similarly in Britain, in February 2002 – at the same time as the British Prime Minister appointed Alan Goulty (a former British ambassador to Sudan) as special envoy for Sudan – the Foreign and Commonwealth Office and the Department for International Development (DFID) established a dedicated 'Sudan Unit', bringing together staff from each department.

130   DARFUR AND THE INTERNATIONAL COMMUNITY

The impact of these inter-departmental initiatives was positive and encouraging, at least to begin with. At the instigation principally of DCHA, the US government explored the possibility of using relief as an entry point for political action, a strategy which it thought was vindicated by its success in 2001–2 in persuading the Sudanese government to agree firstly to USAID relief flights to the Nuba Mountains from El Obeid, and then to the Nuba Mountains ceasefire agreement.[100] Closer relations between foreign-ministry and aid or development ministry officials were also fostered during the peace talks from 2002 onwards. For example, the USAID Assistant Administrator in charge of DCHA, Roger Winter, was closely involved in the US mediation in the talks, along with the principal US mediation representative, Jeff Millington, a State Department official. Likewise, Norwegian foreign and development ministry officials co-operated closely in supporting Norway's mediation role, which itself was led by Hilde Johnson, the Development Minister.

Despite these efforts at policy co-ordination and co-operation, tensions persisted between foreign and humanitarian policy during 2002–4. For the USA, and to a lesser extent Britain, the tensions became more acute when the Darfur conflict escalated, when interests in counter-terrorism co-operation and moving towards the normalisation of relations with Sudan conflicted with pressures to take punitive measures in response to the lack of co-operation from the Sudanese government on resolving the conflict in Darfur and improving the humanitarian situation.[101] With the Darfur situation still far from resolved by the time the CPA was signed, the tensions between foreign and humanitarian policy also continued.

Assessing engagement

Following on from the shift begun in the late 1990s, engagement was the main approach in US and European policy towards Sudan between 2001 and 2004. In concrete terms, the main new element in policy towards Sudan was the undertaking to seek a peaceful settlement of the war by taking a primary mediating role in the IGAD talks. The other two main elements of policy towards Sudan – seeking co-operation on counter-terrorism, and improved access for humanitarian assistance – were essentially a continuation of existing policy.

The shift to engagement brought some new success, but it did not resolve the problems which had previously affected policy towards Sudan. In terms of meeting the objective of bringing about an end to Sudan's civil war, engagement achieved a very mixed result, with the outcome of the CPA being severely compromised by the Darfur conflict. Similarly, while improvements in humanitarian access in the south were achieved through the peace process between the government and the SPLM/A, bureaucratic and security constraints on humanitarian access remained a problem in the Darfur conflict (as discussed in Chapter 3). Set against these results, progress on the objective of improved counter-terrorism co-operation was a modest result.

Finally, the Nuba Mountains ceasefire agreement provided an example of a constructive linkage between political and humanitarian action. However, such linkage was not otherwise attempted, either in the rest of the negotiations between the government and the SPLM/A, or in the Darfur conflict. This remained true in the years after the CPA was signed, when the Darfur conflict continued.

ENGAGEMENT AND CONTAINMENT, 2004 ONWARDS

From 2004 through to 2009 the trend in European and US foreign policy towards greater engagement with Sudan was blocked by renewed pressures to contain, sanction and punish the Sudanese government, primarily on account of the Darfur conflict. In the same period, the African Union, China and the Arab League all became more involved in international responses to Sudan and the Darfur conflict. Simultaneously, the practical forms of the international community's engagement with Sudan grew, as the AU and UN peacekeeping missions in Sudan expanded, as international humanitarian and development aid grew, and as the ICC took up the case of Darfur.

The pressures over Darfur

After rising in prominence only slowly during 2002 and 2003, in 2004 and 2005 the Darfur conflict moved dramatically to the forefront of international attention to Sudan. This was the result of a combination of factors, in particular the intensity of the conflict in this period, the coincidence in April 2004 of the tenth anniversary of the Rwanda genocide, the surge in Western media coverage of the conflict, the rise in international debate about what was happening in Darfur, and the rise in advocacy about what governments and the international community should do in response to the conflict. As a result, Darfur became a challenge to policy that could not be ignored.

The rise in non-governmental advocacy and activism about Darfur was most dramatic in the USA. In July 2004 a group of representatives from various human-rights, political and religious organisations announced the formation of the Save Darfur Coalition (SDC). Over the following two years and beyond, SDC became a small phenomenon in itself in the USA, thanks to a combination of professional advertising, networking, support from celebrities, and outreach to schools and universities, and thanks to the existence of an audience in the USA that was particularly receptive to the organisation's messages. In parallel, a Darfur disinvestment campaign also grew rapidly in the USA, lobbying for investors and companies in the USA and elsewhere to disinvest from Sudan or from companies that were active in Sudan, such as CNPC, Petronas, and European companies active in the oil and power sectors in Sudan.

The campaigns had wide or even delusional aims, if one took at face value the idea of 'saving' Darfur, or that US or other foreign disinvestment would have much impact when US economic sanctions on Sudan had already been in place since 1997.[102] Instead, the impact of the campaigns was largely confined within the USA, to the ways in which the campaigns themselves measured their achievements, such as levels of public communications and mobilisation (what the SDC later called creating a 'constituency of conscience') and influence on US government officials and lawmakers.[103] Subsequently the campaigns were the subject of critiques which argued for example that the campaigns used simplistic or skewed accounts of the Darfur conflict, and that they were in part driven by salvational cause-seeking, accentuated by fervour displaced from the 'cause' of Iraq, and by the tropes and ideas underlying the simplistic accounts of the conflict. Although some of these critiques contained their own flaws, the main elements were justified.[104] In Europe popular activism about Darfur was much weaker, although the approach and methods used in the USA were slowly replicated on a smaller scale. There was also less debate about whether or not the Darfur conflict constituted genocide. Without a single European policy, Britain, France and other EU members states adhered to their own existing policies and approaches to relations with Sudan. Elsewhere in the world, there was much less activism over Darfur.

Internationally the public attention to and advocacy about Darfur prompted governments and the UN Security Council to pay more attention to Darfur, even if the level of attention made little difference to the substance of policy decisions. Targeted by campaigners, even the Chinese government gradually and reluctantly became more engaged in international politics surrounding Sudan, especially when it was faced with the threat that campaigners would try to tarnish the 2008 Beijing Olympics on the grounds of China's economic interests in Sudan.[105] In response to the various pressures on Chinese, European and US policy on Sudan, during 2004–6, the Security Council held frequent meetings on the subject of Darfur and was presented with regular reports from the UN Secretary-General and from a panel of experts monitoring the arms embargo imposed on Darfur by the Security Council. Working within the constraints of Security Council voting and decision-making, the council supported four main forms of response to Darfur: peacekeeping, judicial, humanitarian, and political.

The Security Council's support for humanitarian and political responses to the Darfur conflict essentially meant continuing the existing pattern of support for the work of the UN agencies in Darfur and support for the AU-led peace process for Darfur. On peacekeeping, the Security Council's attention focused firstly on how to bolster AMIS (with extra materiel and funds) and then on how to secure a transition to a UN peacekeeping force in Darfur. The Sudanese government opposed this aim, but on 31 August 2006 the Security Council passed a resolution (UNSCR 1706) calling for UN peacekeepers to be deployed in Darfur, subject to the government's consent. In October the Sudanese government provoked an angry reaction from the Security Council after it sent a letter to potential troop-contributing countries, warning that it would consider participation in a UN force in Darfur a 'hostile act'. The Council was also critical of Sudan's decision in the same month to expel the UN special envoy to Sudan, Jan Pronk. All the same, in December the government agreed to a three-stage plan for UN support to AMIS, which was meant to pave the way for a transition to a UN peacekeeping mission. The government then appeared to abrogate this agreement, but in April 2007 accepted the deployment of a UN 'heavy support package' for AMIS. This led the way to the eventual transition to UNAMID at the end of 2007.

On the judicial side, in September 2004 the Security Council authorised the establishment of an 'international commission of inquiry' to investigate violations of international humanitarian law and human-rights law in the Darfur conflict, to identify perpetrators, to determine whether genocide had occurred, and to suggest what should be done to ensure accountability. In January 2005 the commission submitted its report. According to this, the commission found that all armed parties in the conflict in Darfur, but especially the government and the Janjawid, were guilty of violations, but it judged that the government had not pursued a policy of genocide, although in some instances individuals may have acted with genocidal intent.[106] The report was accompanied by a sealed and confidential list of the names of 51 individuals whom the commission suspected of involvement in violations. Following this, the UN Security Council voted to refer the case of Darfur (and the list of names) to the Office of the Prosecutor in the newly established ICC, which started its investigation in June 2005. The ICC investigation proceeded slowly, but eventually led to the issue in May

2007 of arrest warrants for a Sudanese junior minister, Ahmed Haroun, and a Janjawid leader, Ali Kushayb. The Sudanese authorities rejected the warrants and tried to block the ICC's investigation, saying that Sudan's justice system was itself investigating alleged crimes in Darfur. In 2008 and 2009 the government hardened its rejection of the ICC after the prosecutor announced charges against President Bashir, and the ICC judges in March 2009 issued an arrest warrant for him on charges of war crimes and crimes against humanity.

Complicating factors

The question of how the international community responded to the Darfur conflict and the related pressures was further complicated by other factors. Firstly, in 2005–6 the conflict in Darfur began to be noticeably intertwined with domestic conflict in neighbouring Chad. The two countries had a history of giving shelter and support to each other's rebels or dissidents. But the escalation in tensions between the two countries, the fluctuating relations and repeated failure of reconciliation agreements, led to international concern that the Darfur conflict might widen into a larger regional conflict. It also accentuated differences between Sudan and France, which the Sudanese government saw as supporting the Chadian government of Idris Deby and hosting the SLM/A leader Abdul Wahid Mohammed al-Nur after he left Asmara in late 2006.

A further complicating factor for Britain, the USA and their policy on Darfur was their continuing interest in Sudanese co-operation on counter-terrorism. In 2005 Salah Abdallah Gosh, the head of NSIS, visited the headquarters of the US Central Intelligence Agency in Langley, Virginia, and in 2006 he visited London, where he met with British and American officials, including the US Assistant Secretary of State for Africa, Jendayi Frazer.[107] As Mr Gosh was influential in the government's conduct of its side of the conflict in Darfur (and indeed was alleged to be on the list of 51 names given to the ICC), his contacts with the British and US authorities were widely criticised by campaigners.

More generally, international policy on Darfur was complicated by the international community's need and wish to support the CPA and, after May 2006, by the need at least in principle to support the DPA. Supporting the implementation of the CPA meant that the troika and other donor countries needed to engage bilaterally and multilaterally with the Sudanese authorities, as illustrated by the Oslo donor conference in April 2005, when donors pledged US$4.5bn in aid for Sudan, and a follow-up conference in May 2008, when donors pledged US$4.8bn in aid for the period 2008–11. The desire to support the nascent Government of Southern Sudan and to help the parties overcome the minor crises in CPA implementation that inevitably occurred during 2005–9 also compelled the international community to remain closely engaged with Sudan. Crises included the death of John Garang in July 2005, disputes over the redeployment of troops, the SPLM's temporary suspension of its participation in the national government in late 2007, the dispute over Abyei, and occasional outbreaks of fighting between the SAF and the SPLA. To a much smaller extent, donor countries also tied themselves into supporting the notional implementation of the DPA, even though the agreement was effectively dead at the outset.[108]

Faced with the difficulty of balancing policy on Darfur with policy on the CPA, by 2009 policy advisers and analysts were beginning to recommend that governments adopted policies that treated the whole of Sudan together, rather than having separate policies for Darfur and CPA-Sudan. This led international policy back towards seeing the CPA and the changes that it had brought as the framework within which to address other problems in Sudan, such as the Darfur conflict.

Assessing engagement and containment

Foreign policy towards Sudan from 2004 onwards was not dramatically different from policy in the preceding years, only the tensions in policy were more acute. While the impetus to engage with Sudan strengthened because of the advent and implementation of the CPA, the pressure to contain and punish the government for the Darfur conflict strengthened. Policy was therefore pulled in contradictory directions, which increased confusion and possibly led to missed opportunities. With less heat and more light, the international community might have more consistently supported the CPA, and more consistently supported efforts to negotiate a peaceful settlement to the Darfur conflict.

As it was, despite the awkward mix of engagement and containment, the collective outcome of international policy towards Sudan in this period was not so poor. Within the limitations of their mandate and capabilities, AMIS and UNAMID did have some positive effect in Darfur, helping to dampen down the conflict after the intense phase of 2003–4. Likewise, within its limitations, UNMIS also played a positive role in supporting the implementation of the CPA and preventing larger relapses into fighting. More generally, international support for the CPA helped to keep the agreement alive.

Conclusion

This chapter has examined Western foreign policy towards Sudan during the civil war and the Darfur conflict, with the aim of shedding light on how foreign policy affected decisions about mediation and relief. Overall, the chapter has illustrated how Western policies towards Sudan shifted over time between broadly different strategies or approaches – clientelism, containment and engagement – in response to Western objectives and also to changes in Sudan and the international context. The chapter has furthermore illustrated how conflict resolution, mediation and relief were not themselves the primary objectives of these strategies, but were of varying importance and centrality in the overall policy approaches.

Within this picture, mediation and relief were rarely constructively co-ordinated for the objective of resolving the conflict. In fact, mediation was concertedly pursued only after 2001, as part of the move towards engagement with Sudan. Most of the time, however, relief had the effect (albeit unintentional) of substituting for a more political response to the conflict, such as mediation or other measures to promote conflict resolution. This reflected the fact that for major Western countries resolving Sudan's war was always a lower priority than other interests in Sudan and elsewhere; and while mediation was the one tool of conflict resolution that they sometimes used, relief was never significantly associated with conflict resolution, except in the brief case of the Nuba Mountains ceasefire.

These conclusions lead to a further question. Recognising the interests and foreign-policy constraints on Western countries dealing with Sudan, to what extent could or should they have acted differently, in order to have achieved better results relative to their objectives and the challenges of helping to resolve Sudan's major conflicts and improve the humanitarian situation? This question will be explored in the following chapter.

5

OPTIONS

This chapter looks to answer the questions raised in the conclusions of the preceding three chapters, about the options available to countries that engaged in mediation and relief in Sudan. Those questions are: (i) What could mediators have done to have achieved a better outcome, such as the earlier settlement of the war, or a peace agreement with wider participation or without the accompanying escalation of the conflict in Darfur? (ii) Could relief organisations have done more to prevent the abuse of relief and to bring about a peaceful resolution of the conflict and the associated humanitarian crises? And (iii), could or should Western countries have acted differently in order to have achieved better results relative to their objectives and in particular for resolving the war and improving the humanitarian situation?

MEDIATION

The outcomes of mediated peace talks may be shaped or determined by any of a wide range of context-related and process-related factors, some of them inter-related, as Table 6 below shows.[1] However, two sets of context-related and process-related factors are particularly important to the question of what, if anything, the international community could have done to bring about a better outcome in trying to resolve Sudan's civil war and the conflict in Darfur. These factors are firstly the issues of participation in the talks, and the perception of 'ripeness' and a 'mutually hurting stalemate' (factors which relate to the context of mediation); and secondly the frameworks and principles used by the mediators, and the commitments they made to the peace process and agreement (factors which relate to the mediation process). Some of these factors were partly examined in Chapter 2, but their implications for the question of what options were available to mediators have not yet been directly considered.

Table 6: **Determinants of mediation outcomes**

Overall type of determinant	Area or sub-area of determinants		Possible determinants
Context-related determinants	Characteristics of the conflict	Ripeness for resolution	• Mutually hurting stalemate • Changes in available solutions • Changes in balance of power
		Intensity	• Duration • Magnitude / level of fatalities
		Issues	• Sovereignty • Ideology • Security • Self-determination • Other
	Characteristics of the mediators	(Im)partiality and motives	• Perceived impartiality
		Leverage	• Exercisable power / sticks
		Status	• Rank and moral influence
	Characteristics of the parties and their inter-relationship	Identification of the parties	• Clarity, or lack of, about the key parties
		Cohesiveness	• Ability, or not, to carry supporters / population / constituency
		Type of regime	• Political norms
		Motives to accept mediation	• Relationship with the mediator(s)
		Relationship between the parties	• Type of past relationship/ history
		Balance of power	• Power parity / inequality
	International context	Local factors	• Strength of neighbour(s)
		Regional factors	• Regional organisation and influence
		International factors	• International interest in resolution of conflict
Process-related determinants	Mediator activities and action	Types of behaviour	• Communication • Cultivation • Formulation • Enticement • Manipulation
		Credible commitment	• Provision of guarantees • Enforcement

Participants and spoilers

The question of which parties are included in a peace process tends to be overshadowed by questions of how to counteract the threat posed by potential spoilers to a peace agreement. But in the case of Sudan, the very uncomprehensive nature of the CPA (which excluded Darfur and Eastern Sudan, as well as all the major political opposition parties) and the travails of Darfur peacemaking after 2005, make the question particularly worth asking.

As Chapter 2 showed, the Sudanese government and the SPLM/A were the primary parties responsible for the failure of peace talks during the war. Unsurprisingly, therefore, even in 2004 – two years after the signing of the Machakos Protocol – each party still saw the other as probably the main potential spoiler of any final agreement. This was especially true for the SPLM/A, many of whose senior members attributed the repeated failure of talks in the past overwhelmingly to the government.[2] In the words of one SPLA commander who had participated in most of the IGAD talks as well as at the 1986 Koka Dam talks and the 1989 talks in Addis Ababa, 'All the failure [of talks] was internal failure', and was due to the government 'always wanting 100 per cent for itself and 0 per cent for the SPLM'.[3]

Government officials took a similarly critical view of SPLM/A responsibility for the failure of past talks, though some acknowledged that other factors had played a role. Thus, for example, according to the government's chief negotiator at the 1992 and 1993 Abuja conferences, it was not only the SPLM/A that was responsible for the failure of the conferences, but also conflicting pressures and 'political jealousies' in the government.[4] Similarly, in the view of a government negotiator at Machakos and Naivasha, the presence of Turabi, 'no matter who was doing the negotiations', was one of the reasons why talks before 2000 had always failed to reach a successful settlement.[5] Nonetheless, as of 2004, members of Sudan's past and present ruling parties still saw the SPLM/A as a potential future spoiler of any peace agreement. This view reflected the persistent distrust between the parties, and was consistent with northern perceptions of joint northern and southern responsibility for the failure of the Addis Ababa Agreement, and perceptions of the potential for intra-south conflict ('south–south' conflict between southern groups).[6]

In effect therefore, the government and the SPLM/A were the main potential 'total spoilers' (to use Stephen Stedman's typology of spoilers) both of any final agreement and of the talks.[7] But by virtue of being the two main warring parties they were also essential to any peace process. Given their poor track records in peace talks (particularly the government's record, as it had historically been the less co-operative party), their lack of democratic legitimacy, and the fact that a spectrum of other armed and unarmed political forces also existed, there was therefore a case for mediators to try to broaden the peace process, if possible and if it would improve the outcome. That case was perhaps all the stronger given the potentially dangerous consequences of excluding parties. Retrospectively, the severity of the spoiler threat presented by parties excluded from the talks in Kenya was demonstrated most of all by the conflicts in Darfur and Eastern Sudan.[8]

Mediators at the talks in Kenya professed themselves aware of the dangers of excluding parties from the talks and in some cases talked of the importance of wider participation in implementing the eventual agreement.[9] But in the eyes of critics at the time, they underestimated the motivation and capacity of excluded parties to spoil peace talks or the implementation of a peace agreement. To some degree the risks of exclusion could be seen in what had happened to past bilateral agreements, such as the 1988 DUP–SPLM accord and the 1997 Khartoum Peace Agreement, which both failed largely because they excluded key parties (the former because it excluded the Umma Party, the latter because it excluded the mainstream SPLM/A). Notably, the Addis Ababa Agreement itself provided an example of what could happen to an exclusionary peace agreement negotiated without broader participation. In the Abuja conferences and the IGAD process in the 1990s, exclusion was scarcely controversial, as the talks made no lasting progress. But after 2001, and in particular after the Machakos Protocol, exclusion clearly did become controversial.

Before and during the talks in Kenya, excluded parties publicised their dissatisfaction at being excluded from the talks. As some saw it, IGAD and the troika restricted talks to the government and the SPLM/A only because they could 'exert power over them', which they could not do over other parties such as their own.[10] Although parties such as the DUP and the Umma Party realised early on that the talks would not be broadened, they continued to lobby diplomats from Britain, Norway and the USA to pay attention to their interests and proposals. In return, they received 'nothing except some assurances' that their concerns would be listened to, and offers for them to witness the signing of the final agreement.[11]

In the opinion of some officials in these parties, the mediators thereby missed an opportunity to support democratisation and the achievement of a genuinely comprehensive settlement. Moreover, excluded parties and individuals – northern and southern – felt free to criticise or oppose the agreements coming out of the Kenya talks. An example of this sentiment was the warning (in this case from the DUP) that 'Because we have been excluded, if we come to power at any time during the six [interim] years, we may not be bound by the agreement.'[12] Understandably, many observers and excluded parties feared that their interests were not being served by the bilateral platform.[13] Furthermore, the exclusivity of the talks fed doubts about the international community's commitment to democracy. Thus, for example, in the opinion of Balqis Badri (a Sudanese academic and member of a women's delegation which lobbied the talks at Naivasha), the use of a bilateral platform for the talks was one of the international community's two biggest mistakes in dealing with the war:

> This is what makes us suspicious about the motives of the international community. It is as if it is fine that lack of democracy, absence of human rights, etc, continue, as long as there is a stable, separate south and a stable, separate north.[14]

That the troika and partners stuck with the bilateral platform for the peace talks, rather than attempting to broaden it, reflected a number of factors. These included the government and the SPLM/A's lack of interest in letting other parties join the talks, and the mediators' concern for the talks to produce an agreement sooner rather than later (a prospect which perhaps seemed likelier if there were only two parties to mediate between). In addition, to some extent it appeared that, as of 2002, the government and the SPLM/A increasingly saw the war as having reached a stalemate and were therefore more willing than in the past to resolve the war peacefully. In truth, however, this perception was less significant than it promised to be.

After the CPA was signed, the question of inclusion or exclusion from peace talks narrowed to the Darfur talks, where it became all the more significant after the abortive DPA in May 2006. At the outset that agreement was signed without the most important rebel groups – the mainstreams of JEM and the SLM/A. Mediators then persistently underestimated the determination of the non-signatories, while the rebel factions persistently showed themselves to be weak and selfish about alliances and negotiations. The result was that through the years after 2006 (at least until 2009) efforts to construct a coherent Darfur peace process were repeatedly ineffective and were concentrated too much on the factions, reinforcing the tendency for factionalism which the government simultaneously exploited. By itself, therefore, the Darfur conflict painfully illustrated the high costs exclusion could have.

Perception of ripeness and stalemate

As indicated in Chapter 2, during the internationalised CPA peace process after 2001, some members of the negotiating teams at the talks did think that the war had reached a mutually hurting stalemate and that it was 'ripe' for resolution. In the opinion of one of the government negotiators between 2002 and 2004, both sides had 'realised that it was impossible to win militarily'.[15] The government's lead negotiator during 2002–3, Ghazi Salah al-Din Atabani, likewise believed that a stalemate had been reached and that it played a part in the success of the talks:

> The dynamics within the two negotiating parties have changed, and within the regional parties or actors. ... Both parties have recognised that it is impossible to win militarily. The military situation resembles the first world war in 1916–1917. The military situation has reached a stalemate: one day's gains are reversed the next day.[16]

This view was echoed by the SPLM/A spokesman, Samson Kwaje, who felt that 'war fatigue' on both sides had become acute by the early 2000s.[17]

Objectively, there was good reason to think that there actually was a stalemate: after almost two decades of war neither side was any closer to winning but the war was still blighting the country and the lives of many Sudanese. Some Sudanese observers felt that 'war fatigue' had become more acute by the early 2000s than it had been in the 1990s, and it was sometimes said that every family knew someone who had died in the war or had lost a family member.[18] Aware of this, and influenced by Zartman's stalemate hypothesis, some troika and IPF officials therefore tried to encourage the perception of a stalemate, in order to advance the talks.

In reality, though, the perception of a stalemate did not take root among the parties in a way that satisfied Zartman's hypothesis that it is a necessary condition for negotiating a peace agreement. This can be seen firstly from the variation in the parties' views about the situation in the war, and secondly from their apparent willingness to continue fighting. For example, some senior figures in the SPLM/A believed that although a military stalemate had set in around 1998, a corresponding political stalemate did not come until later.[19] In the opinion of Pagan Amum, an SPLM/A negotiator who participated in the initial IGAD talks in 1994 and the talks from 2002 onwards (but who was on combat duty between 1998 and 2001), the main reason why the talks made little progress after their resumption in 1998 was that the military situation had reached a 'balance' which entailed that the parties 'did not see any serious need to make any concessions' and that 'the talks were also a stalemate'.[20] Furthermore, in his opinion by 2000 the military situation had begun to tilt in favour of the SPLM/A, which prompted the government to try to encourage other countries (such as Egypt and Libya) to mediate in the war, while at the same time trying to move away from IGAD because it felt 'uncomfortable' with it.[21] As he saw it, between 2000 and 2002 the government 'absolutely lost hope in a military victory':

> They had mobilised everything to achieve victory. But by 2002 the military theatre had expanded and there were seven fronts. More opposition forces had become active. The cost of the war had reached 65 per cent of the budget. And with all that they had lost territory.[22]

Regardless of the actual battlefield situation, however, both parties were used to living with the war and its costs, and as of the early 2000s were still willing to continue fighting. The government's economic position had improved substantially since 1999, largely thanks to the rapid growth in oil exports, and the SPLM/A remained confident. In the words of one SPLM/A delegate at Naivasha, 'If we could have had our choice, we would have carried on fighting despite the people's suffering. People had become used to the suffering.'[23] In the opinion of Riek Machar, the SPLM/A could have continued fighting, in part because it was strengthened by the fronts in the east and the west.[24] This willingness to continue fighting was partly demonstrated by the resources and effort which the government then put into the Darfur conflict and, to a lesser extent, by the covert support that the SPLM/A gave to the rebel movements in Darfur.[25] It was also partly shown by the lack of a sense of urgency among the parties at the talks in Naivasha.[26]

In the case of the IGAD talks from 2002–4, and in the peace process in the preceding years, the perception of a mutually hurting stalemate was therefore of limited significance or value.[27] Indeed, there are no good grounds to consider that the perception of a stalemate was a necessary condition for the talks to make progress, let alone to produce the CPA. Rather, as indicated in Chapter 2, what was far more important in determining that the talks made progress and ultimately produced the CPA was the internationalisation of the peace talks (against the government's wishes) and the related changes in the international context that brought the troika to the talks and made it work in concert with IPF members and IGAD. In peacemaking efforts for Darfur the notion of a mutually hurting stalemate was even less helpful. To begin with, the high-level conflict in Darfur between JEM and the SLM/A on the one hand, and the government and the SAF on the other, was new and the material costs to the parties were relatively low (though the human costs were high). By 2008–9 as the conflict dragged on unresolved, but of low intensity, the situation had become a stalemate. But it was a stalemate of low costs to the parties and was certainly not acute enough to be a key to productive peace talks.

Mediation frameworks and principles

More important in determining the outcomes, however, was the process that the troika presided over and, within it, the frameworks and principles that the mediators used or supported in the talks, and the commitments they made to the process and the CPA. Outsiders have often tended to frame Sudan's civil war as a north–south conflict, a representation which is essentially wrong, although it did capture the main manifestations of the conflict. During the IGAD talks the mediators tended to do the same, and the Machakos Protocol – by its focus on self-determination for Southern Sudan – further encouraged this view of the conflict, despite the subsequent protocols for Abyei (an area on the north–south border), and South Kordofan and Blue Nile (two states outside Southern Sudan). But as a framework for representing the conflict, the north–south framework was widely considered to be inadequate and wrong and its use was duly criticised at the time, both by opposition parties and by 'civil society' figures, who for example argued that the conflict was 'centre–periphery', or at root about marginalisation, and that the north–south framework was a 'trap' or a 'limitation' to the IGAD talks.[28] Plainly the framework conflicted with the facts that the SPLM/A had been fighting ostensibly for a 'New Sudan', and that the conflict covered more than just the south. Furthermore, the framework was even criticised by government and SPLM/A delegates at the talks in Kenya. In the opinion of one SPLM/A delegate at Naivasha, the biggest mistake made by Western mediators and principally the troika was to consider Sudan's problem as just north–south.[29]

Up to a point the mediating countries were aware that the war was not just north–south. Britain's DFID acknowledged in its 'country engagement plan' for Sudan for 2004 that the war was 'often simplified into a north–south divide', and that since 1989 the war had included conflict in the north.[30] Similarly in a US Congressional hearing in May 2004 under the title 'The crisis in Darfur: a new front in Sudan's bloody war', the chairman of the hearing declared in his introduction:

> The crisis in Darfur has shown that conflict in Sudan can no longer be viewed in terms of Muslim versus Christian or north versus south. It must be considered in terms of the center of power versus the marginalized periphery.[31]

Nonetheless, as discussed in Chapters 2 and 4, the mediators stuck to the bipartisan framework of the talks in Kenya, or the 'so called north–south peace process', as Danforth later called it.[32] The escalation of conflict in Darfur, and its separation from the peace talks in Kenya, reinforced the convenience of calling the civil war the 'north–south' conflict or war. As a result, by late 2004 officials from the troika countries were frequently referring to the war as 'north–south', and representing it as entirely separate from Darfur. For example, the British minister for international development, Hilary Benn, repeatedly referred to the IGAD peace process as 'north–south'[33] and Danforth (and others) referred to the CPA as the 'north–south agreement'.[34]

Despite having their own criticisms of the north–south framework, the government and the SPLM/A were the main beneficiaries and tacitly contributed to its use, by opposing the widening of the talks to include other parties. This did not stop them holding the mediators responsible for not doing more to deal with the concerns of excluded parties. In the opinion of one SPLM/A delegate, for example, while other parties should not have been included in the talks, the mediators should have 'found a mechanism to carry [their] opinion'.[35] The troika and the IPF did this, to the extent that they canvassed opposition party opinion through their diplomats in Khartoum and Nairobi and provided funding for several non-party delegations (such as a Sudanese women's delegation, and delegations from Abyei and Southern Blue Nile) to visit the talks.[36] However this did not alter the fact that the CPA was ultimately a bipartisan agreement, framed around a central question of unity or secession for Southern Sudan. Some northern opposition parties, such as the Umma Party, felt that the protocols and the CPA gave priority to secession, despite the claims of the signatories and the mediators that the agreements gave priority to unity.[37] Conversely some southerners doubted whether Britain and the USA were ready to accept independence for Southern Sudan and tended to feel that the agreements gave too much priority to unity, despite the claims of the signatories and mediators to be making independence a real possibility by the provision for a referendum at the end of the interim period.[38]

Besides the framework for the talks, the mediators also had influence over a range of principles or issues which were at stake in any eventual agreement, such as approaches to power and wealth sharing, security and disarmament. For the various parties excluded from the peace talks, the most important of these issues were democratisation, reconciliation and justice, which were important because of the government and SPLM/A's lack of democratic legitimacy, and the widespread abuses committed during the war. Moreover, democratisation and reconciliation – although undoubtedly often difficult to ensure at the same time as ending a civil war – were (and still are) important for the longer-term prospects for peace in Sudan. This was commented on in August 2002 by Gerhart Baum, the UN special rapporteur on human rights in Sudan:

> In view of the links between peace and democracy and human rights, peace talks should be more comprehensive and include all stakeholders in what is not simply a North–South conflict. Confidence-building and reconciliation need democracy.[39]

However, Sudanese opposition parties and observers of the talks generally considered that the mediators gave too little priority to democratisation and reconciliation, and some (such as the Umma Party, the DUP and the PCP) felt that the mediators were simply not interested in ending the undemocratic rule of Bashir's government.[40] This opinion persisted despite the inclusion in the protocols and the CPA of provisions for democratic elections. Whether the opinion was justified depended ultimately on the commitment of the parties to implementing the agreement correctly and the commitment of the mediators to holding the parties to it.

A further consequence of using the north–south framework was that the Darfur conflict was framed as something that should be resolved on its own, in its own talks and with little connection to the CPA. This approach was reinforced by the tendency of some outsiders (especially campaigners and people who were new to the story of conflict in Sudan) to decontextualise Darfur and treat it as *sui generis* – an alleged genocide, a conflict beyond comprehension, neither a part of the wider civil war nor even just a 'north–west' conflict. The task of resolving the Darfur conflict did not become easier after the CPA was signed; and it was made more difficult by the fact that the ambitions of JEM reached beyond Darfur and JEM gradually eclipsed the SLM/A as the stronger rebel movement, militarily as well as politically. If John Garang had survived beyond 2005, he would doubtless have been more influential over Darfur than his SPLM successor, Salva Kiir Mayardit. But it is very unlikely that this would have been sufficient to produce a greatly different course of events in Darfur. Meanwhile for Eastern Sudan the consequences of using the north–south framework to conceptualise the civil war and its resolution were less problematic than they were for Darfur. Under the CPA the SPLM/A had to withdraw from the east, politically by ending its alliance with the Eastern Front, and militarily by redeploying SPLA troops out of the east and back to the south. Without the SPLM/A, the scale of the conflict in the east was small, and the ambitions of the eastern groups did not extend beyond the east and the aim of gaining increased representation in the national government.

Commitment and credibility

Evidently the CPA peace process after 2001 made progress largely because of the degree of internationalisation and the involvement of the troika. But the limits to the parties' and the mediators' commitment to the talks, and to implementing an agreement, also influenced the manner of that progress and the prospects of the resulting agreement. In the Darfur conflict the relative weakness and inconsistency of international involvement in peace talks contributed to the poor results of the Darfur peace process.

In general, international mediators could do little about the parties' lack of commitment except note it and bear it in mind in considering how they should support a particular peace process and any resulting agreement. Over the three decades since the Addis Ababa Agreement, most southerners and many other Sudanese had come to be very sceptical about the commitment of any northern-led government to implementing peace agreements. Drawing on his experience of the unsuccessful Khartoum Peace Agreement, Riek Machar, for example, did not expect the Machakos Protocol and subsequent agreements to be honoured unless the international community surmounted the problem of the government's resistance to self-determination.[41] More pessimistically, one commander in the SPLM/A delegation at Naivasha in 2004 felt that the government was buying time and that the mediators had committed 'a grave mistake' by brokering a ceasefire, because it deprived the SPLM/A of its 'only means of pressurising the government'. The consequence, he felt, was that ultimately the mediators would fail and Sudan would go back to war again:

> Most of the mediators don't understand the mentality of this regime. They [the government] haven't abandoned their objectives – of Islamisation, crushing the marginalised, total domination. These talks are just a tactic. And it is not the first time: it happened in 1972, in 1977, [and] in 1997.[42]

Such doubts were echoed by some of the mediators and observers at the talks who had long experience of the Sudanese government, either from involvement in the talks or from diplomatic or humanitarian work in the country, in some cases reaching back to Sadiq's government in the 1980s. Based on experience, some believed (as many Sudanese did) that 'the government always breaks its word'.[43] Appropriately, though, the chair of the talks, Lazaro Sumbeiywo, frequently made it clear that he believed that international support ('both bilateral and multilateral') would be critical for ensuring that the CPA would be implemented successfully.[44]

In the circumstances, therefore, what commitment the mediators showed both to the peace process and to guaranteeing the implementation of any eventual peace agreement, was always likely to be important. And during the CPA talks the mediators did show commitment in a range of ways.

These included trying to enforce deadlines (culminating in the session of the Security Council in Nairobi in November 2004); funding and staffing the JMC and CPMT, which monitored the Nuba Mountains ceasefire and the general ceasefire; endorsing the proposal of a UN peacekeeping mission to support implementation of a final agreement; and supporting the JAM which the government, the SPLM/A, the World Bank and the UN jointly carried out between 2004 and March 2005, to assess Sudan's need for aid following a final peace agreement. In addition, the mediators also bore much of the cost of the CPA talks.

These undertakings and commitments support Barbara Walter's 'credible commitment' theory and the hypothesis that 'security guarantees are a necessary but not a sufficient condition for a settlement'.[45] In Sudan the international community contributed to the development of security guarantees by supporting the security protocol, the ceasefire monitoring bodies and the planned UN peacekeeping mission. These guarantees were not sufficient for the peace process to be fruitful, but it is likely that they were necessary. Nonetheless, the credibility of the international community's wider commitment to peace talks and agreements was weakened by a number of factors which were apparent to the parties at the time. These ranged from the light presence the troika and the IPF had at the talks, to their failure to exert more pressure on the parties to meet deadlines (although both sides criticised the attempt to impose deadlines).[46] As indicated in Chapter 4, the troika and the IPF had less leverage at the talks than was generally assumed, and the carrots and sticks they used were weaker than they hoped. The mediators' decision to prioritise the IGAD talks before taking action over Darfur, and their failure to take stronger action over Darfur, also raised questions about the extent of their commitment to resolving Sudan's conflicts. The mediating and observer countries at the CPA talks were much less present and involved in the separate peace talks for Darfur, when they first started. As the rounds of Darfur talks proceeded, the US and European countries slowly increased their involvement and clumsily pushed the talks to a premature conclusion, the DPA in 2006, which handicapped further US and European involvement in Darfur peace talks in 2007–9. It is fair to say, therefore, that in comparison with the much greater attention it paid to questions about the nature of the violence in Darfur, the use of sanctions and the need for peacekeeping forces, the international community paid insufficient attention to the political process needed to reach an effective peace agreement for Darfur. The limitations to Western countries and IGAD's involvement in the negotiation of peace in Sudan was further illustrated by their very marginal role in the few peace talks for Eastern Sudan.

Implications

The implications of the above are that options were available to the international community which could have helped to bring about a better outcome to efforts to resolve Sudan's conflicts. At the least, mediators could have been more careful in the choice and use of the frameworks through which they represented the civil war and the Darfur conflict and sought to resolve them; and they could have shown stronger commitment to the peace processes and the eventual agreements. Less certainly, mediators could have done more to anticipate the actions of spoilers, for example either by consulting more with excluded parties (such as the northern-based opposition parties and the Darfur rebel groups), or by partly broadening the peace process after the breakthrough at Machakos. A better framework for the CPA talks and more commitment to democratisation could have helped to avoid the escalation in Darfur and have led to a more genuinely 'comprehensive' peace process.

There were other things too that the mediators could have done which might have helped bring about better outcomes. Other factors which members of the Sudanese government and the SPLM/A interviewed by the author commented on included the technical resource staff whom the mediators provided, how the agenda was set, and the level of the talks, meaning who led the negotiations for each side. (In the opinion of one of the troika representatives, the CPA talks became 'dysfunctional' after they were raised to the level of the 'principals' – John Garang and Ali Uthman Muhammad Taha – because neither the IGAD secretariat nor the troika attended the meetings.)[47] In the Darfur talks repeated changes in chief negotiators and international mediators made it difficult to build a concerted and sustained peace process. But in general, looking back over the various peace talks for the CPA, Darfur and the east, the most important factors determining the outcome of those talks (and that were at least partly within the mediators control) appear repeatedly to have been the ways in which the conflicts were framed, the question of who participated and who was excluded, and the commitment of the mediators.

RELIEF

Concern about the outcomes and unintended consequences of prolonged relief in civil war situations has given rise to various arguments, in particular that relief sometimes prolongs war, and that it depoliticises humanitarian crises and has anti-democratic consequences. The following table gives a snapshot of the possible consequences of relief.

Table 7: **Possible consequences of humanitarian relief**

Who or what affected	Type of consequence		
	Economic	Political	Other
Intended beneficiaries of relief	• Longer-term dependency on relief created (e.g. by reduced pressure to re-establish independent sources of food or income)	• Traditional political structures undermined (by dependency on relief agencies, including the warring parties relief organisations)	• Lives saved • Acute suffering reduced
Parties to the conflict	• Increased revenues (e.g. from taxation or duties) • Increased material resources (e.g. from looting or extortion)	• Partial legitimisation, by virtue of co-operation with relief agencies • Reduced pressure to be responsible and accountable for the humanitarian situation	• Increased use of food as a weapon • Tactical encouragement of humanitarian crises (e.g. to benefit from resulting relief or local ceasefire)
Conflict	–	• Political dimensions of conflict are insufficiently recognised	• Conflict prolonged (e.g. by material or tactical advantages gained from relief)
Relief agencies and donors	–	• Donor-country foreign policies advanced	• Interests of relief agencies (to continue doing as before) advanced

In Chapter 3 we found that although relief had been exploited by the warring parties, on balance there was no evidence that it had prolonged the civil war or the Darfur conflict; we also found that relief had sometimes depoliticised the humanitarian crises in Sudan and had had anti-democratic consequences. In considering what relief organisations could have done to better prevent the abuse of relief and to bring about the peaceful resolution of conflict and associated humanitarian crises in Sudan, it will now be useful to consider what options relief organisations had with regard to these arguments.

War duration and relief as a weapon

As seen in Chapter 3, there is no evidence that relief prolonged Sudan's civil war or the Darfur conflict. Despite its massive and sustained scale, relief in Sudan has been only a small part of the economy. As even the government's chief economic adviser acknowledged to the author, the economy was distorted first and foremost by the civil war, on top of which relief was only a further distortion.⁴⁸ Much of the large nominal financial value of relief was consumed in overheads, in particular the costs of delivery by air, road and water, and the costs of international staff. Meanwhile the causes of Sudan's conflicts and the factors which drove and sustained the fighting were not contingent on continued relief.

Nonetheless, it is clear that warring parties in Sudan did abuse relief, by trying to use it as a 'weapon' (by controlling access to relief),⁴⁹ by diverting it for their own use, or by otherwise 'farming' relief aid. In general the warring parties each denied that they exploited or misused relief but accused the other of doing so. Thus the government persistently believed that relief was often intended to help the SPLM/A and went directly to its soldiers; and the SPLM/A believed that the government used 'control over humanitarian access to achieve military objectives', in a way that amounted to using 'food as a weapon'.⁵⁰ Unlike the government, SPLM/A officials did also argue that it was acceptable if its soldiers received relief via their homes and their families. However they invariably denied that anyone had ever diverted relief materials directly to SPLA forces.⁵¹ In Darfur after 2003 the government periodically sought to control humanitarian access to its advantage. But there were no examples of severe manipulation of relief by the rebel groups.

In the civil war the OLS Ground Rules and the various 'technical humanitarian protocols' which the UN negotiated with the parties during the 1990s and early 2000s, provided some guidelines and undertakings for preventing the abuse of relief. But, as seen in Chapter 3, commitments on paper did not translate into practice. As a result, OLS and the UN were frequently confronted with incidents of relief or food being used as a weapon, above all in the form of flight denials and other restrictions on humanitarian access, in response to which OLS would issue formal protests.

In trying to prevent the abuse of relief, one important challenge for OLS and the UN was to avoid complicity with either side, unintentional or otherwise. Some Northern Sector officials considered that they were 'far more neutral in dealing with the GOS than the southern UN were with the SPLM.'⁵² Conversely, some relief workers in the Southern Sector tended to feel that the Northern Sector was too compliant with the government, and sometimes accused it of unintentional complicity. Such accusations may on occasions have been justified, but in general they were not. Some UN chief officials in Khartoum were noted for the resistance they showed to the government. Moreover the fact that some UN heads were designated persona non grata and expelled from Sudan did not mean that those who weren't expelled were supine or soft on the government. In the words of one former UN deputy-head based in Khartoum, 'We constantly battled with the government. Our battle with the government was always about access.

… We fought and squabbled all the way.'[53] Those battles were reflected in the monthly tally of flight denials, which was often recorded in the reports of the UN Secretary General to the Security Council. That record shows that over time, OLS made only faltering progress in persuading the government to improve humanitarian access. In Darfur, pressure from the UN Security Council Resolutions in 2004–5, and then the presence of AMIS and UNAMID, helped to reduce the obstruction of humanitarian relief rapidly and more effectively than had occurred during OLS.

Besides pressuring the parties to improve humanitarian access and comply with their commitments, the other practical measure which relief organisations could take to counteract the abuse of relief was to publicise obstructions, to try to gain international support for improved access, as happened in Darfur. Organisations could also tighten their accounting of how relief was used, so that abuses could be documented and, where possible, countered in the delivery of relief. Insofar as this option was available to relief agencies, it was only partly pursued.

Dependency?

One charge against relief in Sudan which has some bearing on the question of war duration and other arguments, was that it fostered dependency in its beneficiaries. Understandably, this charge was almost never made by relief agencies themselves, but it was sometimes made by government and SPLM/A officials, and by critical observers. For example, in the opinion of one SPLM official, relief agencies were generally reluctant 'to accept that relief changes food systems and fosters dependence'.[54] In truth, though, as with many other dependency theories, generally it was not true that relief induced dependency in Sudan.

As others have observed, the assumption that 'people in distress willingly abandon their coping strategies and independence in the face of crisis' has been shown to be misguided.[55] By extension, the assumption that relief creates dependency is also misguided. This is not to say that relief cannot lead to a measure of localised dependency, such as when some people in IDP camps live principally off relief, or small 'relief ghettoes' arise, or when people have otherwise abandoned or lost their own means for coping with scarcity. But in general, the evidence from Sudan indicates that relief dependency was the exception, rather than the norm, despite relief being provided on a near-continuous basis to many populations.[56] This was well shown by one external assessment of relief in Sudan which estimated that between 1992 and 1998 relief provided on average a maximum of only 7.5 per cent of each target beneficiary's food requirements, a level which does not fit the idea of dependency implicit in claims about relief dependency.[57]

Similar assessments have not yet been made for Darfur. But in light of the evidence from the civil war and the poor targeting of food aid in Darfur,[58] it seems unlikely that relief created significant or widespread dependency in Darfur.

Relief frameworks and approaches

Given the central role played by OLS in relief in Sudan, and the debates that arose about the structure of OLS and the approaches to relief used in Sudan, it is worth considering whether the use of different relief frameworks and approaches in OLS would have produced better results. As described in Chapter 3, the division of OLS into two operating sectors – northern and southern – was a particular area of contention and became a focus of efforts to reform OLS. The division was originally seen as the solution to the challenge of getting relief to both government- and rebel-held territory, but by the mid- to late-1990s it was being seen as an obstacle to maintaining humanitarian neutrality.[59] The fact that it was so difficult to unify OLS even after a decision had been taken to do so (and even though donors such as ECHO supported the unification)[60] was an indication of how connected OLS had become to the political and economic structures prevailing in the north and the south. Bureaucratic inertia and the continuation of the war also contributed to the difficulty of reforming OLS. However the persistence of the north–south relief framework also echoed the persistence of the north–south framework in the peace process, although the relief framework was used to respond to the humanitarian consequences of the war, rather than to try to resolve the war (as the framework used in the talks aimed to do).

Nonetheless, the division of OLS into northern and southern sectors was implicitly seen as an unavoidable condition for large scale relief in war-affected areas (as indeed it had been at the start of OLS). As a framework, it therefore attracted less criticism than the approaches or methodologies for relief which OLS organisations used. One approach which was the object of particular criticism in the 1990s was the 'relief–development continuum'.

The 'continuum' concept was essentially the idea that where possible relief should aim to move towards development, so as to contribute to a sustained improvement in people's lives and to reduce the need for future relief. Despite the intrinsic logic of the continuum, it attracted more criticism than any other policy, and by the mid-1990s was already being attacked as 'simplistic and misleading'.[61] Some of the criticism of the continuum concept was very justified, as for example in the 1996 OLS Review, which argued that the use of the continuum as a programme strategy in the Northern Sector had played into the hands of the government. As critics pointed out, a number of 'area rehabilitation' and 'area development' schemes set up by the UN Development Programme (UNDP) in three war-affected areas had unwittingly supported the government's tactic of forced relocation and resettlement in 'peace villages', which itself was part of the government's overall war strategy.[62]

Other criticisms of the continuum, however, were less justified. Mark Duffield, for example, argued that from the mid-1990s a weakening of donor consensus about relief was 'compounded by an increasing questioning of the role of humanitarian aid within OLS and the attempt to switch to developmental forms of relief', factors which he considers contributed to the 1998 Bahr el-Ghazal famine.[63] In a similar vein, Bradbury argued that the use of the continuum tended to normalise a situation of humanitarian crisis by implying that development work could effectively be undertaken, when in fact the 'emergency' was not over.[64] However, such arguments overstated the impact of the continuum and of donor decisions, as several points show. Firstly, the warring parties had been able to exert some control over relief access and distribution from the outset of OLS, meaning that attempts to control developmental relief were hardly new. Secondly, any questioning in OLS about the role of relief and any attempts to implement developmentalist forms of relief, were surely far less significant factors in the 1998 famine than military factors. Despite the continuum, in 1998 relief was still delivered, and in increased quantities: the total value of relief provided in 1998 was US$314m, which was a marked increase on the US$52m average annual value of relief provided in the three years 1995–7.[65] Furthermore, while it should certainly be recognised that relief and development aid have different political significance or meaning,[66] it should also be acknowledged that relief and development essentially are on a continuum and that it may sometimes be difficult to draw a line between them, especially when it comes to tangible outputs. This is especially true in a context such as Sudan's, in which much of the relief work that was done during the war – ranging from improving conditions in IDP camps and building clinics and schools, to building the capacity of local institutions and promoting increased school enrolment – was developmental, even though it was carried out under the banner of humanitarian action. As the UN Country Team wrote in their collective assessment of the situation in Sudan in 1999:

> [R]elief, rehabilitation, reconstruction and development are, generally, not linear processes. Often, the need for them arises simultaneously in Sudan. This is simply because poor people, devastated by the effects of civil strife, require both relief and development assistance.[67]

The same point has been made elsewhere, including by Mukesh Kapila, the former UN head in Sudan:

> In my view, the only difference between humanitarian work and development work in certain countries is not what you are trying to achieve but the methods by which you achieve them. You do not have development health projects and humanitarian health projects, in the end you have the Millennium Goals that are fundamentally about achieving certain objective targets.[68]

Other points also suggest that the critiques of the relief–development continuum were over-stated, not least the observation that the policy was not new, and that to some extent already in the 1980s there had been a *de facto* policy or practice of linking relief and development in Sudan.[69] However, a wider shortcoming in the critiques of the policy – and in the policy itself – was the fact that they failed to address the question of what the political consequences were of the continuation together of relief and the war.

Relief, depoliticisation and democracy

The analysis of relief in Sudan in Chapter 3 gives support to the argument that relief can have depoliticising and anti-democratic effects. Firstly, from an internal or domestic perspective in Sudan, relief certainly contributed to the depoliticisation of the humanitarian crises during the war. As was noted at the time, the formation of OLS – and its sustained operation – conferred a measure of legitimacy on the SPLM/A and to some extent on the government. And over time, although OLS was responsible neither for sustaining the war nor for the undemocratic character of the warring parties, it contributed to their avoidance of domestic accountability in so far as civilians looked to it (and to international relief in general) rather than to the governing authorities to help them survive. In addition, among the national and local authorities in both government- and SPLM/A-controlled areas, OLS created new power structures, some of which were internal to OLS, others external. In some cases the emergence of these new structures was at the expense of pre-existing power structures or authorities that may have been more locally accountable. As one SPLM official who had spent ten years working on relief and rehabilitation programmes in Southern Sudan put it:

> The OLS structure means that all the resources pass through it. Therefore OLS has become very powerful, and it has taken power

away from traditional power structures and given it to something else. … You don't see this in the short run. But after a while you see it. The traditional leaders lose their influence and ordinary people look to the new relief structures.[70]

Part of the explanation for this was that relief organisations tended to interact principally with the SRRA (or the government's Humanitarian Affairs Commission), rather than local authorities and leaders, and the intended beneficiaries of relief. The fact that relief agencies also tended to import most relief food from abroad rather than buy it on local markets, when available, further distanced the humanitarian crises from local responsibility and, potentially, accountability.[71]

Nonetheless, large-scale international relief did not prevent humanitarian crises gaining local and national political attention, as occurred with the crisis in Darfur from 2003. Then, at the same time as the massive international relief effort, the humanitarian crisis (and the conflict) was the subject of considerable public debate and reporting in the Sudanese media, more so than for many of the other humanitarian crises in previous years. However, the Darfur crisis came in the context of the internationalised IGAD peace process and public debate about the expected peace, and international relief was still a normal or integral feature of Sudan's political landscape. As a result, the massive escalation in relief for Darfur did not provoke public outcry about the failure of the government and local authorities to deal with the humanitarian crisis. In short, the government was no more held to account for the humanitarian crisis in Darfur than it had been for the many crises in the previous two decades.

To the extent that relief helped the government and the SPLM/A to avoid accountability for humanitarian crises, it can therefore be said to have done no favours for democracy. Put another way, it was 'anti-democratic' in its consequences. However, this is not the same as saying that relief was a critical factor in stifling democracy in Sudan. Clearly relief was far from the only or even the main factor causing the warring parties to be undemocratic. As with the reasons for the long duration of the civil war and the Darfur conflict, the fundamental reasons for the lack of democracy lay in the country's recent political history and the political agendas of its warring and opposition parties.

The depoliticising effects of relief domestically in Sudan were mirrored abroad. As indicated in Chapter 3, the provision of relief to Sudan tended to obscure the political causes of the humanitarian crises. By the late 1990s this was less true, as donor governments and aid departments became keener to draw attention to the role of the war in causing the crises. In the Darfur crisis relief did not obscure the role of the war, although in their analyses of the conflict donor governments still tended to avoid emphasising the political causes. This avoidance was manifested in the environmental or natural resource-based explanations which were sometimes advanced for the Darfur conflict,[72] and it was shown by the slow international political response to the conflict. While international political factors were largely to blame for the slowness and weakness of the political response, the large humanitarian response (embodying the need to be seen to do something and to believe that you are doing something) mitigated the shortcomings in the political response. This pattern – of externally depoliticising the war – tended to be exacerbated by aspects of the behaviour and operation of relief agencies.

Relief organisations in Sudan did not wilfully deceive themselves about relief dependency: as indicated above, relief dependency generally did not occur in Sudan. However there was some self-deception or 'functional ignorance' about the impact of relief, with relief organisations often exaggerating the impact of their work and glossing over the abuses of relief. Sometimes bold claims about relief were echoed by the government and SPLM/A – in the opinion of the SRRC director in 2004, for example, relief had 'saved the lives of millions of people in the south who otherwise would not have survived 20 years of war.'[73] Certainly some relief workers and heads of agencies avoided exaggerating the achievements of relief. But more often than not, exaggerated claims about relief went unchallenged.[74] In truth, though, as de Waal argued in the 1980s, relief provides only a small amount of what enables people to live and survive: where people survive displacement and food shortage, it is largely by their own local means and resources.[75]

But in addition to tending to exaggerate their achievements, in their international appeals for funding to respond to particular crises in Sudan, relief organisations typically either did not mention or did not emphasise enough the fact that relief was doing nothing to help stop the war, and that the underlying crisis would continue regardless of how much relief was provided. Instead, as several critical studies have noted, the approach was short-termist, responding to the humanitarian situation in Sudan by means of short-term humanitarian programmes. That the present should have dominated the outlook and approach of relief agencies is largely understandable: it is the role of relief to respond to crises. However, it was a weakness of relief that the present and the very near term (typically the next twelve months) dominated the approach of relief agencies in Sudan for most of the 20-plus years of the civil war and continued to do so during the Darfur conflict.

Ignoring the truth about the effectiveness of relief, ignoring the underlying causes of the humanitarian crises, and continuing with a short-termist approach, focused on responding to crises in the short-term, are all forms of ignorance which suit relief organisations and allow them to continue their work. To say so is not to question the good intentions of relief workers, it is just to point out that relief organisations in Sudan adapted to a system of crisis, response, and continuation of crisis. This system kept them in work and contributed to the persistence of humanitarian approaches to the conflict which understated the limits to their effectiveness and the need for political factors to be better addressed for the overall situation to improve in the longer term.

Implications

The implications of the above are that there were some ways in which relief organisations could have done more to prevent the abuse of relief and to bring about a peaceful resolution of the conflict and the associated humanitarian crises in Sudan, but that these ways were rather limited. As indicated, relief organisations did try to prevent the abuse and obstruction of relief, for example, by protesting against government and rebel actions, by trying to improve their monitoring of relief, and by agreements such as the Ground Rules. In so far as these were all ways to try to improve the impact of relief, UN agencies and INGOs were right to keep using and trying to refine them, although their effectiveness was limited by the relative powerlessness of relief agencies in a war-time context. For its part, OLS might have improved its effectiveness more if it had moved away from its north–south framework. That it failed to do so was not only because of factors external to OLS: it was partly because of internal resistance within OLS to systemic change. In the case of the humanitarian system and operation developed for Darfur, relief organisations could have done more to clarify what relief was and was not doing, to help prevent relief becoming entrenched in the region's political economy and difficult to scale back.

Realistically, though, these 'options' could have brought only minor improvements in the humanitarian response to the war. More helpful would have been if relief organisations had done more to prevent the internal and especially the external depoliticisation of the war. This would have meant seeking more political action from the warring parties, international mediators and donors. As part of this, relief agencies would themselves have needed to pay more attention to the causes of the humanitarian crises that they responded to in the war and Darfur.[76] Ultimately, however, the most important reasons for the deficiencies in international responses to the civil war and the Darfur conflict lay not with humanitarian actors, but in the hands of foreign-policy decision makers. As such, it is in foreign policy that we must look most of all for what options were available to the international community to have helped produce better outcomes in Sudan.

FOREIGN POLICY

In Chapter 4 we saw how Western foreign policy towards Sudan during the war shifted through four broad strategies, from clientelism to containment and then engagement, and finally an awkward mix of engagement and containment during the continuation of the Darfur conflict after the CPA was signed. Within these strategies, support for the resolution of conflict was never the central policy, but varied in importance over the course of the war. Furthermore mediation and relief were never significantly co-ordinated in Sudan, with only one exception, the Nuba Mountains agreement. To see what options were available to foreign policy makers that could have led to better results (relative to their objectives, and for resolving the war and improving the humanitarian situation), it will be helpful now to examine more closely the options for linking mediation and relief, and the frameworks that underlie foreign policy.

Substitutability of mediation and relief

As indicated in Chapter 4, Sudan provides a strong example of what could be called the negative substitution of humanitarian action for political action to resolve conflict. It has been argued that this kind of substitution occurred in other civil wars, such as in the DRC, Rwanda and Yugoslavia. Simply put, this substitution was a dependence on humanitarian action in the absence of concerted political action. Unsurprisingly, too, it has been commented on by senior aid workers, including in Sudan. In the words of Mukesh Kapila, for example, after his term as UN head in Sudan during the escalation of the Darfur conflict:

> [E]very time there is a major political crisis anywhere it is categorised as a humanitarian problem and those who are in charge of humanitarian operations are then burdened with the task of doing something about it and when they inevitably fail the blame is put on the humanitarians and those whose responsibility it is to seek political solutions get off scot-free by saying that the humanitarians did not do their job ....[77]

Sudanese officials as well have held such opinions: in the opinion of one SPLM/A official involved in relief, 'The international community lacked the courage to engage with the causes of the humanitarian situation – which were political.' Relief, in short, was 'to soothe their consciences'.[70]

Evidently though, mediation and relief implicitly serve different objectives, and if those objectives are to be met, it is not possible for one to substitute simply for the other. Moreover, there is no intrinsic or necessary connection between mediation and relief in war, even though there is in principle a common interest in the resolution of conflict. As was seen in Chapter 4, while relief became a constant feature of Western foreign policy towards Sudan, attempts at mediation – and the manner of those attempts – were related to circumstances. After the government of Bashir came to power in 1989, and through most of the 1990s, Sudan's relations with the West were not conducive to fruitful mediation by Western governments; instead, international mediation was, in effect, delegated or left largely to African governments, specifically to Nigeria and IGAD, while relief was looked after by the UN and Western donors (governments and publics). Furthermore, when the prevailing foreign policy approach began to shift from containment to engagement, the increase in Western mediation of the conflict did not substitute for or otherwise alter relief policy. After the CPA was signed international decisions about support for efforts to resolve the conflict in Darfur were unconnected to the prevailing policy and system for humanitarian aid.

Ultimately, therefore, the question of whether mediation and relief were merely 'substitutable' (positively or negatively) as elements of foreign policy towards Sudan is uninformative. More helpful, instead, is to consider what constructive linkages could have been made between them.

Linking political and humanitarian action

The long course of Sudan's war offers examples of when political and humanitarian affairs were linked or co-ordinated, and of when they were not. Between 1983 and 1989, before OLS, Western donor countries made no real linkages between political and humanitarian action; during OLS, however, the role of Western government officials in humanitarian matters tended to grow, with foreign ministry officials and ministers sometimes actively supporting OLS in negotiations over relief access. Finally, as noted in Chapter 3, the Nuba Mountains ceasefire agreement was intended both to improve humanitarian access and to help advance peace talks between the government and the SPLM/A.

A number of arguments have been made against linking political and humanitarian action, either in general or in the case of Sudan. However, such arguments generally do not stand up to scrutiny, as they tend to be motivated either by the assumption that any linkage will compromise humanitarian action, or by other questionable assumptions. Johnson, for example, suggests that the IGAD talks began to 'unravel' in 1999 partly because of a proposal by the IPF 'to link humanitarian relief to a peace agreement between the government and the SPLA'.[79] In truth, though, any potential difficulties raised by the proposal threatened the IGAD talks far less than more immediate factors, such as the parallel Egyptian–Libyan initiative and the distance between the positions of the two parties. More severely, Geoff Loane and Tanja Schümer contend that attempts to link relief and peacebuilding may even cause the intensification of conflict. However, their argument does not explain how this could happen, and it does not consider the many other factors which can lead to an intensification in fighting.[80]

What options, then, were there for constructively linking political and humanitarian action in Sudan? One way of potentially linking political and humanitarian action was by using conditionality.[81] To some extent, over the course of the war, conditions did come to be attached to relief, despite relief agencies' general aversion to using conditions, on the grounds of humanitarian principle.[82] One example of conditionality was the Ground Rules in Southern Sudan, the experience of which led the OLS review team to argue that 'the rule-based conditional approach to relief should be expanded to the Northern Sector, and deepened throughout emergency operations in Sudan.'[83] However, such conditionality was not linked to peace talks: the conditions covered by the Ground Rules affected only relief. Likewise, the agreement of temporary humanitarian ceasefires as a condition for the delivery of relief generally was not connected to firm political action, whether in the form of mediation or progress in peace talks. Sometimes the government and the SPLM/A agreed a temporary ceasefire before talks, other times they agreed one at the end of talks. In either case, though, the talks were usually unsuccessful and humanitarian issues did not play a significant role. Even during the talks in Kenya from 2002 onwards, humanitarian issues did not play a significant part, and nor did participants in the talks who otherwise took a strong interest in humanitarian issues see a need for them to play a role in the talks.[84]

This suggests that the actual scope for successfully using conditions to link political and humanitarian action was small. Nonetheless, the Nuba Mountains ceasefire agreement brokered by John Danforth does offer one example of an apparently effective use of conditions to link political and humanitarian action. The agreement was essentially made on humanitarian rather than political grounds, and it provided an opportunity for the parties to satisfy the conditions Danforth had set for the US to join the IGAD talks. It was therefore with some justification that USAID considered the agreement to have been the fruit of a 'humanitarian-to-political strategy' which its Bureau for Democracy, Conflict, and Humanitarian Assistance (DCHA) had adopted in Sudan in 2001. USAID also felt that the strategy had been boosted by the Sudanese government becoming keener to cooperate with the US after 9/11.[85]

At a local level, the agreement aimed to resolve or 'transform' conflict in the Nuba Mountains through the NMPACT programme, which consisted principally in relief, rehabilitation and development work. True to this aim, the programme did play a small role in peacebuilding. According to one senior NMPACT official (with enough years of experience in aid and in Sudan not to be naïve), the programme did build trust between the government and SPLM/A on tangible issues in the Nuba Mountains, such as health and security:

> For example, MedAir has got the GoS and the SPLM/A to agree similar policies on clinics and medicines (namely that people should contribute [financially] for medicines they use). … For example, not long into the ceasefire in the Nuba Mountains you had soldiers crossing lines, handing their guns in before going to the market, then collecting them when they were ready to leave (a sort of chit system).[86]

All the same, the agreement also had some downsides. In particular, because the ceasefire covered a limited area, it allowed the parties to redeploy troops elsewhere for belligerent purposes, which at least the government did. Thus, for example, in the view of the SPLM/A commander in the Nuba Mountains, the agreement was 'a very good opportunity for the government, as it froze the fourth front in the war and they could redeploy troops to Bentiu', in oil-producing Unity State, where fighting continued in 2002 and 2003.[87]

Such redeployments are liable to occur in many ceasefire situations. In the case of the Nuba Mountains ceasefire, however, the redeployments did not outweigh the benefits of the ceasefire, or the benefits of its use as a confidence-building measure and a starting point for US engagement in the IGAD-led peace process. But in the case of the subsequent overall ceasefire agreement between the government and the SPLM/A during 2003–4, the consequences of redeployments were more problematic: notably, the ceasefire enabled the government to redeploy some of its troops from Southern Sudan (and the Nuba Mountains) to Darfur, where they played a role in the escalation of fighting. The SPLM/A also suspected the government of using the ceasefire to strengthen its position in those parts of Southern Sudan under its control, for example by reinforcing its garrisons in Juba, Malakal and Wau, which constituted a violation of the terms of the ceasefire, which stipulated that the parties could only supply their forces and not strengthen them.[88] Nonetheless, the Nuba Mountains humanitarian ceasefire and the government–SPLM/A ceasefire proved to be lasting achievements, and illustrate how much it was a failure not to conclude an effective, monitored ceasefire in Darfur in 2003 or the years after that. It is realistic to believe that had a humanitarian ceasefire been achieved in Darfur for even a limited area, it could have been used as a basis for building a more successful Darfur peace process.

Leaving aside the issue of the military side effects of ceasefires (humanitarian, conditional, unconditional or otherwise), a general note of caution should be added about the degree to which relief can contribute to conflict resolution. As Neil MacFarlane has commented, 'The capacity of external actors to mitigate or to transform conflict through the use of humanitarian and developmental assistance should not be overestimated.'[89] Relief may sometimes provide an opportunity to reduce local conflicts, as occurred with conflicts between the Toposa in Sudan's south-easternmost corner and the Turkana in neighbouring northern Kenya, where OLS and associated parties helped to broker several temporary truces.[90] However, in a national civil war such as Sudan's, no amount of local conflict 'transformation' or resolution can resolve the overall civil war. The same is true for grassroots conflict resolution initiatives which are not linked to relief or development, but are based on dialogue and reconciliation, such as the Wunlit Agreement in 1999: by themselves, such initiatives could not resolve Sudan's wider war.[91] Instead, the critical elements for conflict resolution lie at a higher political level, and typically require the will to engage in mediation and national peace talks, as was exemplified by US action after the Nuba Mountains ceasefire and the 'humanitarian-to-political strategy' espoused by DCHA. Bearing this example in mind, it will be helpful to look at what options, if any, foreign policy makers had in the choice of frameworks underlying and connecting their foreign and humanitarian policies.

Foreign and humanitarian policy

To discuss foreign and humanitarian policy together is not to assume that Western governments used a common framework dealing with both spheres of policy in the case of Sudan or elsewhere. However, as mentioned above, during the 1990s political actors (typically foreign ministry officials, through embassies) were increasingly involved in supporting humanitarian actors in negotiations over humanitarian access. As one evaluation of relief in Sudan observed, this support contrasted with the example of Bosnia, where military and political actors negotiated humanitarian access on behalf of humanitarian agencies, and, on the other hand, Rwanda and the DRC/Zaire in the 1990s, where political actors left humanitarian agencies to negotiate on their own.[92] Nonetheless, in the case of Sudan foreign policy pressures meant that the tendency of political actors was to leave humanitarian actors to negotiate on their own, and the connection between humanitarian and political actors was therefore not institutionalised.

Occasional or limited political support for humanitarian negotiations in Sudan cannot be said to have constituted 'coherence' of foreign and humanitarian policy.[93] Equally it did not constitute a 'strategic framework' or 'strategic co-ordination' such as the UN – or specifically the UN Office for the Coordination of Humanitarian Affairs (UN OCHA) – ostensibly tried to apply in the Great Lakes region in the late 1990s, in response to earlier experiences in Sudan, Bosnia and Rwanda and Zaire.[94] However, the support was a positive (albeit inconsistent) example of co-ordination, and it did not entail any of the compromises which some humanitarian actors feared 'strategic co-ordination' or policy 'coherence' would have. Such fears largely arose from the presumption that the pursuit of 'strategic co-ordination' and policy coherence would inevitably lead to a harmful politicisation of relief.[95] The presumption can be seen in a comment in the review of relief in Sudan mentioned above:

> 'Strategic co-ordination' is in principle devoted to promoting a rights-based peace, but this may in reality have numerous meanings and hide partisan agendas, as appeared in the case of Afghanistan. To argue that humanitarian and political action always should be coordinated, therefore, implies that the humanitarian actors – and their state sponsors – as a rule should buy into whichever political logic happens to prevail in particular 'strategic frameworks'.[96]

However, the implicit presumption here is wrong, as it rests essentially on humanitarian organisations being disproportionately wary of the political agendas of donor states that engage in efforts to resolve conflict. Certainly such wariness may sometimes be justified: there may and will be cases where humanitarian action may be compromised too much by becoming co-ordinated or associated with political action to resolve a conflict. But in the case of Sudan there was little risk of humanitarian action being so compromised, seeing that donor states did not have strong interests in a particular outcome to the war, and what other economic and political interests they had at stake were small. In short, humanitarian organisations had nothing to lose from calling for or seeking more action from donor governments and the warring parties to resolve the war. As already stated, it would have helped if relief agencies had themselves tried to minimise the depoliticisation of the humanitarian crises they were responding to and been more vociferous about the need for a political solution. Similarly, there was scope for foreign ministries in donor governments to co-ordinate foreign policy more with humanitarian policy, at least to the point of recognising more fully the limitations to what humanitarian assistance could achieve, either in saving lives or resolving the war (for example through 'conflict transformation' and peacebuilding programmes).

Some opportunities for substantive foreign and humanitarian policy co-ordination can be seen when one looks at options in institutional arrangements. As was demonstrated in the early 2000s by the examples of co-operation between the State Department and USAID in the US, and the Sudan Unit in Britain, institutional arrangements could and did help policy co-ordination. It is true that tensions between the two strands of policy persisted (as one official in the US State Department put it, 'It's always going to be a balancing act').[97] But in both the US and British examples, officials believed the efforts at policy co-ordination were worthwhile, and the progress after 2001 in resolving Sudan's civil war supported this view. Furthermore, as these examples suggest, there was surely scope for more such co-ordination, especially so as to have better addressed the policy tensions during the escalation of the Darfur conflict, but also perhaps for such co-ordination to have been attempted earlier on, at least in the second half of the 1990s (when the Sudanese government began to change its policies). In a similar vein, there was some scope for greater policy co-ordination within the UN, between the Department of Political Affairs and the humanitarian and development agencies. Such co-ordination was partly called for by the Brahimi Report in 1999,[98] although it was not until 2005 that the UN established a Mediation Support Unit to help co-ordinate and support mediation initiatives. In its nascent form the Mediation Support Unit would probably have had little impact on the government–SPLM/A peace process, but it was anyway established too late to be involved at all. That this was so, is symptomatic of how the UN system in Sudan tended to be overwhelmingly focused on relief, with very little attention to or role in conflict resolution. After the CPA was signed the UN system in Sudan shifted more towards 'recovery' and development assistance. But what was needed to resolve the conflict in Darfur was obscured by the preoccupation with humanitarian response, the focus on deploying AMIS and UNAMID, the misconceived debate about a non-consensual armed humanitarian intervention in Darfur, and the abortive DPA.

Unfortunately, much of the small stock of theory-oriented literature on the subject of co-ordination or intentional linkages between political and humanitarian action in internal conflicts has tended to assume that any such co-ordination would entail changes only in humanitarian policy and practice, not in foreign policy. Typical of this is the claim of Joanna Macrae, writing in 2002, that following 'a number of experiments in integrating humanitarian and political responses to conflict' in the 1990s in Serbia, South Sudan, Sierra Leone and North Korea, 'humanitarian assistance may no longer be considered to have a significant role to play in conflict resolution'.[99] According to Macrae, the UN too had made mistakes in exploring the possibility of incorporating 'humanitarian action under a political umbrella' or subsuming it under 'a wider peacebuilding agenda'.[100] Such claims, however, are inaccurate and unduly pessimistic. There had, in fact, been no coherent attempt to integrate humanitarian and political responses to the war in Sudan. The Danforth initiative and Nuba Mountains agreement did not constitute the *integration* of humanitarian action into a political agenda; and non-OLS relief (and the tentative US initiatives to support the SPLM/A) had nothing to do with peaceful conflict resolution.[101] More broadly though, and as indicated above, co-ordinating humanitarian action with peacebuilding or peaceful conflict resolution does not require subordinating it to political goals which will necessarily compromise it.

Constructive foreign and humanitarian policy co-ordination (of a sort which could have contributed to momentum to resolve the civil war or Darfur conflict) did not require idealist foreign policy. Indeed, in the late 1990s and early 2000s, US and to a lesser extent European engagement in the peace process for Sudan was partly motivated by the *realpolitik* concern of preventing Sudan becoming a 'failed state' and a 'haven' for al-Qaeda. It was in the context of such interests that the US engaged with the IGAD peace process after 2001. Furthermore, the aim of preventing state failure (for realist, idealist or liberal purposes) did not need to be accompanied by the willingness to undertake an armed humanitarian intervention in Darfur. As Paul Williams and Alex Bellamy have observed, it is true that in the case of Darfur (and Chechnya, for example) 'perceived strategic interests mitigated against an interventionist position'.[102] But in the case of Darfur, armed humanitarian intervention was never the best option for containing or resolving the conflict – not least because such an intervention was not politically feasible when the Sudanese government was engaged in a peace process with the SPLM/A. Instead, a better option was stronger international participation in Sudan's peace process (or processes), and more consistency in foreign policy – for example, to reduce the tension between security interest in counter-terrorism co-operation, and interest in resolving conflict in Sudan.

Implications

The implications of the discussion above are that there were options available to foreign policy makers that could have led to better results, both relative to their policy objectives, and for resolving Sudan's conflicts and mitigating the humanitarian crises. For example, more could have been done in Darfur or earlier in the civil war to try to connect humanitarian ceasefires to political negotiations, along the lines of the example of the Nuba Mountains ceasefire agreement. More generally, foreign and humanitarian policy towards Sudan could have been better co-ordinated, through co-operation and joint policy-making arrangements between foreign ministries and aid or development ministries, as was exemplified by the US and British policy-making initiatives in the early 2000s.

Evidently the potential impact of such initiatives or approaches was limited by external factors, in particular the tractability of the warring parties and the pressures of humanitarian needs. However, the interests of international donors would not have been harmed if they had allocated more financial and human resources to trying to co-ordinate foreign and humanitarian policy towards the common interest of the peaceful resolution of conflict. There is of course no guarantee that donors would this way have had more success in meeting their various objectives. But the very imperfect outcome reached in January 2005 – the CPA combined with the Darfur conflict, and the failure to end that conflict over the following years – speaks in favour of trying to do more rather than less to resolve conflict.

Conclusion

The discussion in this chapter has pointed to a number of inter-connected conclusions about how better outcomes in mediation, relief and foreign policy could have been realised in the international response to Sudan's conflicts. In short, the chapter has argued for more active mediation, for relief organisations to do more to highlight the needs for a political solution, and for foreign policy and humanitarian policy to be better co-ordinated around the mutual interest in the peaceful resolution of conflict. A more accurate framework for representing the civil war and the Darfur conflict, more commitment from the mediators to peace, and possibly more effort to broaden participation and to insist on principles such as democratisation, would have increased the prospect of better outcomes to the CPA and Darfur peace processes (and perhaps even prevented the need for separate processes). A better framework for relief and greater effort to avoid internal and external depoliticisation of humanitarian crises, and to call for political action to resolve the underlying conflicts, would likewise have increased the prospect of peace and breaking the cycle of humanitarian crises. Finally, more constructive co-ordination of foreign and humanitarian policy – through policy frameworks and institutions – would have increased the prospect of a better outcome, both in terms of saving lives and ending the war, and in terms of the interests of donors and mediators.

Evidently these 'options' are only possibilities or likelihoods, not guarantees. However their merits will be considered further in the following chapter, the conclusion of this book, which will consider more broadly the overall outcomes in Sudan, some comparisons with other conflicts, and the implications for conflict resolution.

6

CONCLUSION

This chapter – the conclusion of the book – reflects on the overall outcomes of international efforts to resolve conflict in Sudan, the reasons for the outcomes, and the possible impact of the options discussed in the previous chapter. It considers briefly how the case of Sudan compares with other cases of internal conflicts involving humanitarian crises, and then looks at the prospects for peace in Sudan. The chapter concludes by considering what theoretical or practical lessons can be drawn from or for the case of Sudan in conflict resolution and international relations.

THE OUTCOMES IN SUDAN

As indicated at the beginning of this book, the outcomes of international mediation in Sudan were very mixed: this was evident in the paradoxical juxtaposition of the signing of the CPA in January 2005 and the simultaneous continuation of the Darfur conflict; but it could also be seen in the longer history of unsuccessful efforts to resolve conflict and the never-ending provision of relief and the loss of life during much of the preceding two decades.

Successes, failures, reasons

Broadly speaking, the international community's engagement with Sudan between 1983 and 2009 had some successes in mediation, relief and foreign policy. The limited or partial success of international mediation in Sudan was embodied in the CPA, its subsidiary protocols, and the permanent cessation of hostilities between the Sudanese government and the SPLM/A. The main reasons for this success lay in the internationalisation of the Sudan peace talks and, linked with this, the changes in the international context which encouraged international convergence on the objective of ending the conflict. Relief was rarely linked successfully with conflict resolution. But it was effective or successful to the unmeasured extent that it saved lives and reduced suffering, mitigating but not resolving conflict. So far as relief did this (which it did), the main reasons for its success lay in the systematisation of relief embodied by OLS and then the Darfur humanitarian operation, and the persistence in the provision of relief, year after year, crisis after crisis. Lastly, through its support for three peace-support or peacekeeping missions in Sudan after 2005 (UNMIS, AMIS and UNAMID), the international community made a very valuable contribution to supporting the implementation of the CPA and containing the Darfur conflict (deterring further escalation, though not resolving it in the manner of a peace agreement).

Evidently, though, the international community's engagement with Sudan between 1983 and 2009 also met with significant failures. The thwarted initiatives of Carter and Cohen, and the 'track two' diplomacy of Norway in the early 1990s, were modest failures in mediation. Larger failures were the botched mediation of the DPA and the haphazard mediation efforts in the following years. But the largest failures in Western engagement were the inability or unwillingness for many years to become involved in peace talks, and then the failure to prevent the positive outcome of the talks in Kenya from 2002 to 2004 being accompanied in Darfur by the escalation of a violent conflict and a major humanitarian crisis. Certainly the key reasons and responsibility for the failure of many talks lay with the warring parties.[1] But international mediators made mistakes too, such as using inappropriate frameworks for talks, accepting an exclusive two-party platform for talks without adequately addressing the needs of excluded parties, and not showing stronger commitment to reaching a credible political settlement and effective ceasefire in Darfur, and guarantees for their implementation.

The failures or shortcomings of relief in Sudan were the reverse side of the coin of its success: broadly they were the failure to do better – to save more lives, to reduce suffering more effectively, to better prevent the abuse of relief. However, they were also the failure to prevent the domestic and external depoliticisation of the civil war and the humanitarian crises to which relief organisations were trying to respond. The reasons for these shortcomings lay in the way that relief organisations worked (including their short-termist approach), and the north–south OLS framework. Lastly, the shortcomings in US and European foreign policy towards Sudan were embodied in the repeated deteriorations in relations and the repeated need to change the overall foreign-policy approach, shifting from clientelism, through containment, to engagement, and finally to a complex combination of containment and engagement. From 2003, the shortcomings in overall policy were illustrated by the conflicting pressures of trying to push negotiations towards a comprehensive peace agreement and pursue co-operation on counter-terrorism issues, at the same time as witnessing the Darfur conflict escalate. Across the span of the civil war and the Darfur conflict, foreign policies towards Sudan generally failed to give enough priority to direct efforts to resolve conflict.

Options and opportunities

The very mixed outcomes in Sudan mean that it is not idle speculation to consider what opportunities there were to have achieved better outcomes. Evidently the combination of the CPA and the Darfur conflict was not a 'best-case scenario', of a kind that foreign-policy decision makers would have aimed for. Equally it was not a 'worst-case scenario': worse outcomes were possible, such as, for example, the collapse of the government–SPLM/A peace process in parallel with the Darfur escalation, or a wider state collapse, both of which were realistic possibilities. However, even if we take the Darfur conflict only in the period between 2003 and the CPA signing on 9 January 2005 (and leave aside the fact that it continued beyond then), the conflict was plainly disastrous, and if policy makers could have foreseen how bad the conflict would be, they surely would have given greater priority to trying to deal with it. Considering the options discussed in Chapter 5 – in particular those that were available to the mediators in Kenya – the sustained escalation and continuation of the conflict could quite possibly have been prevented. Moreover the options that were available – such as efforts to widen participation in the talks, the use of a more appropriate framework, and better policy co-ordination – did not require special foresight about the likelihood of severe conflict in Darfur.

That some of those options in mediation and foreign policy could have been pursued before 2002 points to missed opportunities to have brought about a better outcome. That some of these options were not taken during 2002–4 points to a missed opportunity to have better contained and limited the escalation in Darfur. Furthermore, the escalation of the Darfur conflict illustrates how a missed opportunity for conflict prevention or resolution can be followed by a dramatic deterioration both in events and in the prospects for resolving that conflict. As Zartman has argued, early diplomatic or political action to prevent or resolve conflict is 'more effective and more efficient, and less costly and less constrained, than delayed action'.[2] By the start of 2005, the losses incurred by the warring parties in Darfur and by the civilian population were already very large, and international actors had little influence over the situation.

In short, therefore, the options discussed in Chapter 5 for mediation, relief and foreign policy in dealing with Sudan's conflicts were important.

All of the options meet appropriate criteria such as feasibility, relevance and likely beneficial effectiveness, so it is fair to consider them as opportunities.[3] Widening participation in the talks in Kenya after the Machakos protocol and/or avoiding using a north–south framework for the talks could well have mitigated escalation in Darfur (so that the conflict resembled more the small-scale conflict in the east). Avoiding the depoliticisation of relief (domestically and externally) could have helped to bring about more prompt and substantial international action to address the civil war, and could have encouraged greater domestic pressure on the governing authorities – the government and the SPLM/A – to deliver basic services and end the war. Finally, more or better foreign-policy co-ordination could have brought more timely political action on Darfur. This would have increased the chances of peace talks for Darfur during 2003–4 being more effective than the weakly mediated talks that were held and which resulted only in ineffective ceasefire agreements.

Other questions

Many questions can be asked about Sudan's civil war and the Darfur conflict which are not directly explored in this book. However, one pair of questions which is more relevant than others to the core questions of this book is (i) Why did the conflicts go on for so long? and (ii) why was the CPA concluded when it was? These questions are interesting in themselves, and in the light of academic literature focusing on the economic dimensions of internal conflict and the motivations of warring parties.[4] Having reached the conclusions above, about the outcomes of mediation and relief in Sudan, it is worth making some direct responses to these two questions.

It is hard to give a short and adequate answer to the question of why Sudan's major conflicts went on for so long. In truth, there was a host of primarily internal but also external factors, of varying causal priority and magnitude, which caused the civil war and then the Darfur conflict to go on for so long. In one respect the war lasted so long because the two main parties – the successive governments in Khartoum and the SPLM/A – were willing to keep fighting. Although each party sometimes gained external assistance, the involvements and interests of external actors fluctuated and were not sufficient to sustain more than two decades of conflict: rather, the determining factors were internal. At the root of these factors was the government's historical unwillingness to share power and resources in a way that was sufficient to satisfy politically and economically marginalised populations in the south and other parts of the country, including South Kordofan, Blue Nile, Darfur and parts of Eastern Sudan. This unwillingness was a product of history, ideologies and perceptions (of self and others); and it was compounded by ideologies, policies and actions during the war itself. Conflicting explanations of the country's conflicts, and conflicting visions of peace, further impeded the search for a negotiated end to the conflicts.

Certainly, on both sides of the civil war and the Darfur conflict, some individuals and parties profited, economically and politically. Examples ranged from opportunist militia leaders and businessmen, to senior figures in politics, the military and the security apparatus. Certainly, too, anyone who was able to reduce such profiteering and thereby increase the chances of ending a conflict should ideally have taken action to do so. However it would be both wrong and unconstructive to emphasise the economic dimensions of the conflicts over all other dimensions. It would be wrong because the evidence does not support the claim; and it would be unconstructive because, in the case of Sudan, the external actors involved in mediation and relief had much less control or influence over economic factors (such as war profiteering or the development of the oil sector) than they had over decisions about mediation and relief (about the *what, when, who, how* and *where* of mediation and relief).

The limited use of focusing on the economic dimensions of the conflicts is evident when one considers whether the war would have gone on for so long if there had been no oil (exploited or not). Very probably, the war would have gone on for as long as it did. In the first war, the exploitation of actual or potential oil reserves was not a matter of contention, but the war still went on for more than a decade until 1972. In the war after 1983, oil was known to be a potential resource, but it was not extracted and exported in significant volumes until after 1998, some 15 years into the war. In Darfur oil was not a significant motivating factor for the rebels or the government (there were no proven reserves, nor was there believed to be great potential), but conflict still arose in Darfur in the 1990s and escalated violently from 2003 onwards. Lastly, when one looks further back into the history of modern Sudan – for example to the arguments before independence about the north and the south, the hegemonic interest of Egypt, and past internal conflicts – one sees plenty of capacity for prolonged conflict without oil or another sole natural resource being the primary cause of conflict or peace.

The limited explanatory power of economic factors is further confirmed by what Sudanese themselves say. It was not the intention of this book to show this, but it was repeatedly evident in the interviews carried out during its research. Interviewees' opinions about the causes of the civil war and the Darfur conflict, and the successes or failures of attempts to end them, varied.[5] But they all pointed towards the complex of internal causes of conflict, rather than giving primacy to economic factors or single economic resources such as oil, land or water.

Concerning the conflict in Darfur, in the words of a former governor of Darfur, Tijani el-Seisi: 'The problem has been there a long time: marginalisation and exclusion from power and wealth.'[6] A member of the JEM negotiating delegation to the Darfur talks explained the failure of the talks and the continuation of the conflict by saying: 'The government has no wish to reach a peace agreement. They are treating it only as a security problem. ... From the beginning the government has refused to recognise that there is a political problem.'[7] Furthermore, the fact that the war and talks could go on for so long did not greatly surprise people. As one Sudanese peace activist saw it, the government took every opportunity to delay negotiations, simply because 'they are sitting on top of power, and peace will mean losing some of that power. ... They have every interest to delay, and they have succeeded.'[8] One important reason for the government to be intransigent about the war was the perceived public and political support for unity, at least in the north. As one former SPLM member put it, 'In sum, the government feels that the majority is for unity and only a minority for separation, so why give in?'[9]

Much as the conflicts and their duration were not the result of a single cause, the advent of the CPA was not the result of a single factor. Instead, as indicated in Chapters 2 and 5, the most important determinants of the progress in the CPA peace talks between 2002 and 2004 were the international context, the widened international mediation, and domestic political changes in Sudan. The result was an agreement concluded exclusively between the government and the SPLM. In some ways the CPA was ultimately a 'deal'[10] or 'an accommodation between the two warring parties'.[11] However, it would be wrong to reduce the political complexity which produced the CPA to a matter of economics. As was evident from the research conducted for this book, and from other points, economic factors were not at all the primary determinant of the advent of the CPA. As several interviewees remarked, the government was getting all the oil revenues, so why should it settle for a negotiated peace? Between 1998 and 2002 it had been able to increase output, and as long as talks continued, it did not have to share revenues with the SPLM/A.[12] Certainly oil was a more significant factor by 2002–4, by virtue of Sudan's growing output and revenues. But why should oil have been a critical determinant in 2002–4, but not in 1999, 2000 or 2001, for example? Oil-revenue sharing figured as one element of the negotiations at Naivasha, but there was no sense that the availability of increased oil revenues, or for the SPLM/A the prospect of gaining a share of revenues, was the real reason why the talks converged on the CPA.

Besides being wrong, the suggestion that economic factors were the primary cause of the advent of the CPA does not provide useful ideas about the options available to external actors in mediation and relief. External actors responding to Sudan's war and the Darfur conflict had negligible control over the warring parties' perceptions of economic incentives during the conflicts. This was because those actors interested or involved in mediation and relief had little influence over Sudan's economy (economic sanctions proved ineffective), and still less over the development of Sudan's oil industry during the 1990s (which was led by Chinese and Malaysian companies). If these actors had been the sole or lead developers of Sudan's oil industry in the 1990s, the equation could have been different: they could perhaps have had significant leverage over part of the economic stakes in the war. As it was, they had next to none.

As indicated in Chapters 3 and 4, during the IGAD talks the troika did try to use aid (in particular debt forgiveness, but also the JAM and the expected international donor conference) as a 'carrot'. However these incentives were still relatively small and were not critical determinants of the outcomes of the talks or, still less, of the situation on the ground (as was shown by the escalation of the conflict in Darfur and its continuation beyond the signing of the CPA). In contrast, the troika, the EU and the UN had much control over their actions in mediation and relief, and over their policies towards Sudan. It is therefore with good reason that this book has focused on questions about the role of mediation and relief in the civil war and the Darfur conflict, and has explored more broadly what determined the outcomes of peace talks and what options there were to have brought about better outcomes.

COMPARISONS AND PROSPECTS

It is instructive to compare the case of Sudan briefly with other cases of internal conflicts involving prolonged or large-scale humanitarian crises. Among the conclusions that are sometimes drawn concerning mediation, relief and foreign policy in other conflicts, there are both similarities and dissimilarities with the case of Sudan. Bearing these in mind, it will be useful also to consider briefly the future prospects of Sudan, before drawing final conclusions about conflict resolution and the case of Sudan.

Similarities and dissimilarities

The two decades after the end of the Cold War offer many examples of internal conflicts and civil wars which have involved major humanitarian crises, from Angola, Burundi, the DRC and Liberia, to Rwanda, Somalia, Tajikistan and the former Yugoslavia. These conflicts and the associated humanitarian crises have varied in many ways, not least in terms of the causes, actors, intensity, magnitude and duration, but also in terms of the international responses (in overall foreign policy and in specific undertakings such as mediation and relief) and the outcomes. Nevertheless, many of the issues focused on in the discussion above and in Chapter 5 were also relevant in these conflicts. This is particularly so in mediation and conflict resolution, where the lessons drawn in research have often concerned the questions of who participates in peace talks (and the consequences of this), and what commitments or guarantees are offered by external actors.

The case of Rwanda, for example, inevitably begs the question of what would have happened had a more inclusive approach been used at the peace talks that led to the August 1993 Arusha Accords for Rwanda. Although the international mediation at the talks was effective in bringing about a theoretically good agreement, the talks were fundamentally 'flawed' by the fragmented condition of the Rwandan government, which meant that it was unable to fulfil its side of the agreement.[13] The question that has therefore sometimes been asked is whether the Hutu extremists excluded from the Arusha talks might not have carried out their genocidal plans had they been included in the peace process. Like most counterfactual arguments, it is essentially unprovable that they would not have done so. But the possibility that inclusion would have helped to avert the genocide is tantalising, although hindsight has tended to focus instead on perceived missed opportunities in deploying international armed forces in Rwanda, and on the facts of the genocide itself.

In other cases, however, arguments in favour of greater inclusivity in peace processes have been made with more confidence. For example, in the case of the civil war that began in Tajikistan in 1992, Kathleen Collins has argued that the main mistake made by the UN and the Organisation for Security and Co-operation in Europe (OSCE) – the two main international actors involved in mediating the bilateral peace agreement which formally ended the war in 1997 – was essentially to have allowed the exclusion of other parties from the peace process:

> The major failure of the UN and the OSCE was their endorsement of negotiations and a peace agreement that excluded not only numerous minor clan factions and militias but also Khodjent – an entire region of Tajikistan including over 25 percent of the country's population.[14]

George Kieh has similarly argued that one of the lessons from the peace initiatives for Liberia during its two bouts of civil war (between 1989 and 2003) is that 'effective peacemaking must include civil society', and that in

Liberia 'the peacemaking efforts marginalized the citizenry and civil society and focused exclusively on the warring factions'.[15] Similarly, in the case of the peace process for Burundi between 1993 and 2001 Mohammed Maundi has argued that the most important transferable policy lesson from Burundi is that inclusion is worthwhile:

> [W]hile multilateral negotiations can be very difficult, they nonetheless help in building confidence among the negotiating parties. The long and arduous negotiations in Arusha, surprisingly, acted as a confidence-building exercise by the negotiating parties. ... Hostility and distrust eventually gave way to tolerance and even camaraderie.[16]

However in Burundi the approach to peace talks was only partly and incrementally inclusive. At first, talks included political parties and factions but excluded armed groups. Gradually armed groups were included in subsequent phases of talks, but other factions were excluded or not brought to the table. The result was a succession of political agreements and ceasefires in the years after 2001, through to 2008, which cumulatively brought peace.[17] Somewhat differently, in the case of the conflicts in Zaire/DRC, Tatiana Caryannis and Herbert Weiss have argued that the exclusion of opposition parties from mediation efforts in 1996–7 was a mistake, and that inclusiveness was vital to the relative success of the talks that led to the Lusaka Agreement in 1999.[18]

Contrasting with these examples is the case of Somalia's 'national reconciliation' process in the early 2000s, which was convened by IGAD and led to the formation of the Transitional Federal Government (TFG) in 2004. This was an inclusive process: so inclusive, in fact, that in 2004 the mediators and donors paying the costs of the peace talks demanded that the large number of participants be reduced, although some observers at the time argued that the process should instead be broadened.[19] As it was, the large number of participants in the talks was no guarantee of success. Unusually for a national peace process, there was no effective party of government at the talks, and partly as a result of this the TFG was unable to establish its authority across anything but a small part of Somalia after it took office.

In many cases lessons have been drawn about the roles of commitment and guarantees, especially from external actors, in resolving conflict. Drawing on the case of Liberia, for example, Kieh argues that political will and 'staying power' from 'interveners' are critical for success, and that there must be commitment to enforcing ceasefires and implementing agreements.[20] Stettenheim argues that the 'prestige, moral authority, and leverage' of Western countries (principally the USA and France) were central to bringing about the Arusha talks for Rwanda, although he also attributes the holding of the talks to the 'ripeness of the conflict'.[21] Similarly, Walter argues that the case of Rwanda partly validates her 'credible commitment theory', although she acknowledges that it also challenges some of the assumptions underlying the theory, not least by showing that the world is more complex than a few 'variables' can describe.[22] The limits to what external actors can do are also noted in the case of Burundi by Maundi, who suggests that full success in peacefully ending a war may depend on 'the firm support and active involvement of all the major parties to the conflict'.[23] Angola during the 1990s provides a further example of a situation in which external commitments to the peace process (in the form of UN observer and peacekeeping missions) were not matched by adequate domestic commitment to disarmament, demobilisation and implementation of the existing peace accords, a situation which led to a re-escalation of the war.[24]

Other conflicts and peace processes have also raised questions about the role of democratisation and the commitment of mediators and international actors to democratisation. The argument has been made both ways: in the case of Tajikistan, Collins argues that the UN and the OSCE risked jeopardising the democratisation they had pushed for during the peace process by subsequently giving their approval to elections (in 1999 and 2000) that were neither free nor fair.[25] Taking examples from Angola, Bosnia, Burundi and Sierra Leone, Ben Reilly warns more generally about the risk that 'early and ill thought-through elections' after a peace process and peace agreement may undermine progress on democratisation.[26]

Understandably, most scholarship on humanitarian action in protracted internal conflicts has focused on humanitarian aspects and lessons, and not the actual or possible relationship between relief and conflict resolution. It has sometimes been argued that relief can serve as a negative substitute for political action to deal with a conflict, for example in the DRC and the former Yugoslavia.[27] Also, the argument that externally provided relief tends to reduce local accountability has often been made, and the question of whether relief depoliticises a conflict domestically has sometimes been explored.[28] But these arguments aside, there has been little examination of whether or to what degree relief depoliticises a conflict externally and thereby diminishes the prospects of external pressure for the conflict to be resolved peacefully. Furthermore, because relief has usually been provided on an *ad hoc* basis, rather than by a more systematic framework such as OLS, the question of the role played by relief frameworks in the overall dynamics of a conflict has usually not been relevant. The main exception to this is the case of the former Yugoslavia, where relief corridors were negotiated on a similar basis to the 'corridors of tranquillity' of OLS. However, in Yugoslavia the humanitarian crises were not as protracted as in Sudan, and the relief system ultimately did not hinder calls for political action to end the war, and nor did it have any bearing on the frameworks used for negotiations to end the conflict.

Similarly, accounts of Western foreign policy towards countries going through protracted internal conflicts have tended to focus only on inter-state relations, rather than the implications for the prospects of resolving the conflicts. The broad foreign-policy approaches adopted vis-à-vis Sudan – clientelism, containment and engagement – were used in other cases, albeit not in the same sequence and not necessarily with the same implications. For example, Cold War clientelist approaches entailed that the USA undertook only limited mediation in Angola in the 1980s, and that it avoided taking action over the fall of Mohamed Siad Barre in Somalia, until it attempted an interventionist approach in 1993–4. Clientelism also shaped French and Belgian policy towards Burundi, the DRC and Rwanda during the early stages of the escalation of the conflicts in each country, hampering their willingness or ability to act as impartial agents for resolving the conflicts. Examples of early co-ordination of foreign policy with humanitarian policy and the objective of conflict resolution are rare, although policies did sometimes eventually converge. In the case of Yugoslavia, for example, the variations in European and US policies in the early 1990s had important implications for the conflict, exemplified by Germany's unilateral recognition of Croatia and Slovenia, and it was only slowly between 1991 and 1995 that European and US policy converged on a concerted approach to resolving the conflict. However, as argued in Chapter 5, attempts at 'strategic co-ordination' of relief with political objectives in the Great Lakes region in the late 1990s, and elsewhere, did not entail a sudden co-ordination of foreign and humanitarian policy (and still less the subordination of humanitarian policy to foreign policy), although in the case of the DRC the search for 'strategic co-ordination' may have added to the slow momentum towards a more concerted international effort to resolve the conflict.

Co-ordination of foreign policy with the objective of conflict resolution has therefore been rare. Reflecting this, it has been argued that opportunities for potentially valuable international efforts at conflict prevention or resolution have often been missed. Zartman, for example, argues that there were various specific opportunities in the conflicts (or the preludes to the collapse of the state) in Haiti, Lebanon, Liberia, Somalia, Yugoslavia and Zaire (before 1996).[29] The cost of missing these opportunities was high, particularly because a missed opportunity was sometimes followed by a long period in which there were no promising opportunities for resolving the conflict. This, claims Zartman and others, was the case for Somalia after a period of opportunities between 1989 and 1993,[30] and it is telling that even when the 2004 reconciliation agreement was reached it had limited international backing. The agreement had only the support of IGAD and promises of new international aid, rather than, say, the level of US, European and UN backing that was accorded to Sudan's CPA. Notable too was the absence of the USA from the Somali peace process (either in an official mediating capacity or in a behind-the-scenes capacity), although during the peace process the USA had been pursuing an active policy in and around Somalia, which was focused on combating perceived terrorist activity in the region.

The prospects for Sudan

As this book has argued, when the CPA was signed at the start of 2005, the outcome of efforts to resolve Sudan's civil war and the Darfur conflict was very mixed. Furthermore, the prospects for the CPA and for lasting peace in Sudan were fragile. As of 2005, the Darfur conflict and the lower-level conflict in the east were still continuing; the CPA did not have the full support of parties that had been excluded from its negotiation; and the commitment of the government to the CPA was far from certain. Five years later, as of early 2010 (the time of writing), the situation had not fundamentally changed. The CPA and the eastern agreement had held, but the Darfur conflict remained unresolved and, with the scheduled end of the CPA approaching, the risk of renewed conflict on a larger scale was still significant. The threats entailed by the original exclusion of other parties from the negotiation of the CPA were also still present. Although the main excluded parties officially supported the CPA, they also continued to search for a share of power on terms other than those offered by the CPA. In differing ways, the NCP and the SPLM both continued to counterbalance their continued implementation of the CPA with threats and overtures of new political agreements and arrangements.

During its first five years, the CPA provided the ruling NCP and the SPLM with a measure of legitimacy and licence to rule, by virtue of their being the only parties to an agreement which many inside and outside Sudan wanted to see hold. Despite much distrust, and intermittent crises (for example over troop redeployments, the sharing of cabinet positions, the boundaries of Abyei, the census, and elections), the NCP and the SPLM maintained the CPA, co-existing in the NCP-led Government of National Unity (GONU) and the SPLM-led Government of Southern Sudan (GOSS) that were formed in mid-2005. However, the relationship and co-operation between the two parties remained uneasy – as much a cold war as a peace – and this brought little confidence about the future, even after the elections in 2010.

It is possible that the CPA will prevail over its deficiencies, for example if it leads to the intended referendum on self-determination for Southern Sudan, and if the outcome of that referendum is credible and is peacefully implemented. But if the agreement is ultimately subverted or fails, and if conflict widens again in Sudan, this will in large part be a result of the intrinsic problems in the CPA and its negotiation, as discussed in Chapter 5. Fundamentally, it was because of the exclusive and non-comprehensive nature of the CPA, and the fact that the agreement had been shaped around a north–south framework, that as of 2010 more talks were still needed for Darfur, and a political settlement between the government and the northern-based opposition parties which had refused to join the GONU was still missing. In short, the exclusive and non-comprehensive nature of the CPA meant that the country's conflicts were still not resolved, and that there was still a risk that future political bargains or agreements would compromise the CPA, perhaps eventually fatally, just as the 1977 reconciliation undermined the Addis Ababa Agreement.

Meanwhile, as of 2010, the dynamics of humanitarian action in Sudan remained largely unchanged. International relief continued to be provided on an immense scale for Darfur, with little scrutiny of its effects and effectiveness, and little prospect of change in sight. Although efforts to end the conflict in Darfur were continuing, the provision of relief remained the principal form of international response to the conflict. Within Sudan a well-established pattern of avoided responsibility therefore continued, whereby the government faced little domestic pressure over the humanitarian situation in Darfur, and international relief agencies took primary responsibility for providing assistance to IDPs. In short, the government was no more at risk of being brought to account by the Sudanese public for humanitarian crisis and the needs of civilians than it had been during the wider war in the preceding decades. This situation is unlikely to change until there is a transformation in Sudan's politics and the economy in which the country's poor live.

CONFLICT RESOLUTION

Evidently, similarities and differences exist between mediation, relief and foreign policy in the case of Sudan and other cases. Evidently too, there are other similarities and differences between Sudan's conflicts and other cases. The country is politically and socially complex (divided and united by far more than a simple African–Arab dichotomy); it has acute poverty and new wealth derived from natural resources; it is strategically important but not indispensable to regional and international powers; and its major conflicts – the civil war and the Darfur conflict – have been especially long and costly (lasting more than two decades, and costing an unknown number of lives). The same conflicts will not be repeated elsewhere, although they may be echoed; and Sudan itself may in the future suffer from continued or renewed internal conflict and civil war. What then are the most important lessons from Sudan about the resolution of conflict, and what are the most important lessons for Sudan?

Lessons from Sudan

Sudan does not offer any unprecedented answers or lessons for conflict resolution. However, the lessons that it offers about mediation, relief and foreign policy in relation to the objective of resolving conflict are important and worth restating.

On mediation, the following lessons should be drawn from the case of Sudan:

(i) Although the idea of necessary and sufficient conditions for conflict resolution is attractive, the case of Sudan shows that the perception of a 'mutually hurting stalemate' should not be considered a necessary condition for peace talks to make progress or be successful. In the late 1980s, when breakthroughs in Sudan were almost achieved, there was no perception of a stalemate; and in the period leading up to and during 2002–4, when peace talks for Sudan did make progress, it is not clear that the parties perceived such a stalemate.

(ii) In contrast, credible commitments and guarantees from external actors (in this case, mediators and their supporters) do appear to have been essential to bringing about the positive outcome of the IGAD peace talks. In short, external commitment was a necessary but not a sufficient condition for producing the CPA. Thus, Sudan supports the argument of Walter that 'Outside powers can play a critical role in the resolution of civil wars, but only if they are willing to make a solid commitment and bear the necessary costs'.[31]

(iii) Sudan illustrates how unevenly opportunities for successful mediation may be distributed.[32] While there were opportunities for fruitful mediation in the late 1980s, during the revolutionary heyday of Hasan al-Turabi in the early to mid-1990s there was little or no scope for

(iv) Conflict resolution is sometimes best pursued 'in concert',[33] with international actors co-ordinating their efforts to mediate a conflict, as exemplified by the co-ordination between the troika and IGAD in the internationalised peace process for Sudan between 2002 and 2004. Uncoordinated or unconcerted mediation is less likely to be successful, as was illustrated by the competition between the Egyptian–Libyan initiative and the IGAD talks between 1999 and 2002, by the weak mediation of the Darfur conflict from late 2003 through to 2005, and by the disarray in Darfur mediation efforts between 2006 and 2009. Similarly, mediation that aims at a 'quick fix' is also unlikely to be successful in a protracted internal conflict, and may potentially backfire – as seen with the DPA and its aftermath. In Sudan, international ultimatums tended to lead to missed deadlines and draft texts that the parties did not accept.

(v) Mediation and conflict resolution based on inappropriate frameworks or understandings of a conflict can be dangerous. In the case of Sudan, the tendency to use a bilateral, north–south framework contributed to the CPA being 'comprehensive' only in a technical sense that the document covered all the substantive matters (from ceasefire through to implementation). The agreement was singularly uncomprehensive in that it excluded the conflict in Darfur and the remnants of conflict in the east, and in that it excluded major unarmed parties which had a significant spoiler potential. This had consequences which resonated through the Darfur conflict, and through to the dangers which the CPA was ultimately likely to face. Meanwhile in mediation in Darfur, the use of a framework which underestimated the excluded parties was counterproductive.

On humanitarian relief, Sudan offers the following lessons:

(i) The extent to which large-scale relief fuels a protracted internal conflict is less than has often been assumed. Even in the case of Sudan, the very high levels of relief provided through OLS and the Darfur operation were still only a small part of the wider economy. While relief certainly can distort motives, behaviour and local economies (and can alter the dynamics of conflict in localised areas), overall it has less impact – positive or negative – than is often claimed or assumed.

(ii) Claims about the harmful consequences of using a 'relief–development continuum' or transition approach in situations of protracted internal conflict and humanitarian crisis, and arguments against using such an approach, are somewhat exaggerated. Often relief cannot be entirely separated from development, especially in situations of acute poverty and absence of basic services, as in much of Southern Sudan during the war. As OLS and the Darfur relief operation illustrate, the greater problem is that relief systems become entrenched and take longer to scale back than they should, and that this happens at the expense of support for development.

(iii) More serious is the risk of relief internally and externally depoliticising conflict and humanitarian crises. In Sudan, relief tended to depoliticise the humanitarian crises, reducing domestic pressure for the government to be accountable for them. In other words, relief had anti-democratic effects, though it was not responsible for the absence of democracy. During the civil war, relief agencies tended to ignore the role that the war played in causing Sudan's humanitarian crises, encouraging the belief abroad that Sudan's problems were primarily humanitarian, not political. During the Darfur conflict, it was widely recognised that the conflict was the cause of the humanitarian crises. In both cases, however, the narrative of relief, and its vast scale, tended to obscure the need for political action to resolve the conflict.

(iv) Organisations providing relief in conflict situations such as Sudan's have an interest in the resolution of the conflict, and should advocate for action towards this end. Co-ordination of relief and foreign policy oriented towards conflict resolution need not compromise humanitarian action: instead, relief organisations should seek changes in foreign policy, bringing it more into line with humanitarian policy and objectives. This should not be confused with the exploitation of humanitarian action to serve self-interested foreign-policy objectives (which is characterised by a tendency for foreign policy to shape humanitarian policy, rather than vice versa).

(v) There is some scope for relief to be used as an entry point for constructive political action, as the case of the Nuba Mountains agreement shows. However, relief organisations should be realistic and transparent about the limitations to what relief can achieve. Exaggerating the ability of relief to 'transform' or resolve conflict risks reducing impetus for a political solution, when a political solution is typically what is needed in major conflicts.

On foreign policy, Sudan offers the following lessons:

(i) There is a genuine risk that humanitarian action in response to protracted internal conflicts will be used as a tacit substitute for political action, and that this will be at the expense of pursuing a more coherent and effective foreign policy. In the case of Sudan, international donors depended on UN organisations to lead the international humanitarian response to the war and the Darfur conflict. But because of their responsibilities in managing OLS and the Darfur humanitarian operation, the UN organisations in Sudan were unable to take a leading role in trying to resolve the conflicts.

(ii) It is possible to co-ordinate foreign policy with humanitarian policy constructively and to the benefit of the objective of resolving conflict peacefully. This was demonstrated by the examples of US and British inter-departmental co-ordination and co-operation in policy towards Sudan during 2002–4. These two examples show that simple changes in institutional arrangements (such as in the structure of departments, or the methods for making and implementing policy) can help to make policy more co-ordinated and more effective.

(iii) Conventional foreign-policy approaches towards strategically significant countries going through protracted internal conflict, can be inappropriate. In the case of Sudan, Western foreign policy generally failed to address the fact of the civil war adequately, and overarching foreign-policy approaches (such as clientelism and containment) tended to struggle to achieve their objectives, necessitating successive shifts in policy. This continued to be the case during the Darfur conflict. Furthermore, the belated but weak engagement between Western and Asian countries (in particular China) over Sudan, illustrates the need for better international co-ordination in such situations, cutting across conventional divisions between international actors and assumed spheres of influence.

(iv) Theories in the academic field of International Relations tend to overlook the interests of outside states in the resolution of internal conflicts. Realist and liberal or cosmopolitan outlooks may have greater common interest in the resolution of civil wars than tends to be assumed, as was shown during the shift towards international engagement in the IGAD peace process for Sudan. International norms favouring more active conflict resolution for its own sake are likely to gain ground only slowly. But concerns about development, international security and the purported failure of states may encourage increased interest in conflict resolution – although such interest may not necessarily be compatible with disinterested support for conflict resolution.

Other issues

This book has focused on the role of international mediation and relief in Sudan's war, the role of foreign policy, and their relationship with the challenges of resolving conflict. There are of course other issues relating to conflict resolution which the book has touched on but not directly addressed. Three such issues which are the subject of particular interest and debate are grassroots conflict resolution, the role of natural resources in conflict, and the idea of 'liberal peace'. What, in conclusion, does Sudan say about these issues?

Firstly, Sudan does offer examples of the positive role that grassroots or 'bottom–up' conflict resolution can play in addressing local tribal conflicts. However, the civil war and the Darfur conflict also show that grassroots conflict resolution is no substitute for national-level conflict resolution. The 1999 Wunlit Agreement and efforts to replicate it elsewhere in Sudan, especially in the south, could never have been effective substitutes for the national-level, 'top–down' peace talks convened through IGAD and international mediation. Somewhat differently, the January 2006 Juba agreement between the SPLA and the South Sudan Defence Force, a rival southern militia, was not an example of grassroots conflict resolution. It is possible that grassroots initiatives, especially those that aim at reconciliation, may ultimately be essential for a 'top–down' peace agreement in a protracted and complex civil war to succeed. However, the intrinsic relevance of grassroots conflict resolution is to local conflict, and Sudan has not offered any model for connecting it with top–down conflict resolution. The largely futile 'Darfur–Darfur Dialogue and Consultation' after 2006 and the failed DPA were far from being examples of a successful combination of bottom–up and top–down conflict resolution.

Secondly, Sudan shows how natural-resource wealth – in its case oil – can be a reason both for fighting and for settling. As was well documented, the development of Sudan's oil industry in the late 1990s led to an intensification of fighting in the oil fields in Western Upper Nile and Unity State. Conversely, the idea that peace could facilitate the exploitation and expansion of the oil sector was implicit in some of the negotiations between 2002 and 2004 about wealth sharing. However, this is not the same as oil being the primary or even the main cause of fighting or pursuing a peaceful settlement. Sudan underwent many years of civil war before 1972, when oil was not even a prospect, and for much of the war after 1983 oil was not a central issue of contention: the best evidence for this is that oil and wealth sharing did not figure in peace talks until around 2002, and even after that, as discussed above, they were only one element in a larger set of issues which had to be negotiated. Meanwhile in the Darfur conflict, notwithstanding conspiracy theories about purported oil reserves, natural-resource wealth was far from the main causes of the conflict, and scarcity of basic resources such as water and fertile land was only relevant to local conflict, not the high-level conflict seen in the region after 2002–3. In short, therefore, Sudan does not support reductivist, mono-causal claims about the role of natural-resource wealth in civil conflict.

Finally, the history of conflict resolution in Sudan between 1983 and 2009 does not show problems with the concept of the 'liberal peace'. There was little that was inappropriately 'liberal' in Sudan's various peace talks and agreements, and even in the CPA, for example, there was no requirement for rapid democratisation, let alone the implementation of liberal economic reforms. Key elements of the CPA, such as power sharing and the right to self-determination, were tabled in the various peace talks by the SPLM/A and the IGAD mediators (and by Nigeria at the talks in Abuja in 1992 and 1993), not by UN or Western proponents of a 'liberal peace'. Furthermore, while the CPA contains many provisions associated with recent models for peace agreements which might be called 'liberal' (for example for wealth sharing, power sharing and elections), such provisions had also featured in earlier agreements such as the 1997 Khartoum Peace Agreement, which was negotiated without external mediation, and the 1972 Addis Ababa Agreement.

Lessons for Sudan

Certainly the history of peace talks, peace agreements and international relief in Sudan offers lessons which Sudanese who are involved in trying to end conflict in their country could do well to heed. The record of partial agreements between factions and the government points to the need for unity in negotiations (within and between parties opposing the government). The long list of fruitless or near-fruitless talks points to the need to avoid using a zero-sum approach to negotiations. The repeated changes in mediators and forums, and the many attempts by mediators to impose deadlines, highlight the need for the Sudanese parties in peace talks to understand better the limits to mediators' patience and understanding. And the inability of international relief to put an end to humanitarian crises points to the need for concerned Sudanese to press for greater domestic responsibility and accountability for those crises and their causes.

But if there is one overall lesson for Sudan about conflict resolution, it is that leaders, politicians and the public in Sudan must take ultimate responsibility for the continuation of war or peace. As this book has shown – and as at least some government and SPLM/A officials have acknowledged – the primary causes of the failure of past peace talks and agreements for Sudan have been overwhelmingly internal. The same goes for the CPA: if the peace that it brought ultimately collapses, it will primarily be the fault of the parties to the agreement and not, for example, because of any purported liberal framework underlying the agreement or the process by which it was reached (flawed though this was).

Given the weakness of the parties' commitment to the CPA (which was apparent before it was signed and in the following years), the survival of the peace that it brought will therefore depend at least in the short term on the international community working to keep the parties to the agreement negotiating a peaceful path for Sudan. This means that China, Europe and the USA, and the Arab League, the AU, IGAD and the UN must show commitment to seeing peace maintained and to seeing the future of the CPA, or what comes after it, negotiated peacefully. However, external commitment and guarantees are still not an adequate substitute for domestic commitment: in the longer term, peace in Sudan can be secured only internally, by domestic commitment. Such commitment will probably come about only when domestic political changes happen – when new leaders and new or reformed political parties emerge, and when (although it can only happen gradually) the public, who bear the brunt of armed conflict, can more effectively hold the government to account.

Expectations

In drawing final conclusions about conflict resolution in Sudan, one can make judgements about the outcomes and point to comparisons and lessons, as above. And one can pose questions about theory and future practice. How, for example, should the relationship between foreign policy, humanitarian or aid policy, and the search to resolve conflict be conceived? In practice the relationship has usually been one of disjuncture and discontinuity (scarcely a relationship at all), but constructive co-ordination is possible, as seen at brief moments in Sudan. Furthermore, what theories or perspectives in international relations would best capture the constructive co-ordination of foreign policy, humanitarian policy and conflict resolution? At present, theoretical and practical frameworks for constructively co-ordinating or associating foreign policy, humanitarian action and conflict resolution barely exist.

But if there is a single, overall conclusion about conflict resolution that the international community can draw from Sudan's civil war and the Darfur conflict, it is surely about the need to have realistic expectations but to persevere nonetheless. Mediation and relief are typically subject to high expectations, as too are other kinds of intervention that aim to resolve or ameliorate a problem. It should not be a surprise if they do not fulfil these expectations, given the difficulty of what they seek to do. In the case of Sudan, the story of mediation, relief, foreign policy, and conflict resolution is neither one of great success, nor one of unmitigated failure. The overall failures of peace processes and peace agreements, and the continuation of conflict, have been the result primarily of internal factors. The failures and shortcomings have also shown some of the limits of international influence or power, be it exercised from Africa, Europe, the UN, the USA or elsewhere.

Ultimately, therefore, Sudan's civil war and the Darfur conflict are hard examples of how difficult it can be for outsiders – even with the best of intentions – to stop conflicts or to save lives in other countries. Not that proof is needed, they illustrate how difficult it can be to help other people make peace – as, too, it is usually difficult to help people in another country who are suffering from poverty, famine or war. There are no easy answers. Equally, though, Sudan is an example of why outsiders should not give up their efforts to help to resolve conflicts and save lives, or give up looking for ways to improve their actions.

NOTES

INTRODUCTION

1. On this, see for example Michael E. Brown (ed.), *The International Dimensions of Internal Conflict* (Cambridge: MIT Press, 1996), p. 27.
2. Roy E. Licklider, 'The consequences of negotiated settlements in civil wars, 1945–1993' in *American Political Science Review*, vol. 89, no. 3 (1995), p. 687.
3. On the uncertainties of the overall estimates, see Chapter 1; and on the basis of mortality estimates, see Chapter 3.
4. In 1999 Barbara Walter noted that since 1945 '57 percent of civil war settlements failed to prevent the reemergence of conflict'. Barbara F. Walter and Jack L. Snyder (eds.), *Civil Wars, Insecurity, and Intervention* (New York: Columbia University Press, 1999), pp. 306–7.
5. Steven Wondu and Ann Mosely Lesch, *Battle for Peace in Sudan: An Analysis of the Abuja Conferences, 1992–1993* (Lanham: University Press of America, 2000).
6. Stephen J. Stedman, 'Negotiation and mediation in internal conflict', in *The International Dimensions of Internal Conflict*, edited by Brown (Cambridge: MIT Press, 1996), p. 358.
7. Ibid., p. 361.
8. Wondu and Lesch, *Battle for Peace in Sudan*, p. 18.
9. Douglas H. Johnson, *The Root Causes of Sudan's Civil Wars* (Oxford: James Currey, 2003), p. 143.
10. Ibid., p. xix and p. 143.
11. Alex de Waal, *Famine Crimes: Politics and the Disaster Relief Industry in Africa* (Oxford: James Currey, 1997a), p. 1 and p. 4; and p. 77.
12. For example, see Alex de Waal (ed.), *Food and Power in Sudan: A Critique of Humanitarianism* (London: African Rights, 1997b), p. 7 and *passim*.
13. Johnson, *The Root Causes*, p. 176.
14. Brown (ed.), *The International Dimensions of Internal Conflict,* p. 29.
15. See for example Department for International Development (DFID), Foreign and Commonwealth Office (FCO) and Ministry of Defence (MOD), *The Global Conflict Prevention Pool: A Joint UK Government Approach to Reducing Conflict* (London: FCO, 2003).
16. On the concept of 'ripeness', see I. William Zartman, *Ripe for Resolution: Conflict and Intervention in Africa* (Oxford: Oxford University Press, 1989).

CHAPTER 1 Conflict, War and Peace

1. Examples of works focusing on identity questions include: Francis Mading Deng, *War of Visions: Conflict of Identities in the Sudan* (Washington DC: Brookings Institution, 1995); Hervé Bleuchot, Christian Delmet and Derek Hopwood (eds.), *Sudan: History, Identity, Ideology* (Reading: Ithaca Press, 1991); and Ann Mosely Lesch, *The Sudan: Contested National Identities* (Bloomington: Indiana University Press, 1998), ch. 1.
2. The 2008 census did not include questions about tribe and religion. The last full census which gave detailed information on ethnic background was conducted in 1956. It indicated that there were 19 major ethnic groups and 597 sub-groups – Arab groups constituting 40 per cent of the total population, Dinka 12 per cent, Beja 7 per cent and other groups lesser shares. Economist Intelligence Unit, *Country Profile: Sudan, 2004* (London: EIU, 2004a), p. 28.
3. For a good summary of the 'moveable and slippery concept' of ethnicity in Darfur, see R. S. O'Fahey, *The Darfur Sultanate: A History* (London: Hurst, 2008), pp. 9–20.
4. For examples of different estimates for the current population share by religion, see Lesch, *The Sudan*, p. 20; and Economist Intelligence Unit, *Country Profile: Sudan, 2004*, p. 28.
5. Although essentially correct, it is of course a simplification to say that the fundamental causes of more than thirty years of civil war lie in the distribution of 'political and economic power'. For a fuller summary of historical causal factors, see Johnson, *The Root Causes*, pp. xvii–xix.
6. Ibid., pp. 27–32.
7. Cecil Eprile, *War and Peace in the Sudan, 1955–1972* (Newton Abbot: David & Charles, 1974), p. 96.
8. Abel Alier, *Southern Sudan: Too Many Agreements Dishonoured* (Exeter: Ithaca, 1990), p. 33.
9. Johnson, *The Root Causes*, pp. 36–37.
10. Ibid., p. 37.
11. Alier, *Southern Sudan*, p. 79.
12. Ibid., p. 75
13. Johnson, *The Root Causes*, p. 39.
14. For a substantial account of the process and agreement, see Alier, *Southern Sudan*, chapters 6–8. According to Joseph Lagu, 'There was no carrot and stick' at the talks. Interview with Joseph Lagu, former leader of SSLM and former vice-president for the south under Nimeiri; London, 9 December 2003.
15. Alier, Southern Sudan; and 'The Addis Ababa Agreement on the Problem of South Sudan', in Appendix B of Mohamed Omer Beshir, *The Southern Sudan: From Conflict to Peace* (London: C. Hurst, 1975), pp. 158–77.
16. J. Bowyer Bell, 'The Sudan's Africa policy: problems and prospects', in *Africa Today*, vol. 20, no. 3 (1973).
17. Beshir, *The Southern Sudan*, p. 123.
18. Ibid., pp. 123–24.
19. Ibid., p. 125.
20. The 'Grass Curtain' was the title of an Anyanya newsletter; see Edgar O'Ballance, *The Secret War in the Sudan, 1955–1972* (London: Faber, 1977), p. 13.
21. Christopher S. Clapham, *Africa and the International System: The Politics of State Survival* (Cambridge: Cambridge University Press, 1996), p. 237.
22. Interview with Joseph Lagu, London. According to Lagu, the Anyanya lost its

bases in Uganda after Idi Amin's pro-Arab shift and break with Israel.
23 Indeed, it was the only example until the early 1990s. See Clapham, *Africa and the International System*, p. 237.
24 Johnson, *The Root Causes*, p. 39.
25 Alier, *Southern Sudan*, p. 124.
26 Johnson, *The Root Causes*, p. 56.
27 Ibid., pp. 57–58.
28 Quotations from speech by Garang on 3 March 1984. The imposition of *sharia* in September 1983 did not form part of the immediate causes of the war, although it later came to be a compounding cause. See John Garang, *The Call for Democracy in Sudan* (London: Kegan Paul International, 1992), pp. 19–25.
29 See for example a speech by Garang on 22 March 1985. Ibid., pp. 25-36. On the goals of the SPLM, see also Alier, *Southern Sudan*, chapter 14.
30 Sadiq al-Mahdi is commonly referred to simply as Sadiq, and this usage is followed in this book.
31 The fullest account of the war is in Johnson, *The Root Causes*. Other accounts covering military and political aspects of substantial parts of the war include Edgar O'Ballance, *Sudan: Civil War and Terrorism, 1956–99* (Basingstoke: Macmillan Press, 2000); Lesch, *The Sudan;* de Waal (ed.), *Food and Power in Sudan*; Alier, *Southern Sudan*; Peter Adwok Nyaba, *The Politics of Liberation in South Sudan: An Insider's View* (Kampala, Uganda: Fountain Publishers, 1997); and Peter Woodward (ed.), *Sudan after Nimeiri* (London: Routledge, 1991).
32 de Waal (ed.), *Food and Power in Sudan*, p. 62.
33 Johnson, *The Root Causes*, pp. 67–69.
34 Ibid., pp. 83–84; Alier, *Southern Sudan*, p. 265.
35 Even a government official (Angelo Beda, the Chairman of the Southern Council) estimated this toll to be at least 200,000 by September 1988. See Alier, *Southern Sudan*, p. 261. A higher toll is implied by Burr's estimates. See Millard Burr, *Quantifying Genocide in the Southern Sudan, 1983–1993* (Washington DC: US Committee for Refugees, 1993).
36 By 1989 some one million southerners had moved to the north, many of them to Kordofan and Khartoum, while around 400,000 were in Ethiopia and 40,000 in Kenya and Uganda. Alier, *Southern Sudan,* p. 265.
37 Millard Burr and Robert O. Collins, *Requiem for the Sudan: War, Drought, and Disaster Relief on the Nile* (Boulder: Westview, 1995), p. 27; Alex de Waal, *Famine that Kills: Darfur, Sudan* (Oxford: Oxford University Press, 2005), p. 176.
38 Alier suggests that the war was costing the government the equivalent of US$2m per day by April 1989. In contrast in the late 1990s and early 2000s – when the war was no less intense – it was commonly claimed in Sudan that the war was costing the government US$1m per day. This figure was perhaps as much a convenient number as an estimate based on the government's total official defence budget, which in 2002 was equivalent to US$390m. See Alier, *Southern Sudan*, p. 266; Peter Verney, *Raising the Stakes: Oil and Conflict in Sudan* (Hebden Bridge, England: Sudan Update, 1999), p. 6; and Economist Intelligence Unit, *Country Profile: Sudan, 2004*, p. 37.
39 Johnson, *The Root Causes*, p. 71.
40 Simultaneously, the UN secretary-general forbade UN agencies to have any dealings with the SPLA.
41 Alier, *Southern Sudan*, p. 270.
42 Johnson, *The Root Causes*, p. 84.

43 As Alier argues, their opposition to the accord was driven by domestic rivalries, exacerbated by the Umma Party's fear that the DUP peace initiative was backed by Egypt, which was historically the ally of the DUP. This prompted the Umma Party (and the NIF) to sign a new unity pact with Libya – which was opposed by the DUP. Alier, *Southern Sudan*, p. 272.
44 Because of the importance of the Nile waters interest, Egyptian policy on Sudan has long been in the hands of Egypt's president and the external intelligence service, rather than the foreign ministry.
45 Under the Addis Ababa Agreement, Sudan had been required to withdraw from the union with Egypt and Libya.
46 Despite the protocol, in October 1985 the Egyptian defence minister Othman Abdullah claimed that the joint defence agreement between Egypt and Sudan was still intact. See 'Othman Abdullah: the events in Khartoum have not closed the door to dialogue with the south', *Al-Sharq al-Awsat*, 4 October 1985.
47 Interview with Hussain Musharrafa, former Egyptian ambassador to Sudan (1985–9); Cairo, 11 May 2004.
48 G. Norman Anderson, *Sudan in Crisis: The Failure of Democracy* (Gainesville: University of Florida Press, 1999), pp. 236–37.
49 Alex de Waal (ed.), *Islamism and its Enemies in the Horn of Africa* (London: Hurst, 2004), p. 185.
50 A number of people interviewed for this book (such as Mansour Khalid, a senior political adviser to Garang and former foreign minister of Sudan) felt that the DUP–SPLM accord was the largest 'missed opportunity' to end the war, until the peace process after 2002. Others, such as Joseph Ukel Abango, a minister in the March 1989 unity cabinet, were less confident of this. (Interview with Mansour Khalid, senior political adviser to Garang and formerly foreign minister under Nimeiri; Naivasha, Kenya, 12 April 2004. Interview with Joseph Ukel Abango, secretary-general of NDA and chairman of USAP; Naivasha, Kenya, 19 April 2004. Lesch, *The Sudan*, p. 167.)
51 Lesch, *The Sudan*, p. 168.
52 Gérard Prunier, *Darfur: The Ambiguous Genocide* (London: Hurst, 2005), pp. 72–74.
53 The NDA had been formed by opposition parties and activists in the wake of the 1989 coup. It included the Umma Party, DUP and Sudan Communist Party, which were banned in Sudan after the 1989 coup. In March 1990 the SPLM signed an accord with the NDA to unite their efforts to overthrow the regime, restore democracy and hold the previously planned constitutional conference. See Lesch, *The Sudan*, pp. 149–50, and p. 187.
54 Ibid., pp. 156–59.
55 Johnson, *The Root Causes*, p. 103.
56 Lesch, *The Sudan*, pp. 193–96.
57 These tactics and the campaign in the oilfields were widely documented. See in particular: Christian Aid, *The Scorched Earth: Oil and War in Sudan* (London: Christian Aid, 2001).
58 Burr, *Quantifying Genocide in the Southern Sudan*, 1983–1993; and Millard Burr, *Quantifying Genocide in Southern Sudan and the Nuba Mountains*, 1983–1998 (Washington DC: US Committee for Refugees, 1998).
59 For examples of questioning of such estimates, see Johnson, *The Root Causes*, p. 143; and de Waal (ed.), *Food and Power in Sudan*, p. 352.
60 UN, 'Situation of Human Rights in the Sudan', A/49/539, interim report prepared by Gaspar Biro (Special Rapporteur of the UN Human Rights Commission), New York, 19 October 1994b, paragraph 52.

61 Ibid., paragraph 20.
62 Ibid., paragraph 21.
63 Ibid., paragraph 56.
64 Ibid., paragraph 60.
65 UN, 'Emergency Assistance to the Sudan: Report of the Secretary-General', New York, 24 October 1997, paragraph 11.
66 UN, 'Situation of Human Rights in the Sudan', New York, 20 August 2002, paragraph 27.
67 Ibid., paragraphs 18–24.
68 'Sudan: Displaced in Shilluk kingdom in urgent need of aid, says rebel leader', IRIN report, 11 May 2004.
69 UN, 'Situation of Human Rights in the Sudan [1994]', paragraph 84.
70 UN, 'Situation of Human Rights in the Sudan [2002]', paragraph 86.
71 de Waal (ed.), *Food and Power in Sudan*, chapter 9.
72 For example, one Southern group, the South Sudan Civic Forum, and its successor, the South Sudan Democratic Forum, considered the goal of a 'New Sudan' to be 'too difficult' and 'an obstruction to self-determination'. (Interview with Martin Lomuro, chairman of South Sudan Civic Forum; London, 5 February 2004. See also Prunier, *Darfur: The Ambiguous Genocide*, p. 72.)
73 A prominent example was Mansour Khalid, a northerner who had served in Nimeiri's government as foreign minister, but who joined the SPLM and became a close political adviser to Garang early in the war. For an account of this, see Garang, *The Call for Democracy in Sudan,* prefaces and introduction.
74 For example, the conventional causes of 'monopolization of power and wealth' by 'riverain Sudan's dominating establishment' were invoked in the SLM/A political declaration published on 13 March 2003 (archived at www.sudan.net/news/press/postedr/214.shtml).
75 Johnson, *The Root Causes*, pp. 140–41.
76 Johnson, *The Root Causes*, pp. 140–41.
77 Interviews with SPLM officials, Naivasha, April 2004. See also Julie Flint and Alex de Waal, *Darfur: A Short History of a Long War* (London: Zed Books, 2005), pp. 81–84; and UN, 'Report of the Panel of Experts Established Pursuant to Paragraph 3 of Resolution 1591 (2005) Concerning the Sudan', S/2006/65, New York, January 2006c
78 Flint and de Waal, *Darfur: A Short History of a Long War,* pp. 38–39.
79 The contribution of environmental factors to conflict in Darfur should not be exaggerated (for example, by arguing that Darfur was the first war of climate change, or was caused by lack of rainfall). For a more sober view, see Michael Kevane and Leslie Gray, 'Darfur: rainfall and conflict', in *Environmental Research Letters*, no. 3 (2008).
80 After one attack by the nascent Darfur Liberation Front on Golo, in Jebel Marra, in August 2002, the government arrested some 70 Fur men, including Abdul Wahid Mohamed al-Nur, a future leader of the SLM/A, who was subsequently released.
81 Prunier, *Darfur: The Ambiguous Genocide*, p. 91.
82 The numbers 100,000–300,000 became a fixture of reporting of the conflict, for the number of deaths during 2003–4, typically without differentiation between deaths by violence and deaths because of deterioration in health. This book is not the place for debating the reliability of various mortality estimates for Darfur.
83 UN, *Report of the International Commission of Inquiry on Darfur to the United*

Nations Secretary-General (Geneva: UN, 2005d), p. 68 and p. 76.
84 Ibid., p. 69.
85 Ibid., pp. 81–83.
86 Ibid., p. 74.
87 Ibid., pp. 66–70.
88 Ibid., p. 75.
89 UN, 'Report of the Secretary-General on the Sudan Pursuant to Paragraphs 6, 13 and 16 of Security Council Resolution 1556 (2004), Paragraph 15 of Security Council Resolution 1564 (2004) and Paragraph 17 of Security Council Resolution 1574 (2004)', S/2005/68, New York, 4 February 2005e, p. 3.
90 UN, 'Monthly Report of the Secretary-General on Darfur', S/2005/240, New York, 12 April 2005c, p. 2
91 UN, 'Monthly Report of the Secretary-General on Darfur', S/2005/825, New York, 23 December 2005b, p. 2.
92 UN, 'Monthly Report of the Secretary-General on Darfur', S/2006/430, New York, 21 June 2006b, pp. 1–2.
93 UN, 'Monthly Report of the Secretary-General on Darfur', S/2006/870, New York, 8 November 2006a, pp. 1–3.
94 UN, 'Report of the Secretary-General on the Deployment of the African Union–United Nations Hybrid Operation in Darfur', S/2007/759, New York, 24 December 2007, pp. 9–10.
95 Ibid., pp. 9–10.
96 UN, 'Report of the Secretary-General on the Deployment of the African Union–United Nations Hybrid Operation in Darfur', S/2008/781, New York, 12 December 2008, paragraph 19.
97 UN, 'Report of the Secretary-General on the Deployment of the African Union–United Nations Hybrid Operation in Darfur', S/2009/201, New York, 14 April 2009, pp. 2–3.

CHAPTER 2 Mediation

1 'Sudan seeks Egypt's help for talks with rebels', Reuters, 14 November 1989.
2 Burr and Collins, *Requiem for the Sudan*, p. 249.
3 *Al-Sudan al-Hadith*, 2 December 1989.
4 Wondu and Lesch, *Battle for Peace in Sudan*, p. 15.
5 Ibid., Appendix E, p. 223.
6 Ibid., p. 224.
7 See Chapter 4; and Sudan United News Agency (SUNA), 'Daily Bulletin', 7 January 1990.
8 Mohammed el-Amin Khalifa, *Ten Years of Peace Making in Sudan, 1989–1999: Documents and Facts* (Khartoum: COFPA, 2003), p. 75 and p. 38.
9 Ibid., p. 76.
10 Interview with Deng Alor, SPLM/A delegate to peace talks (1989–2004); Naivasha, Kenya, 22 April 2004.
11 Interview with Hussein Abu Saleh, former foreign minister of Sudan (1988 and 1993–5); Khartoum, 7 April 2004.
12 The government had held a 'dialogue conference', but this was not a constitutional conference, and besides had excluded opposition parties. See Wondu and Lesch, Battle for Peace in Sudan, p. 16.

13 Ibid., p. 16.
14 Interview with Busho Ndinyenka, Ugandan diplomat and special envoy for Sudan peace talks; Naivasha, Kenya, 16 April 2004.
15 Interview with Kjell Hødnebø, representative of Norway at the peace talks in Kenya; Naivasha, Kenya, 20 April 2004.
16 Lesch, *The Sudan*, p. 172.
17 Wondu and Lesch, *Battle for Peace in Sudan*, p. 58.
18 Ibid., p. 26; and Lesch, *The Sudan*, p. 173.
19 Wondu and Lesch, *Battle for Peace in Sudan*, p. 83.
20 Ibid., p. 147.
21 Ibid., pp. 146–47.
22 Ibid., p. 149: 'Composition of the Cease-fire Commission', Paragraph 5.4.
23 Ibid., p. 175.
24 Interview with Peter Nyaba, former captain in the SPLA; Nairobi, 26 April 2004.
25 Interview with Deng Alor, Naivasha.
26 Interview with Ghazi Salah al-Din Atabani, former lead Sudanese government negotiator at peace talks (1994–2003); Khartoum, 4 May 2004.
27 Deng left Sudan in December 1993 and gained asylum in Britain, like a number of other former politicians. Interview with Aldo Ajo Deng, cabinet minister under Sadiq and political adviser to Bashir on peace and dialogue on the south (1989–1993); London, 5 February 2004.
28 Wondu and Lesch, *Battle for Peace in Sudan*, p. 174.
29 Johnson, *The Root Causes*, p. 101.
30 Lesch, *The Sudan*, p. 179. The IGAD member states were Djibouti, Eritrea, Ethiopia, Kenya, Somalia, Sudan and Uganda.
31 Johnson, *The Root Causes*, p. 102.
32 Ibid., p. 102; Lesch, *The Sudan*, pp. 179–85.
33 Interview with Ghazi Salah al-Din Atabani, Khartoum.
34 Ibid.
35 Interview with Pagan Amum, SPLM/A commander and delegate at peace talks and former secretary for trade and aid; Naivasha, Kenya, 14 April 2004.
36 Lesch, *The Sudan*, p. 182.
37 Johnson, *The Root Causes*, p. 102.
38 The SSIM/A was Machar's new name for his SPLM/A-United faction.
39 Paragraphs 2 and 3, Government of Sudan and SSIM/A, 'Political Charter', Khartoum, 10 April 1996; and Lesch, *The Sudan*, p. 164.
40 In the agreement, the various southern signatories collectively went under the umbrella name of the South Sudan United Democratic Salvation Front. The agreement was formally called the Sudan Peace Agreement, but came more commonly to be known as the Khartoum Peace Agreement. See Government of Sudan and UDSF, 'Sudan Peace Agreement', Khartoum, 21 April 1997, section 2.1.
41 Johnson, *The Root Causes*, p. 123.
42 Government of Sudan, 'The Attitude of the Government Delegation towards the SPLM-Main Stream Proposal', Nairobi, November 1997.
43 IGAD, 'Proceedings of the 6th Ordinary IGAD Summit of Heads of State and Government', Djibouti, 16 March 1998, p. 9 and *passim*.
44 IGAD Ministerial Subcommittee, 'Communiqué issued in Nairobi on 6 May 1998', Nairobi, 6 May 1998b, paragraphs 4–7.

45 Government of Sudan, 'Updated Sudan government position', Nairobi, May 1998.
46 IGAD Ministerial Subcommittee, 'Communiqué issued at Addis Ababa on 7 August 1998', Addis Ababa, 7 August 1998a.
47 IGAD, 'The Proceedings of the Summit of Heads of State and Government of IGAD Member States for the Launching of Revitalized IGAD', Djibouti, 25–26 November 1996, p. 6 and p. 9.
48 IGAD Partners Forum, 'First Ministerial Meeting of the Joint IGAD Partners Forum', Rome, 19–20 January 1998.
49 During 1999 the Secretary General of the Arab League made several statements of support for the Egyptian–Libyan initiative, and also expressed support for the IGAD initiative. See, for example, BBC (SWB) ME/D3676/MED, 'Arab League head appeals to USA to help solve Sudan's problem', Sudan TV, Omdurman, 27 October 1999.
50 According to one NDA official, the NDA agreed to the initiative because it held out the prospect of participation of all parties in peace talks, unlike the IGAD talks. Interview with Hashim Muhammed Ahmed, member of NDA leadership council and former president of National Union of Engineering and Trades Unions; Oxford, 17 December 2003.
51 It was also said by members of the Umma Party and the DUP that the initiative was initially only a Libyan initiative (albeit fostered or instigated in Sudan), but that Egypt quickly joined the initiative. Interview with Mudawwi Turabi, assistant secretary-general of DUP-Hindi faction; Khartoum, 6 March 2004.
52 'Egypt–Libya agree new steps in peace initiative', IRIN, 6 October 1999.
53 Umma Party, 'Message to Co-Chairman and Honorable Members of IPF Conference', Rome, 18 October 1999.
54 IGAD, 'Proceedings of the 8th Ordinary IGAD Summit of Heads of State and Government', Djibouti, November 2000a, p. 48.
55 IGAD, 'Resolution on the Sudan Peace Process', Khartoum, 23 November 2000b.
56 Egypt and Libya's inertia was largely the result of the contradictory pressures from the DUP, the Umma Party and the Sudanese government, concerning the best way to take the initiative forward. For example, according to the DUP-Hindi faction, Egypt and Libya disagreed with its insistence that the initiative support multiparty democratisation. Interview with Mudawwi Turabi, Khartoum.
57 Johnson, *The Root Causes,* p. 176.
58 For one picture of the tensions between the NDA, the Umma Party and the SPLM, see Mansour Khalid, *War and Peace in Sudan: A Tale of Two Countries* (London: Kegan Paul, 2003), pp. 379–401.
59 IGAD, 'Declaration of the 7th IGAD Summit of Heads of State and Government', Djibouti, 26 November 1999, paragraph 3.3, p. 6.
60 Between 1999 and 2002, IPF instigated a 'Planning for Peace' project, which was intended to support the IGAD-led talks. See IGAD Partners Forum, *Facing up to the Realities of Future Peace: First Outline of the Integrated Planning for Peace (PfP) Framework* (Rome: IPF, 2002), pp. 2–16.
61 IGAD, 'Proceedings of the 9th Summit of the Assembly of Heads of State and Government of IGAD', Khartoum, 10–11 January 2002, p. 42.
62 International Crisis Group, *God, Oil and Country: Changing the Logic of War in Sudan* (Nairobi/Brussels: ICG, 2002c), p. viii.
63 IGAD, 'Proceedings of the 9th Summit of the Assembly of Heads of State and Government of IGAD', p. 8.

64 Ibid., p. 8.
65 Don Petterson, *Inside Sudan: Political Islam, Conflict, and Catastrophe* (Boulder: Westview, 2003), p. 147.
66 John C. Danforth, *Report to the President of the United States on the Outlook for Peace in Sudan* (Washington DC: 2002), pp. 4–5.
67 Ibid., p. 20.
68 CARE, Christian Aid, International Rescue Committee (IRC), Oxfam, et al., *The Key to Peace: Unlocking the Human Potential of Sudan* (London: CARE et al., 2002), p. 5.
69 International Crisis Group, *Capturing the Moment: Sudan's Peace Process in the Balance* (Nairobi/Brussels: ICG, 2002a), p. ii.
70 Interview with Sayyid el-Khatib, Sudanese government delegate at peace talks and director of Centre for Strategic Studies; Naivasha, Kenya, 12 April 2004.
71 Interview with Lazaro Sumbeiywo, chair of the IGAD peace talks for Sudan (2001–5); Naivasha, Kenya, 16 April 2004.
72 Government of Sudan and SPLM/A, 'Nuba Mountains Cease-Fire Agreement', Bürgenstock, Switzerland, 19 January 2002c.
73 Interview with Suleiman Musa Rahhal, director of Nuba Survival (NGO); London, 18 December 2003.
74 Government of Sudan and SPLM/A, 'Machakos Protocol', Machakos, Kenya, 20 July.
75 Government of Sudan and SPLM/A, 'Memorandum of Understanding on Cessation of Hostilities', Kenya, 15 October 2002b; 'Sudan: Landmark aid deal signed', IRIN, 28 October 2002; and 'Sudan: Government and rebels extend truce', IRIN, 19 October 2002.
76 Interview with Yasser Arman, SPLM/A spokesman and delegate at peace talks; Naivasha, Kenya, 11 April 2004.
77 Interview with Hussein Abu Saleh, Khartoum.
78 Interview with Busho Ndinyenka, Naivasha.
79 Interview with Yasser Arman, Naivasha.
80 Joint Military Commission, 'The Nuba Mountains Experience', report by Brigadier General Jan Erik Wilhelmsen, Chairman of the JMC, in 2004, www.jmc.nu/en/0301.htm (accessed on 23 October 2004); and Joint Military Commission, 'Facts and figures', information on the JMC in the Nuba Mountains, including data on ceasefire violations, www.jmc.nu/en/0302.htm (accessed on 23 October 2004).
81 Economist Intelligence Unit, *Country Report: Sudan, June 2002* (London: EIU, 2002), p. 16.
82 Civilian Protection Monitoring Team, 'CPMT Final Report: Military Events in Western Upper Nile, 31 December 2002 to 30 January 2003', Khartoum, Sudan 2003, pp. 1–2.
83 Ibid., p. 5.
84 Mortality estimates for the Darfur conflict were highly contentious, and media reports on the conflict commonly conflated all types of deaths and resorted to single rough estimates or projections (in particular the figure 300,000). One careful study estimated that in the period September 2003 to December 2004 the total number of violent deaths caused by the Darfur conflict was around 35,000, while a further 85,000 excess deaths (above usual mortality rates) were attributable to the deteriorated health conditions. See Debarati Guha-Sapir and Olivier Degomme, *Darfur: Counting the Deaths. Mortality Estimates from Multiple Survey Data* (Brussels: University of Louvain, 2005), p. 6 and passim;

and US Government Accountability Office (GAO), *Darfur Crisis: Death Estimates Demonstrate Severity of Crisis, but Their Accuracy and Credibility Could be Enhanced* (Washington DC: GAO, 2006), pp. 19–20 and *passim*.
85 Interview with Lazaro Sumbeiywo, Naivasha.
86 Interview with Abd al-Aziz al-Hilu, SPLM/A commander and delegate at peace talks; Naivasha, Kenya, 14 April 2004; the largest such business was a conglomerate of partly government-owned industries, known as GIAD.
87 Interview with Joseph Duer Jakok, Sudanese government delegate at peace talks; Naivasha, Kenya, 16 April 2004. The interviewee was the only southerner in the government delegation at the time of the interview.
88 Interview with Peter Marwa, member of IGAD secretariat resource staff for Sudan talks; Naivasha, Kenya, 12 April 2004.
89 Interview with Lazarus Sumbeiywo, chief mediator in the peace talks', IRIN, 30 May 2003.
90 'Sudan: Peace deal expected by end of 2003', IRIN, 22 October 2003.
91 Interview with member of troika; Naivasha, Kenya, 20 April 2004 and other interviews.
92 Economist Intelligence Unit, *Country Report: Sudan, March 2004* (London: EIU, 2004b), p. 14.
93 'Sudan: Darfur rebels keen to extend ceasefire', IRIN, 17 October 2003.
94 A JEM official justified JEM's non-participation in these rounds of talks on the grounds that the international community did not participate in the talks, and JEM knew that the Sudanese government would not honour any agreement coming from such talks. Interview with Ahmed Hussain, member of JEM delegation to Darfur peace talks and JEM representative in Britain; London, 19 March 2005; and 'Sudan: Deadlock in Darfur peace talks', IRIN, 31 October 2003.
95 'Sudan: Darfur MPs urge international intervention', IRIN, 15 December 2003.
96 Government of Sudan, SLM/A and JEM, 'Humanitarian Ceasefire Agreement on the Conflict in Darfur', N'djamena, Chad, 8 April 2004; followed by an agreement on modalities for the ceasefire commission, May 2004, and protocols on enhancing the humanitarian and security situation, November 2004.
97 One problem facing the various Darfur talks was the different capacities and priorities of JEM and the SLM/A – JEM having more of a national agenda, the SLM/A being more focused only on Darfur. One NGO tried to help the SLM/A to improve its negotiating capacities, but this did not resolve the differences between the two movements. Interview with Hafiz Mohammed, Justice Africa staff member; London, 18 March 2005.
98 Although factionalism is endemic to Sudanese politics (and politics elsewhere), the government actively fomented it. As a result of the various internal and external pressures, by 2004 there were, for example, some five DUP factions, three Umma Party factions, and splits within the Sudan Communist Party. Interview with Mohammed Zain Osman, DUP political affairs officer; Khartoum, 5 March 2004.
99 Egypt gained 'observer' status during the internationalised IGAD talks, but in practical terms this meant that it took no real part in the talks. Despite Egypt's non-participation in the talks, in the view of the British ambassador at the time, Egypt was 'reconciled' to self-determination for Southern Sudan. A Sudan government delegate to the Machakos and Naivasha talks judged that Egypt would have seen matters at the talks not from the GoS perspective, but 'from the northern perspective'. The non-participation of Libya, however, was

'probably a good thing'. Interview with William Patey, British ambassador to Sudan (2002–5); Khartoum, 1 April 2004; Interview with Sayyid el-Khatib, Naivasha.

100 The DUP and the Umma Party, for example, signed an agreement (nominally known as the Cairo Declaration) with the SPLM/A in early 2003 in Cairo, which in theory recognised them as genuine participants in the peace process. In practice, the agreement was quickly forgotten and ignored.
101 'Sudan: Opposition leaders warn against bilateral peace deal', 17 December 2003.
102 International Crisis Group, *Darfur Rising: Sudan's New Crisis* (Nairobi/Brussels: ICG, 2004b), p. i.
103 See, for example, the recommendations of Crisis Group to Britain, Italy, Norway and the USA in March 2004. Ibid., p. iii.
104 'Sudan: Peace talks resume after brief interlude', IRIN, 28 January 2003.
105 Christian Aid, *The Scorched Earth,* p. 11, footnote 8.
106 International Crisis Group, *Sudan: Towards an Incomplete Peace* (Nairobi/Brussels: ICG, 2003), p. ii.
107 UN Security Council Resolutions 1547 (11 June 2004), 1556 (30 July 2004), 1564 (18 September 2004) and 1574 (19 November 2004). The AU mission gradually became known as the AU Mission in Sudan (AMIS).
108 The UN Advance Mission in Sudan was deployed in June 2004. In March 2005, the advance mission became the UN Mission in Sudan (UNMIS), with an initial mandated strength of 10,000 military personnel and civilian support. UN Security Council, 'Resolution 1590', New York, 24 March 2005.
109 The third round of AU Darfur talks ran from September to October 2004; the fourth round from 11 to 21 December 2004. See AU, 'Report of the Chairperson of the Commission on the Situation in the Darfur Region of the Sudan', AU Peace and Security Council document PSC/PR/2(XXVIII), Addis Ababa, 28 April 2005; Flint and de Waal, *Darfur: A Short History of a Long War*, pp. 119–20.
110 Laurie Nathan, *No Ownership, No Peace: The Darfur Peace Agreement* (London: LSE, 2006), pp. 3–4.
111 Jeremy Brickhill, *Protecting Civilians through Peace Agreements: Challenges and Lessons of the Darfur Peace Agreement* (Pretoria: Institute for Security Studies, 2007), p. 2.
112 SLM/A and JEM, 'Joint Statement', Abuja, 14 April 2006.
113 For a rather personalised and not self-critical account of the final stages of the mediation that produced the DPA, by one of the AU mediation advisers, see Alex de Waal, '"I will not sign"', *London Review of Books,* 30 November 2006.
114 Abaker Mohamed Abuelbashar, 'On the failure of Darfur peace talks in Abuja', *Sudan Tribune*, 25 August 2006.
115 Brickhill, *Protecting Civilians through Peace Agreements: Challenges and Lessons of the Darfur Peace Agreement*, p. 3.
116 Nathan, *No Ownership, No Peace,* p. 3.
117 Ibid., p. 3.
118 International Crisis Group, *Darfur: Revitalising the Peace Process* (Nairobi/Brussels: ICG, 2007), pp. 6–8.
119 Ostensibly the mediators were following a 'road map' for 're-energising the political process'. As with other 'road maps' in notional peace processes, such as the Israeli–Palestinian process in the same period, the supposed map was a delusion. AU and UN, 'The Chairmen's conclusions from the Arusha

consultations', Arusha, Tanzania, 6 August 2007.
120 As the US special envoy for Sudan acknowledged at the time, many ceasefires had previously been announced and then broken by both the government and the rebels. 'Sudanese government announces unilateral ceasefire in Darfur', AP, 27 October 2007.
121 The focuses of international attention during this period, and the implications, are discussed in more detail in Chapter 4.
122 The list of agreements included Tripoli agreement, 8 February 2006; Jeddah agreement, 3 May 2007; Dakar agreement, 13 March 2008; Doha agreement, 3 May 2009.
123 For further information, see John Young, *The Eastern Front and the Struggle Against Marginalization* (Geneva: Small Arms Survey, 2007), pp. 37–43.
124 In the post-mortem analyses in the aftermath of the Abuja talks, there was a tendency for those who had invested more in the DPA to blame Abdul Wahid and JEM for the agreement's failure. Others took a more impartial line. Laurie Nathan judged that despite all of Abdul Wahid's weaknesses, he was not an opportunist, but 'sought an agreement that satisfied the needs of his constituency and he was convinced that the DPA did not do this'. (Nathan, *No Ownership, No Peace,* pp. 11–12.)

CHAPTER 3 Relief

1 de Waal (ed.), *Food and Power in Sudan*, p. 36.
2 Burr and Collins, *Requiem for the Sudan,* p. 28; and de Waal (ed.), *Food and Power in Sudan,* p. 55.
3 At this time there was a severe lack of systematic studies of famine mortality in Sudan and elsewhere in Africa. See de Waal (ed.), *Food and Power in Sudan,* p. 56.
4 Ibid., p. 56. See also Burr and Collins, *Requiem for the Sudan,* p. 27.
5 de Waal (ed.), *Food and Power in Sudan,* p. 57.
6 Ibid., pp. 40–50.
7 Reproduced in: UN, 'Emergency Assistance to the Sudan: Summary of Urgent Humanitarian Requirements. Report of the Secretary-General', New York, 27 October 1988a, paragraph 32.
8 de Waal (ed.), *Food and Power in Sudan,* p. 88.
9 See for example David Keen, *The Benefits of Famine: A Political Economy of Famine and Relief in Southwestern Sudan, 1983–1989* (Princeton: Princeton University Press, 1994); and Alex de Waal, 'Starving out the South', in *Civil War in the Sudan,* edited by Daly and Sikainga (London: British Academic Press, 1992).
10 Keen, *The Benefits of Famine,* p. 212.
11 John Garang, *John Garang Speaks* (London: Kegan Paul, 1987), p. 71.
12 de Waal (ed.), *Food and Power in Sudan,* p. 89; and *Sudan Times,* 29 November 1988.
13 Ibid., p. 104.
14 Burr and Collins, *Requiem for the Sudan,* p. 43.
15 Michael Medley, 'Humanitarian assistance in Sudan: a chronological analysis of shifting mandates', in *The Wider Impact of Humanitarian Assistance: The Case of Sudan and the Implications for European Union Policy,* edited by Loane and Schümer (Baden-Baden: Nomos Verlagsgesellschaft, 2000), p. 175.

16 de Waal (ed.), *Food and Power in Sudan*, p. 106.
17 Ibid., p. 108.
18 UN, 'Emergency Assistance to the Sudan [1988]', paragraph 36.
19 Ibid., paragraph 34.
20 In 1986 the total refugee population was estimated to be 1.16m, comprising 786,000 from Ethiopia, 250,000 from Uganda, 123,000 from Chad, and 5,000 from Zaire. See UN, 'Situation of Refugees in the Sudan: Report of the Secretary-General', New York, 8 April 1986, paragraph 22.
21 For UN use of the term 'civil strife' instead of conflict or war, and the government's estimate, see: UN, 'Situation of Refugees in the Sudan: Report of the Secretary-General', New York, 29 August 1988b, paragraphs 10, 11 and 21.
22 As one interviewee put it simply, 'In 1985 Nimeiri had run out of alliances and a lot of problems were mounting up, including the famine.' It is worth noting too that Sudan had previously experienced a popular uprising and overthrow of a military ruler – the 'October Revolution' in 1964 – when there was no famine. Interview with Mahjoub Mohammed Salih, editor of *Al-Ayaam* newspaper; Khartoum, 11 March 2004.
23 de Waal (ed.), *Food and Power in Sudan*, p. 38.
24 Ibid., p. 115.
25 UN, 'Emergency Assistance to the Sudan: Operation Lifeline Sudan. Report of the Secretary-General', New York, 27 September 1989a, paragraphs 13 and 23.
26 UN, 'Plan of Action: Sudan Emergency Relief Operations', Khartoum, 14 March 1989b.
27 de Waal (ed.), *Food and Power in Sudan*, p. 119.
28 Burr and Collins, *Requiem for the Sudan*, p. 246.
29 UN, 'Emergency Assistance to the Sudan [1989]', paragraph 79.
30 UN, 'Operation Lifeline Sudan: Draft Plan of Action', Khartoum, 28 March 1990.
31 Retroactively, the operation of OLS from April–October 1989 became referred to as OLS I, and the resumption of OLS in April 1990 as OLS II.
32 For data for assessed requirements and actual contributions between 1993 and 2002, see UN Office for the Coordination of Humanitarian Affairs, *Consolidated Inter-Agency Appeal 2003: Sudan* (Geneva: UN OCHA, 2002), p. 6.
33 Ataul Karim, Mark Duffield, Susanne Jaspars, Aldo Benini, et al., *Operation Lifeline Sudan (OLS): A Review* (Geneva: UN Department of Humanitarian Affairs, 1996), p. 16; and UN, 'Emergency Assistance to the Sudan: Report of the Secretary-General', New York, 31 August 1999a, paragraph 51.
34 The first such flight out of El Obeid was on 6 June 1998. See UN, 'Emergency Assistance to the Sudan: Report of the Secretary-General', New York, 4 September 1998, paragraph 10.
35 Ibid., paragraph 39; and UN, 'Emergency Assistance to the Sudan [1999]', paragraphs 19 and 54–57.
36 In truth, both the government and the SPLM/A sometimes managed to 'piggyback' arms deliveries on relief deliveries, despite the efforts of relief agencies generally to avoid this happening. Ultimately, the GOS and the SPLM/A had much more control over relief access than did OLS and relief agencies. For Khalifa's claim, see Burr and Collins, *Requiem for the Sudan*, pp. 259–60, citing *Al-Quwat al-Musalaha* (Khartoum), 8 December 1989; SUNA, 'Daily Bulletin', 8 December 1989; and *Al-Sudan al-Hadith* (Khartoum), 9 December 1989.

37 Ibid., p. 263, citing SUNA 'Daily Bulletin', 31 December 1989; and Reuters, 'Sudan's leader accuses relief workers of arming rebels', 31 December 1989
38 Colonel Salah el-Din Karrar, chairman of the economic affairs committee, quoted by Associated Press on 29 October 1990; quoted in de Waal (ed.), *Food and Power in Sudan*, p. 132; see also p. 137.
39 Government of Kenya, 'Relief Supplies and Humanitarian Assistance to the War Affected Areas', Nairobi, 23 March 1994b; and Government of Kenya, 'Agreement on Operation Lifeline Sudan (OLS) Corridors for Relief Supplies and Humanitarian Assistance to War Affected Areas', Nairobi, 17 May 1994a.
40 Karim, Duffield, Jaspars, Benini, et al., *Operation Lifeline Sudan (OLS): A Review*, p. 28.
41 SPLM/A, 'Resolutions of the SPLM/SPLA Torit Conference, 1991', Sudan, SPLM/A 1991.
42 Interview with Elijah Malok, director of SRRC; Naivasha, Kenya, 13 April 2004.
43 Karim, Duffield, Jaspars, Benini, et al., *Operation Lifeline Sudan (OLS): A Review*, pp. 51–52.
44 Ibid., p. 54.
45 UN, 'Emergency Assistance to the Sudan [1997]', paragraph 9.
46 de Waal (ed.), *Food and Power in Sudan*, p. 326.
47 UN, 'Emergency Assistance to the Sudan: Report of the Secretary-General', New York, 22 September 1995, paragraph 20.
48 Ibid., paragraph 20.
49 Ibid., paragraph 20.
50 UN, 'Emergency Assistance to the Sudan [1997]', paragraph 12.
51 UN, 'Emergency Assistance to the Sudan [1998]', paragraph 13.
52 Ibid., paragraph 13.
53 UN, 'Humanitarian Assistance to the Sudan: Report of the Secretary-General', New York, 27 September 2001, paragraph 17.
54 Ibid., paragraph 17.
55 Ibid., paragraph 17.
56 Ibid., paragraph 17.
57 For specific examples, see UN, 'Emergency Assistance to the Sudan [1998]', paragraph 18.
58 Ibid., paragraph 38.
59 Ibid., paragraph 19.
60 Ibid., paragraphs 18–19.
61 UN, 'Emergency Assistance to the Sudan [2001]', paragraph 8.
62 UN, 'Emergency Assistance to the Sudan [1999]', paragraph 44.
63 UN, 'Emergency Assistance to the Sudan [2001]', paragraph 22.
64 Burr and Collins, *Requiem for the Sudan*, pp. 76–80.
65 UN, 'Emergency Assistance to the Sudan [1989]', paragraph 46.
66 Burr and Collins, *Requiem for the Sudan,* p. 268.
67 Karim, Duffield, Jaspars, Benini, et al., *Operation Lifeline Sudan (OLS): A Review*, p. 64.
68 de Waal (ed.), *Food and Power in Sudan*, pp. 279–81.
69 Mark Duffield, Jok Madut Jok, David Keen, Geoff Loane, et al., *Sudan: Unintended Consequences of Humanitarian Assistance* (Dublin: Trinity College, University of Dublin, 2000), p. 33.

70 UN, 'Situation of Human Rights in the Sudan [1994]', paragraph 73.
71 UN, 'Emergency Assistance to the Sudan: Report of the Secretary-General', New York, 12 September 1994a, paragraph 23.
72 UN, 'Emergency Assistance to the Sudan [1999]', paragraph 44.
73 de Waal (ed.), *Food and Power in Sudan*, p. 297.
74 Duffield, Jok, Keen, Loane, et al., *Sudan: Unintended Consequences*, p. 43; for a detailed example see footnote 223, p. 177.
75 Karim, Duffield, Jaspars, Benini, et al., *Operation Lifeline Sudan (OLS): A Review*, p. 64.
76 Burr and Collins, *Requiem for the Sudan*, p. 225.
77 Medley, 'Humanitarian assistance in Sudan', p. 175.
78 Ibid., p. 181.
79 Nyaba, *The Politics of Liberation in South Sudan: An Insider's View*, p. 174.
80 Interview with Peter Nyaba, Nairobi.
81 Interview with Cirino Hiteng, SPLM/A delegate at peace talks; Naivasha, Kenya, 13 April 2004; the speaker, an academic as well as a member of the SPLM, wrote a PhD on the EPLF and EPRDF.
82 Conversations with various UN staff; Khartoum, March and October 2004.
83 UN, 'Situation of Human Rights in the Sudan [1994]', paragraphs 69 and 72.
84 UN, 'Emergency Assistance to the Sudan [1995]', paragraph 11.
85 UN Office for the Coordination of Humanitarian Affairs, *Consolidated UN Inter-Agency Appeal for Sudan, January–December 1996* (Geneva: UN OCHA, 1995), Executive Summary.
86 UN, 'Emergency Assistance to the Sudan: Report of the Secretary-General', New York, 4 September 1996, paragraph 8.
87 Karim, Duffield, Jaspars, Benini, et al., *Operation Lifeline Sudan (OLS): A Review*.
88 Ibid., p. 263 and p. 266.
89 Ibid., chapters 2.3, 9.4.2, 9.4.3 and 9.5.
90 Ibid., chapters 7.1–7.3; on the 'relief–development continuum', see in particular chapter 7.2; and also Joanna Macrae, Susanne Jaspars, Mark Duffield, Mark Bradbury, et al., 'Conflict, the continuum and chronic emergencies: a critical analysis of the scope for linking relief, rehabilitation and development planning in Sudan', in *Disasters*, vol. 21, no. 3 (1997), p. 231 and *passim*.
91 Karim, Duffield, Jaspars, Benini, et al., *Operation Lifeline Sudan (OLS): A Review*, p. 276.
92 Ibid., p. 277.
93 Macrae, Jaspars, Duffield, Bradbury, et al., 'Conflict, the continuum and chronic emergencies', p. 240; this conclusion is not explicit in the review itself but is consistent with it.
94 Larry Minear, 'Time to pull the plug on Operation Lifeline Sudan?', in *Crosslines Global Report* (1997), pp. 59–60.
95 Although the report gives extensive consideration to questions of access, assessed needs and ex-depot delivery volumes, it does not directly address the issue of diversion and abuse during delivery, for example by examining instances or assessing overall levels, patterns or consequences. The issue is only incidentally touched on in discussions of the 'Criticisms and concerns of the warring parties', the distribution of relief, and programming (Karim, Duffield, Jaspars, Benini, et al., *Operation Lifeline Sudan (OLS): A Review*, sections 2.4, 3.3 and 5.4).

96 UN, 'Emergency Assistance to the Sudan [1997]', paragraph 69.
97 UN, 'Emergency Assistance to the Sudan [1998]', paragraph 21.
98 UN, 'Emergency Assistance to the Sudan [1996]', paragraph 10.
99 UN, 'Emergency Assistance to the Sudan [1998]', paragraphs 6–7 and 35.
100 UN, 'Emergency Assistance to the Sudan [1999]', paragraph 20.
101 UN, 'Emergency Assistance to the Sudan [2001]', paragraph 16.
102 UN, 'Emergency Assistance to the Sudan [1999]', paragraph 21.
103 IGAD Ministerial Subcommittee, 'Communiqué issued at Addis Ababa on 7 August 1998', paragraphs 6–7.
104 See, for example, Mark Bradbury, Nicholas Leader and Kate Mackintosh, *The 'Agreement on Ground Rules' in South Sudan* (London: Overseas Development Institute, 2000), p. 11.
105 Medley, 'Humanitarian assistance in Sudan', p. 181.
106 Although not an OLS agency, the ICRC also sometimes resorted to suspending operations in Sudan. For example, after three staff were taken hostage in November 1996, the ICRC suspended operations in Sudan until June 1998.
107 UN, 'Emergency Assistance to the Sudan [1998]', paragraph 19.
108 'Scraps in Sudan', *The Economist*, 4 March 2000, p. 70.
109 By the late 1990s, UNICEF and WFP treated most of their relief activities as OLS relief. For example, of a total of 12,516 tons of food relief delivered in December 1998, WFP labelled only 54 tons delivered to the Red Sea Hills as 'non-OLS', while food delivered to Kassala, Khartoum, Kosti, South Darfur and West Kordofan was counted as OLS. See World Food Programme, *WFP in Sudan: Emergency Food Assistance to War and Drought Affected Populations – Monthly Overview* (Khartoum: WFP, 1998), appendix.
110 de Waal (ed.), *Food and Power in Sudan*, p. 345.
111 UN, 'Emergency Assistance to the Sudan [1999]', paragraph 24; and see UNICEF, 'Country Note: Sudan', New York, 20 November 2000, paragraph 12, on proposed UNICEF 'Rights, protection and peace-building programme'.
112 UN, 'Emergency Assistance to the Sudan [2001]', paragraph 9.
113 Ibid., paragraph 75.
114 Ibid., paragraph 76.
115 de Waal (ed.), *Food and Power in Sudan*, p. 129.
116 Interview with Christoph Jaeger, former UN and UNDP head for Sudan (1994–8); Juba, Sudan, 26 October 2005.
117 UN Resident Co-ordinator in Sudan, *Annual Report 2000* (Khartoum: Office of the UN RC in Sudan, 2001), p. 10. Interview with Maxwell Gaylard, former head of UN OCHA Sudan; Nairobi, 23 April 2004.
118 Interview with Maxwell Gaylard, Nairobi.
119 Interview with Jake Hamm, UN field co-ordinator for Nuba Mountains and aid worker in Sudan since 1989; Khartoum, 22 October 2004.
120 UN, 'Emergency Assistance to the Sudan [1999]', paragraph 98.
121 UN Office for the Coordination of Humanitarian Affairs, *Consolidated Inter-Agency Appeal 2003: Sudan*, p. 14.
122 International Crisis Group, *Ending Starvation as a Weapon of War in Sudan* (Nairobi/Brussels: ICG, 2002b), p. i.
123 See, for example, UN Office for the Coordination of Humanitarian Affairs, *Sudan: Mid-year Review* (Geneva/New York: UN OCHA, 2003b), pp. 2–3.
124 UN Office for the Coordination of Humanitarian Affairs, *Sudan 2004: Consolidated Appeal for the Sudan Assistance Programme* (Geneva: UN OCHA,

2003a), p. 12 and p. 18.
125 UN, *Darfur Humanitarian Profile no. 7* (Khartoum: Office of the UN Resident and Humanitarian Co-ordinator, 2004), p. 6; and UN Office for the Coordination of Humanitarian Affairs, *Sudan 2004: Consolidated Appeal for the Sudan Assistance Programme*, pp. 96–97.
126 UN, *Darfur Humanitarian Profile no. 10* (Khartoum: Office of the UN Resident and Humanitarian Co-ordinator, 2005a), p. 5.
127 US$720m of the projected total was for food aid. See UN Office for the Coordination of Humanitarian Affairs, *United Nations and Partners 2005 Work Plan for the Sudan* (Geneva: UN OCHA, 2004), p. 3.
128 'Sudan: Peace talks, humanitarian action', IRIN, 31 January 2003.
129 UN Office for the Coordination of Humanitarian Affairs, *Consolidated Inter-Agency Appeal 2003: Sudan*, p. 13. Problems over appointments also continued. At the end of 2002 the designated UN head in Sudan, Mike Sackett, was forced to leave the country after being unable to formally present his credentials during some six months in post.
130 On travel restrictions, see UN Security Council, 'Resolution 1556', New York, 30 July 2004a, paragraph 1, p. 3; on military flights, see UN Security Council, 'Resolution 1564', New York, 18 September 2004b, paragraph 11, p. 3.
131 UN Office for the Coordination of Humanitarian Affairs, *United Nations and Partners 2005 Work Plan for the Sudan*, p. 3.
132 Ibid., p. 100.
133 UN, Darfur Humanitarian Profile no. 10, pp. 5–7.
134 For example, in early 2005 a backlog of 250 truckloads of aid built up between Ed Daein and Nyala in South Darfur, because of insecurity. UN, 'Monthly Report of the Secretary-General on Darfur [April 2005]', p. 7.
135 World Food Programme, *Full Report of the Evaluation of EMOP 10339.0/1: Assistance to Populations Affected by Conflict in Greater Darfur, West Sudan* (Rome: WFP, 2006), p. 33.
136 Ibid., p. 34.
137 UN Office for the Coordination of Humanitarian Affairs, *United Nations and Partners 2006 Work Plan for Sudan* (Geneva: UN OCHA, 2005), p. 3.
138 Planned humanitarian and early recovery assistance for Southern Sudan in 2008 totalled US$632m. By October 2008, overall funding secured for the 2008 Work Plan stood at US$1.41bn, compared with a revised funding target of US$2.48bn. UN Office for the Coordination of Humanitarian Affairs, *United Nations and Partners 2008 Work Plan for Sudan* (Geneva: UN OCHA, 2007), pp. v and 23–24.
139 UN Office for the Coordination of Humanitarian Affairs, *United Nations and Partners 2009 Work Plan for Sudan* (Geneva: UN OCHA, 2008), p. x.
140 'Darfur crisis: situation as of 11 June 2009', WFP website statement, www.wfp.org/countries/Sudan.
141 UN, 'Report of the Secretary-General', p. 8.
142 UN agencies and some of the many Sudanese and international NGOs that remained in Darfur took on what work was needed of the expelled organisations, so that no crisis occurred. In fact, expelling aid organisations was not new: the government had intermittently done this in the 1980s and 1990s.
143 Helen Young and Daniel Maxwell, *Targeting in Complex Emergencies: Darfur Case Study* (Medford, MA: Feinstein International Center, 2009), p. 34.
144 In 2006 the UN received a total of US$1,277m against its appeal for UN$1,731m. Of the funds received, 90 per cent was marked for humanitari

aid; US$633m for aid in Darfur; and US$356m for aid in Southern Sudan.
145 Estimates drawn from various editions of Economist Intelligence Unit *Country Report: Sudan*.

CHAPTER 4 Foreign Policy

1. Peter Woodward, *The Horn of Africa: Politics and International Relations* (London: I.B.Tauris, 2003), pp. 142.
2. Ibid., pp. 142–44.
3. Ibid., p. 144.
4. This also meant that by 1985 debt servicing accounted for around half of budgeted government expenditure. Economist Intelligence Unit, *Country Profile: Sudan, 1986–87* (London: EIU, 1986), p. 41.
5. Anderson indicates that the cumulative total up to 1983 was US$350m. See Anderson, *Sudan in Crisis*, p. 18 and p. 49; and US Library of Congress Federal Research Division, *Sudan: A Country Study* (Washington DC: Library of Congress, 1991).
6. In Operation Bright Star, see Gayle Smith, 'George Bush in Khartoum', in *MERIP Reports*, no. 135, 'Sudan's Revolutionary Spring' (1985), p. 26.
7. Anderson, *Sudan in Crisis*, p. 49.
8. Statement of Kenneth Brown, US Deputy Assistant Secretary of State for Africa. See US Congress, 'Ethiopia and Sudan: Warfare, Politics, and Famine', hearing before the Select Committee on Hunger, House of Representatives, 100th Congress, second session, 14 July 1988 (Washington DC: US GPO, 1988), pp. 19–20.
9. 'Sudan: war and peace', *Africa Confidential*, vol. 30, no. 10, 12 May 1989; and Anderson, Sudan in Crisis, p. 225.
10. The agreement covered training assistance and the provision of Egyptian-assembled Brazilian 'Toucano' fighter jets. See 'Overcoming differences… and integration one day', *Al-Tadamon* magazine, 9 November 1985.
11. 'Sudan: battle lines', *Africa Confidential*, vol. 26, no. 20, 1 October 1985, p. 3.
12. Despite the replacement of the Joint Defence Agreement with the Brotherhood Treaty, Egyptian strategic interest in Sudan of course remained fundamentally unchanged. In the words of the Egyptian ambassador to Sudan at the time, 'We never asked [Sudan's leaders] for anything … Our overall concern is security. Our fear is instability affecting the south of our country. In comparison with this [risk], joint venture projects don't matter.' Interview with Hussain Musharrafa, Cairo.
13. See 'Sudan: sleight of hand', *Africa Confidential*, vol. 26, no. 2, 16 January 1985.
14. Ann Mosely Lesch, 'Sudan's foreign policy: in search of arms, aid and allies', in *Sudan: State and Society in Crisis*, edited by Voll (Bloomington, Ind.: Indiana University Press, 1991), pp. 51–52. Relations with the IMF also deteriorated because of a failure to pay off rescheduled arrears, and as a result in February 1986 the IMF declared Sudan ineligible for further borrowing. See Economist Intelligence Unit, *Country Profile: Sudan, 1986–87*, p. 42.
15. Libya also provided four MIG-23 fighter jets to Khartoum in April 1987, which arrived ironically on the day when Sadiq delivered a 'peace speech' on the second anniversary of Nimeiri's overthrow. As part of the military and economic relationship with Libya, in September 1988 Sadiq also agreed a 'unity project' between Sudan and Libya. But like most such plans, the project was

only symbolic. See Anderson, *Sudan in Crisis*, p. 108.
16 Macrae, Jaspars, Duffield, Bradbury, et al., 'Conflict, the continuum and chronic emergencies', p. 241.
17 US Congress, 'Emergency Famine Relief Needs in Ethiopia and Sudan', hearing before the Subcommittee on Africa of the Committee on Foreign Affairs, House of Representatives, 99th Congress, first session, 19 September 1985 (Washington DC: US GPO, 1985), p. 7.
18 de Waal (ed.), *Food and Power in Sudan*, p. 37.
19 Ironically, one person at the hearing noted that for the Ethiopian government fighting the war was the first priority, while feeding people in the cities came second, and feeding people in the country came third. As the speaker remarked, fighting or waging the war would also be the first priority of the USA if it were under attack. However the truth of this for Sudan too was not noted. See US Congress, 'Emergency Famine Relief Needs in Ethiopia and Sudan', p. 14.
20 US Congress, 'Ethiopia and Sudan: Warfare, Politics, and Famine', p. 1 and p. 10.
21 The words of the co-chair of a Congressional hearing. See US Congress, 'Politics of Hunger in the Sudan', joint hearing before the Select Committee on Hunger and the Subcommittee on Africa of the Committee on Foreign Affairs, House of Representatives, 101st Congress, first session, 2 March 1989 (Washington DC: US GPO, 1989), p. 2.
22 Concrete details are scarce, but it is certain that, for example, a number of southern Sudanese went to Cuba for education and military training. There is no firm evidence that Israel provided any support for the SPLM/A in the 1980s, unlike in the first war when it had clearly supported the Anyanya.
23 'Sudan: the SPLA in focus', *Africa Confidential*, vol. 29, no. 8, 15 April 1988.
24 Indeed, the only notionally peacemaking action for Sudan taken by the USA between 1983 and 1989 was some token efforts to end 'external influence in Sudan' through talks with the Soviet Union about peace in the Horn. By March 1989, however, the USA had not even been able to discuss peace issues in the region with the Soviet Union at an 'operational level', because (according to the then US Deputy Assistant Secretary of State for Africa, Kenneth Brown) Soviet officials had been unwilling to do so, although the USA expected discussion to happen 'in the near future'. See US Congress, 'Politics of Hunger in the Sudan', p. 23 and p. 34.
25 Herman J. Cohen, *Intervening in Africa: Superpower Peacemaking in a Troubled Continent* (Basingstoke: Macmillan, 2000), p. 63.
26 Hasan Hajj Ali, '*Al-Siyasa al-Kharijiyya l-il-Inqadh tujah Duwal al-Jiwar al-Ifriqi*' ('The Foreign Policy of the Salvation towards Neighbouring African States'), paper read at 'Erkowit conference', at Erkowit, Sudan, 2000, p. 3.
27 'Sudan: the Islamic Front in power', *Africa Confidential*, vol. 32, no. 14, 12 July 1991, p.3.
28 'Sudan: guns not butter', *Africa Confidential*, vol. 32, no. 25, 20 December 1991, p. 8; and Verney, *Raising the Stakes*, p. 53.
29 Cohen, *Intervening in Africa*, p. 67.
30 US Congress, 'Impending Famine and Recent Political Developments in the Sudan', hearing before the Subcommittee on Africa of the Committee on Foreign Affairs, House of Representatives, 101st Congress, second session, 25 October 1990 (Washington DC: US GPO, 1990), p. 1 (referring to remarks at US Congressional hearing on Sudan in March 1990).
31 Petterson, *Inside Sudan*, pp. 25–33.
32 Ibid., pp. 85–90.

33 Ibid., p. 52. In retrospect it is interesting to note that during Petterson's term in Khartoum (August 1992–July 1995), neither Osama bin Laden nor al-Qaeda was included in the list of organisations or individuals that the US State Department provided him to challenge the Sudanese authorities about. This was because at the time the USA saw bin Laden only as a financer of terrorist organisations and not as being directly involved. See Petterson, *Inside Sudan*, p. 117; and 9/11 Commission, *The 9/11 Commission Report: Final Report of the National Commission on Terrorist Attacks upon the United States* (New York: WW Norton, 2004), pp. 108–09.
34 Petterson, *Inside Sudan*, p. 111.
35 Ibid., p. 86.
36 Ibid., p. 108.
37 Ibid., p. 110.
38 US Congressional Research Service, *Sudan: Humanitarian Crisis, Peace Talks, Terrorism, and US Policy* (Washington DC: CRS, 2004), p. 13.
39 US Congress, 'The Crisis in Sudan', hearing before the Subcommittee on Africa of the Committee on International Relations, House of Representatives, 104th Congress, first session, 22 March 1995 (Washington DC: US GPO, 1995), p.12.
40 Interview with Hussein Abu Saleh, Khartoum.
41 US Congress, 'The Crisis in Sudan', p. 1.
42 Three UN Security Council resolutions on Sudan were passed in 1996. UNSCR 1044 required Sudan to extradite to Ethiopia for prosecution three suspects for the assassination attempt and to desist from 'activities of assisting, supporting and facilitating terrorist activities and from giving sanctuary to terrorist elements'. UNSCR 1054 imposed travel restrictions on Sudanese government officials, and UNSCR 1070 threatened a ban on government-controlled flights.
43 US Congress, 'Terrorism and Sudan', hearing before the Subcommittee on African Affairs of the Committee on Foreign Relations, United States Senate, 105th Congress, first session, 15 May 1997 (Washington DC: US GPO, 1997), p. 18.
44 Combined with the decision by the Sudanese Ba'ath party to join the opposition, these executions appeared to give even Iraq second thoughts about its relationship with the new government. However, Iraqi satisfaction with Sudan was shortly afterwards bolstered by Sudan's position on the Gulf crisis. See 'Sudan: losing friends?', *Africa Confidential*, vol. 31, no. 10, 18 May 1990, p. 8.
45 Verney, *Raising the Stakes*, p. 52.
46 For example, 'The Gulf Crisis has unveiled the self-interested opportunists', *Al-Sudan al-Hadith*, 10 October 1990; 'King Fahd calls for end to media campaign', SUNA, 2 May 1991; and 'The ignorance of Riyadh', *Al-Inqadh al-Watani*, 22 November 1991.
47 'Sudan: fundamentalist economics', *Africa Confidential*, vol. 30, no. 2, 25 January 1991, pp. 6–7.
48 Lesch, *The Sudan*, p. 152.
49 'Sudan: global condemnation', *Africa Confidential*, vol. 33, no. 21, 23 October 1992.
50 Nonetheless the Legitimate Command was linked to coup plots reported in Sudan in 1990 and 1991. See Lesch, *The Sudan*, pp. 151–52.
51 SUNA report, 4 June 1992.
52 For an account of the proxy fighting between Sudan and Uganda, see Gérard Prunier, 'Rebel movements and proxy warfare: Uganda, Sudan and the Congo

(1986–99)', in *African Affairs,* vol. 103, no. 412 (2004), pp. 366–67 and passim.
53 US Congress, 'Terrorism and Sudan', pp. 38–40.
54 The US administration was unable to substantiate the CIA claim that a soil sample from the vicinity of Al-Shifa had tested positive for EMPTA, a precursor chemical for VX, a nerve gas, and that Osama bin Laden had 'invested in' and 'almost certainly' gained access to VX produced at a plant in Sudan. See 9/11 Commission, *The 9/11 Commission Report,* p. 117. In a slightly different vein, by 2000 various investigations and tests by the UN, Britain and Finland of soil samples from alleged incidents of chemical-weapons use by the Sudanese government in the war had all found no evidence to support the allegations. See for example Applied Science and Analysis Inc., 'Analysis of samples from Sudan', in *The ASA Newsletter,* no. 79 (2000); and UK Minister of State for Defence Procurement, 'Regarding the testing of Sudan samples at the Chemical and Biological Defence Agency', letter to the President of CSI, Baroness Cox, from the UK Minister of State for Defence Procurement, Baroness Symons, 5 June 2000.
55 Notable examples include 'Slavery in Sudan', a two-part documentary broadcast by the US television station CBS on 1–2 February 1999; and 'For such a time as this', a CBS 'Touched by an Angel' programme, broadcast on 26 September 1999.
56 US Congress, 'Crimes against Humanity in Sudan', joint hearing before the Subcommittee on International Operations and Human Rights and Subcommittee on Africa, 106th Congress, 27 May 1999 (Washington DC: US GPO, 1999), p. 2. Ironically this debate had largely been forgotten when debate began in the USA about whether genocide was occurring in Darfur after 2003.
57 US Commission on International Religious Freedom, *Annual Report 2000* (Washington DC: US CIRF, 2000), p. 25.
58 US Congress, 'House Resolution 2906: To Facilitate Famine Relief Efforts and a Comprehensive Solution to the War in Sudan', mark-up before the Sub-committee on Africa of the Committee on Foreign Relations, 106th Congress, first session (Washington DC: US GPO, 2000).
59 Ibid., p. 4.
60 These included Verney, *Raising the Stakes;* John Harker, *Human Security in Sudan: The Report of a Canadian Assessment Mission* (Ottawa: 2000); Amnesty International, *The Human Price of Oil* (New York: Amnesty International, 2000); and Christian Aid, *The Scorched Earth.*
61 European Coalition on Oil in Sudan, 'Statement of background', 2001, www.ecosonline.org/back/history.html (accessed on 20 January 2004).
62 The charm offensive included the 'Peace from within' strategy and Sudan's return to the IGAD talks, and was seen by the Sudanese government as breaking the international 'blockade' against it. See Government of Sudan, *Al-Taqrir al-Istratigi al-Sudani, 1999* ('The Sudan Strategic Report, 1999') (Khartoum: Centre for Strategic Studies, 1999), p. 453.
63 Interview with Abd al-Rahim Ali, academic and member of NCP council who mediated in NCP split in 1999; Khartoum, 31 March 2004.
64 For an account of these policy reversals, see Human Rights Watch, *Sudan, Oil, and Human Rights* (New York: HRW, 2003), pp. 483–84, and 496–99.
65 Petterson, *Inside Sudan,* pp. 237–38.
66 The State Department was also responsible for providing relief to refugees, through its Bureau for Population, Refugees and Migration. However this

amounted to much less relief than USAID provided to Sudan for Sudanese populations
67 Burr and Collins, *Requiem for the Sudan*, p. 238.
68 Petterson, *Inside Sudan*, p. 109.
69 Judith Randel and Tony German, 'Trends in the financing of humanitarian assistance', in *The New Humanitarianisms: A Review of Global Trends in Humanitarian Action*, edited by Macrae (London: Overseas Development Institute, 2002), p. 27. The EU had suspended development aid to Sudan in April 1990 on human-rights grounds.
70 Department for International Development (DFID), 'Sudan: Country Engagement Plan', London 2004, section 3.1.
71 Interview with Maxwell Gaylard, Nairobi.
72 Abby Stoddard, 'Trends in US humanitarian policy', in *The New Humanitarianisms: A Review of Trends in Global Humanitarian Action*, edited by Macrae (London: ODI, 2002), p. 43.
73 Human Rights Watch, *Sudan, Oil, and Human Rights*, p. 508.
74 Emery Brusset, 'Sudan's foreign policy environment: some implications for humanitarian assistance', in *The Wider Impact of Humanitarian Assistance: The Case of Sudan and the Implications for European Union Policy*, edited by Loane and Schümer (Baden-Baden: Nomos Verlagsgesellschaft, 2000), pp. 157–58.
75 US Congress, 'America's Sudan Policy: A New Direction?', joint hearing before House Committee on International Relations, Subcommittee on Africa and Subcommittee on International Operations and Human Rights, 28 March 2001 (Washington DC: US GPO, 2001).
76 Center for Strategic and International Studies, *US Policy to End Sudan's War: Report of the CSIS Task Force on US–Sudan Policy* (Washington: CSIS, 2001), pp. 2–3.
77 One example was Congressman Tom Payne. See US Congress, 'America's Sudan Policy', pp. 138–40.
78 Ibid., pp. 33–34.
79 It was not until early 2002 that the slave-redemption story began to be widely discredited in the US media, although some reports maintaining the basic claims of the story continued to circulate. See, for example, 'Ripping off slave "redeemers": rebels exploit Westerners' efforts to buy emancipation for Sudanese', *Washington Post*, 26 February 2002; 'The slave trade and mass redemptions hoax in Sudan', CBS television '60 Minutes' programme, 16 May 2002; and, in contrast, 'Meanwhile it takes 2 goats, or $33, to free a slave in Sudan', *International Herald Tribune*, 11 June 2002.
80 US Congress, 'Implementing US Policy in Sudan', hearing before the Subcommittee on African Affairs of the Committee on Foreign Relations, 107th Congress (Washington DC: US GPO, 2002), pp. 10–11. US policy remained framed around these three goals or 'pillars' through 2003 and beyond. See US Agency for International Development, 'Interim Strategic Plan for Sudan, 2004–2006', Washington DC, June 2003, p. 4.
81 Some Sudanese officials also claimed that the USA had spurned a Sudanese offer to share this intelligence back in 1997, after the departure of bin Laden from Sudan. See David Rose, 'The Osama files', *Vanity Fair*, January 2002, pp. 50–56.
82 US Congressional Research Service, Sudan: *Humanitarian Crisis, Peace Talks, Terrorism, and US policy* (Washington DC: CRS, 2002).
83 It is also claimed that even before 9/11 the USA had intended to abstain from the UN Security Council vote on Sudan, which was initially scheduled for 17

Notes to pp. 124–32   213

September. See de Waal (ed.), *Islamism and its Enemies,* p. 229 and p. 241.
84 'Ghazi Salah al-Din: *Khalal manhaj al-tafawud dafa'ni l-il-istiqala*', interview by Daya' al-Din Bilal with Ghazi Salah al-Din, Al-Jazeeranet, 23 December 2003.
85 It is striking how in the years after 9/11 the US or Western idea of the 'failed state' largely replaced the idea of the 'pariah state', with implications for policy towards states categorised this way, such as Sudan.
86 The words of the Acting Assistant Secretary of State for Africa, Charles Snyder. See US Congress, 'Sudan: Peace Agreement Around the Corner?', hearing before the Subcommittee on Africa of the Committee on International Relations, House of Representatives, 108th Congress, second session (Washington DC: US GPO, 2004b), p. 49, and see p. 27.
87 For one analysis of the failure to better heed the warnings, see Sharath Srinivasan, *Minority Rights, Early Warning and Conflict Prevention: Lessons from Darfur* (London: Minority Rights Group, 2006), pp. 6–7.
88 International Crisis Group, *Darfur Rising: Sudan's New Crisis,* p. 14.
89 UK International Development Committee, 'Darfur, Sudan: Crisis, Response and Lessons', minutes of evidence taken before the House of Commons International Development Committee, 22 February 2005 (London: The Stationery Office, 2005b), Q200.
90 Ibid., Q191. Understandably, the Darfur rebels also felt that the Naivasha talks were being prioritised over Darfur. According to one SLM/A official, the SLM/A tried to lobby the troika representatives but felt that 'they didn't want to hear about Darfur … they were more interested in getting a peace agreement for the south.' Interview with Abdel Latif Ismael, SLM/A representative in Britain; London, 19 March 2005.
91 UK International Development Committee, 'Darfur, Sudan: Crisis, Response and Lessons', Q200.
92 Ibid., Q201.
93 Ibid., Q204.
94 Words of Charles Snyder. US Congress, 'The Crisis in Darfur: A New Front in Sudan's Bloody War', hearing and mark-up before the Committee on International Relations, House of Representatives, 108th Congress, second session (Washington DC: US GPO, 2004a), p. 22.
95 'Ambassador: Sudan accords only one step in peace process', interview with Michael Ranneberger, Christianitytoday.com, 4 June 2004.
96 BBC, '"Never Again"', edited transcript of interview with John Danforth, Panorama television programme, 3 July 2005.
97 Ibid.
98 Ibid.
99 UK International Development Committee, 'Darfur, Sudan: Crisis, Response and Lessons', minutes of evidence taken before the House of Commons International Development Committee, 23 February 2005 (London: The Stationery Office, 2005a), Q239.
100 Interview with Roger Winter, USAID assistant administrator responsible for DCHA bureau; Naivasha, Kenya, 20 April 2004.
101 Interview with David Rhoad, USAID liaison official at US State Department 'Sudan Programs Group'; Washington DC, 30 March 2005 and other interviews.
102 The USA also imposed restrictions on its foreign aid to Sudan in 1988, because of accumulating arrears in Sudan's debt servicing to the USA; in 1993 the USA imposed further restrictions after it listed Sudan as a supporter of terrorism. See US Congressional Research Service, Sudan: *Economic Sanctions* (Washington

DC: CRS, 2005).
103 SDC's total expenditure in the financial year 2007–8 was only US$9.3m. From this small sum and the tens of thousands of Americans who were drawn to the 'cause' of Darfur, a lot of noise was made. See Save Darfur Coalition, *Annual Report 2008* (Washington DC: SDC, 2008), pp. 3 and 14.
104 Mahmood Mamdani's *Saviors and Survivors* contained a powerful and important critique of the SDC. But it also suffered from serious flaws, in particular a neglect of the wider context of the civil war and CPA, and some exaggerated theorising to the effect that aspects of the international response to the conflict were driven by a 'big power agenda' to re-colonise Africa. See Mahmood Mamdani, *Saviors and Survivors: Darfur, Politics, and the War on Terror* (London: Verso, 2008), p. 300.
105 Campaigners initially focused on Chinese arms sales to Sudan and the role of Chinese oil companies in Sudan, and targeted the latter for disinvestment by Western investors. Partly in response, in May 2007 China appointed a special envoy for Darfur, the first time it had appointed such an envoy for Sudan. For an account of China's growing relations with Sudan, see Dan Large, 'From non-interference to constructive engagement? China's evolving relations with Sudan', in *China Returns to Africa: A Rising Power and a Continent Embrace*, edited by Alden, Large and Soares de Oliveira (London: Hurst, 2008), pp.295–317.
106 UN, *Report of the International Commission of Inquiry on Darfur*, pp. 2–6.
107 'Gosh again', *Africa Confidential*, 8 September 2006, p. 8.
108 For example, in 2006 DFID paid for a British communications and public-relations company to run a publicity campaign for the DPA in Darfur. An elaborate campaign was subsequently embedded in AMIS and UNAMID, and broadened into supporting a notional 'Darfur–Darfur Dialogue and Consultation'. But no amount of orchestrated publicity and spin could bring the DPA to life.

CHAPTER 5   Options

1 This table draws on Marieke Kleiboer, 'Understanding success and failure of international mediation', in *Journal of Conflict Resolution*, vol. 40, no. 2 (1996), p. 362.
2 Interview with Yasser Arman, Naivasha, and other interviews.
3 Interview with Malik Agar, SPLM/A commander and delegate at peace talks; Naivasha, Kenya, 11 April 2004.
4 Interview with Mohammed el-Amin Khalifa, former government negotiator and PCP official; Khartoum, 16 March 2004.
5 Interview with Sayyid el-Khatib, Naivasha.
6 Interview with Ali Mahmoud Hassanein, DUP secretary-general; Khartoum, 9 March 2004.
7 See Stephen J. Stedman, 'Spoiler problems in peace processes', in *International Security*, vol. 22, no. 2 (1997).
8 Later on, other matters such as militia activity in the south and the mainstream northern opposition parties' resistance to the CPA also illustrated the spoiler threat.
9 For example, one of the mediation resource staff, Fink Haysom, argued that while the bilateral nature of the talks was effective, the implementation of the eventual agreement would 'need to be multilateral'. Interview with Nicholas 'Fink' Haysom, member of IGAD secretariat resource staff for Sudan talks;

Naivasha, Kenya, 15 April 2004.
10 Interview with Ali Mahmoud Hassanein, Khartoum and other interviews; and see chapter 3.3.
11 Interview with Hassan Abdelgadir Hilal, DUP official and businessman; Khartoum, 14 and 20 March 2004. Interview with Sadiq al-Mahdi, Umma Party leader; Khartoum, 15 March 2004.
12 Interview with Ali Mahmoud Hassanein, Khartoum.
13 For example, a Nuba Mountains NGO, Nuba Survival, feared that both the government and the SPLM/A would use the Nuba Mountains as 'a bargaining chip'. Interview with Suleiman Musa Rahhal, London.
14 For Badri, and for several other interviewees, the other 'biggest mistake' was the failure to do more to support the period of democracy from 1986 to 1989. Interview with Balqis Badri, director of Institute of Women, Gender and Development Studies, Ahfad University, and member of women's delegation to Naivasha talks; Khartoum, 9 March 2004.
15 Interview with Sayyid el-Khatib, Naivasha.
16 Interview with Ghazi Salah al-Din Atabani, Khartoum.
17 Interview with Samson Kwaje, SPLM/A spokesman and delegate at peace talks; Naivasha, Kenya, 12 April 2004.
18 Interview with Abd al-Rahim Ali, Khartoum, and other interviews.
19 Interview with Lam Akol, former leader of SPLM/A breakaway faction and successor groups; Nairobi, 28 April 2004.
20 Interview with Pagan Amum, Naivasha.
21 Ibid.
22 Ibid.
23 Interview with Abd al-Aziz al-Hilu, Naivasha.
24 Interview with Riek Machar, former leader of SPLM/A breakaway faction and successor groups; Nairobi, 28 April 2004.
25 Covert SPLM/A military support to the Darfur rebel groups was rumoured at the time and credible reports of SPLM/A support until at least August 2004 were later noted in a UN investigation of the international arms embargo on Darfur. UN, 'Report of the Panel of Experts', p. 4. and p. 28.
26 The parties themselves showed no sense of urgency or any great impatience with the talks. Many observers felt that the slow progress was due primarily to GoS intransigence, and that the SPLM/A often took the initiative. In contrast, a central mediating 'resource person' at the talks, Fink Haysom, felt that the SPLM could have offered more concessions, though he did not feel that the talks were more drawn out than was reasonable, in the context of the past fifty years in Sudan. Interview with Nicholas 'Fink' Haysom, Naivasha.
27 Affendi has argued similarly that the importance of a stalemate was 'exaggerated' for Sudan. See Abdelwahab el-Affendi, 'The impasse in the IGAD peace process for Sudan: the limits of regional peacemaking?', in *African Affairs*, vol. 100, no. 401 (2001), p. 596.
28 Interview with Abdullah Hasan Ahmed, PCP deputy secretary-general and former minister of finance (1993–6); Khartoum, 17 March 2004. Interview with Sayyid el-Khatib, Naivasha. Interview with Abd al-Nabi Ali Ahmed, Umma Party secretary-general and former governor of Darfur; Khartoum, 20 March 2004. Other interviews.
29 Interview with Yasser Arman, Naivasha. Another interviewee (not from the parties) described the north–south framework as a 'false start' and a 'trap' which IGAD and the troika had fallen into. Interview with Guma Kunda, Sudanese

inter-faith peace activist; Khartoum, 13 March 2004.
30 Department for International Development (DFID), 'Sudan: Country Engagement Plan', section 2.1.
31 US Congress, 'The crisis in Darfur', p. 8.
32 BBC, '"Never Again"'.
33 UK International Development Committee, 'Darfur, Sudan: Crisis, Response and Lessons', minutes of evidence taken before the House of Commons International Development Committee, 21 December 2004 (London: The Stationery Office, 2004), e.g. in answers to Qs 103, 107, 109, and 114.
34 BBC, '"Never Again"'.
35 Interview with Yasser Arman, Naivasha.
36 Several of these delegations were funded by the Netherlands. Interview with Balqis Badri, Khartoum. Interview with Southern Blue Nile delegation, including Stephen Missa, Elhadi Eltinjour (Chairman of North and South Funj Union), and others; Naivasha, Kenya, 19 April 2004.
37 Interview with Sadiq al-Mahdi, Khartoum.
38 In the opinion of an SCC official, for example, 'neither Britain nor the US intend the referendum to be a [genuinely] free choice for Southern Sudan.' Interview with Jeremiah Swaka, SCC National Coordinator for Peace and Advocacy; Khartoum, 23 March 2004.
39 UN, 'Situation of Human Rights in the Sudan [2002]', summary, p. 2.
40 Sadiq considered the mediators' failure to 'stop the dictatorship' of Bashir to be one of their three main failures, the other two being the failure to broaden the peace talks and the failure to bring Egypt into the peace process. Interview with Sadiq al-Mahdi, Khartoum; and other interviews.
41 Interview with Riek Machar, Nairobi.
42 1972 was the year of the Addis Ababa Agreement, 1977 the 'national reconciliation', and 1997 the Khartoum Peace Agreement. Interview with Abd al-Aziz al-Hilu, Naivasha.
43 Interview with Roger Winter, Naivasha and other interviews.
44 Interview with Lazaro Sumbeiywo, Naivasha. In an interview in 2003, Sumbeiywo said: 'We do not want another agreement like the Addis Ababa agreement of 1972. We want an agreement which can be guaranteed internationally, possibly by the UN, the African Union, and bilateral countries.' 'Interview with Lazarus Sumbeiywo', IRIN, 30 May 2003.
45 Barbara F. Walter, 'The critical barrier to civil war settlement', in *International Organization*, vol. 51, no. 3 (1997), p. 362.
46 By April 2004 at least five deadlines had been set and not complied with. Interview with Kjell Hødnebø, Naivasha.
47 Taha was vice-president to Bashir, and in 2003 replaced Atabani as head of the government delegation at the talks. Interview with member of troika, Naivasha.
48 Interview with Badr el-Din Suleiman, economic adviser to President Bashir and former minister of finance under Nimeiri; Khartoum, 6 April 2004.
49 See de Waal, *Famine Crimes*; and de Waal (ed.), *Food and Power in Sudan;* and for example, Duffield, Jok, Keen, Loane, et al., *Sudan: Unintended Consequences,* pp. 30–33.
50 Interview with Elijah Malok, Naivasha. Interview with Anne Itto, SPLM agriculture and natural-resource development adviser and delegate at peace talks; Naivasha, Kenya, 13 April 2004. Other interviews.
51 Interview with Elijah Malok, Naivasha.
52 Interview with Maxwell Gaylard, Nairobi.

53 Ibid..
54 Interview with Anne Itto, Naivasha.
55 M. Bradbury, 'Normalising the crisis in Africa', in *Disasters*, vol. 22, no. 4 (1998), p. 333.
56 Duffield, Jok, Keen, Loane, et al., Sudan: *Unintended Consequences*, pp. 194–96.
57 Ibid., pp. 195–96.
58 Young and Maxwell, *Targeting in Complex Emergencies: Darfur Case Study*, p.34.
59 One senior UN official considered that the division was OLS's biggest flaw and that it led to OLS prolonging the war. Interview with Maxwell Gaylard, Nairobi.
60 Duffield, Jok, Keen, Loane, et al., Sudan: *Unintended Consequences*, p. 220.
61 Larry Minear and Thomas G. Weiss, *Mercy under Fire: War and the Global Humanitarian Community* (Boulder: Westview, 1995), p. 15.
62 The schemes in question were in Kadugli (Nuba Mountains), and Juba and Wau (Southern Sudan). See Macrae, Jaspars, Duffield, Bradbury, et al., 'Conflict, the continuum and chronic emergencies', p. 231 and footnotes 6–9, pp. 241–42.
63 Mark Duffield, 'Humanitarian conditionality: origins, consequences and implications of the pursuit of development in conflict', in *The Wider Impact of Humanitarian Assistance: The Case of Sudan and the Implications for European Union Policy*, edited by Loane and Schümer (Baden-Baden: Nomos Verlagsgesellschaft, 2000), p. 114.
64 Bradbury, 'Normalising the crisis in Africa'.
65 The 1998 figure of US$314m included relief 'carried over' from 1997. See UN Office for the Coordination of Humanitarian Affairs, *Consolidated Inter-Agency Appeal 2003: Sudan*, p. 6.
66 Macrae, Jaspars, Duffield, Bradbury, et al., 'Conflict, the continuum and chronic emergencies', p. 241.
67 UN Country Team Sudan, *The Common Country Assessment for the Sudan, 1999* (Sudan: UN, 1999), pp. 4–5.
68 UK International Development Committee, 'Darfur, Sudan: Crisis, Response and Lessons', Q190.
69 Duffield, Jok, Keen, Loane, et al., Sudan: *Unintended Consequences*, p. 82.
70 Interview with Anne Itto, Naivasha.
71 Western Equatoria is often cited as an example of a region which sometimes produced a food surplus which relief agencies could have bought for delivery to areas of need, but did not.
72 The worst example of such explanations was the claim that the conflict in Darfur was the first conflict of the twenty-first century caused by global warming. Local-level conflicts over resources had long existed in Darfur (as elsewhere in Sudan), but were not the same as the much larger and higher-level conflict fought by JEM and the SLM/A.
73 Interview with Elijah Malok, Naivasha.
74 One example during the Darfur conflict can be seen in the UN appeal for funding for 2005, which claimed that in 2004 the UN and INGOs had 'prevented the loss of hundreds of thousands of lives' in Darfur. To their credit, UN agency staff drafting the appeal did not make this claim themselves, and in fact tended to be more critical of the UN response in Darfur; instead the claim was inserted at the last minute by an assistant to the UN deputy head in Sudan, who wanted to represent the achievements of the UN and INGOs in Darfur in a better light. See UN Office for the Coordination of Humanitarian Affairs,

United Nations and Partners 2005 Work Plan for the Sudan, p. 13.
75 de Waal, *Famine that Kills*, p. 8 and *passim*.
76 cf. Randolph C. Kent, 'International humanitarian crises: two decades before and two decades beyond', in *International Affairs*, vol. 80, no. 5 (2004), p. 867.
77 UK International Development Committee, 'Darfur, Sudan: Crisis, Response and Lessons', Q185.
78 Interview with Anne Itto, Naivasha.
79 Johnson, *The Root Causes*, p. 176.
80 Geoff Loane and Tanja Schümer (eds.), *The Wider Impact of Humanitarian Assistance: The Case of Sudan and the Implications for European Union Policy* (Baden-Baden: Nomos Verlagsgesellschaft, 2000), pp. 26–27.
81 This is not the same as 'peace conditionality' after a negotiated end to a civil war, as discussed for example by Boyce. See James K. Boyce, *Investing in Peace: Aid and Conditionality after Civil Wars* (Oxford: Oxford University Press, 2002).
82 Joanna Macrae, *The New Humanitarianisms: A Review of Global Trends in Humanitarian Action* (London: Overseas Development Institute, 2002), p. 2.
83 Macrae, Jaspars, Duffield, Bradbury, et al., 'Conflict, the continuum and chronic emergencies', p. 240.
84 For example, SPLM/A officials who otherwise dealt with relief but were involved in the talks in Kenya, tended to accept that the talks should deal with the fundamental causes of the war and then with issues of reconstruction and development, especially the return, resettlement and reintegration of displaced persons. Interview with Anne Itto, Naivasha and other interviews.
85 Interview with Roger Winter, Naivasha.
86 Interview with Jake Hamm, Khartoum.
87 Allegedly the redeployment was done in the gap between the signing of the agreement and the arrival in the field of the JMC. Interview with Abd al-Aziz al-Hilu, Naivasha.
88 Interview with George Garang, journalist and editor of *SPLM Update*; Naivasha, Kenya, 15 April 2004.
89 S. Neil MacFarlane, *Humanitarian Action: The Conflict Connection* (Providence RI: Watson Institute, 2000), p. 61.
90 Duffield, Jok, Keen, Loane, et al., *Sudan: Unintended Consequences*, pp. 178–79.
91 Conversely, as proponents of grassroots conflict resolution could argue, a 'top-down' approach to conflict resolution failed to bring peace in Sudan for more than two decades. Interview with Michael Ouko, New Sudan Council of Churches peace advocacy co-ordinator; Nairobi, 29 April 2004.
92 See for example Danida and Overseas Development Institute, *Evaluation of Danish Humanitarian Assistance to Sudan, 1992–98* (Copenhagen: Ministry of Foreign Affairs / Danida, 1999), chapter 4.4.
93 Joanna Macrae and Nicholas Leader, *Shifting Sands: The Search for 'Coherence' between Political and Humanitarian Responses to Complex Emergencies* (London: Overseas Development Institute, 2000), *passim*.
94 Danida and Overseas Development Institute, *Evaluation of Danish Humanitarian Assistance to Sudan, 1992–98*, ch. 4.4.
95 Macrae and Leader, *Shifting Sands*, p. 6.
96 Danida and Overseas Development Institute, *Evaluation of Danish Humanitarian Assistance to Sudan, 1992–98*, ch. 4.4.
97 Interview with David Rhoad, Washington DC.
98 The report assigned responsibility for this to DPA's 'nascent Peace-building

Support Unit'. UN, *Report of the Panel on United Nations Peace Operations* (New York: UN, 1999b), p. 40.
99 Macrae, *The New Humanitarianisms,* pp. 6–7.
100 Ibid., p. 9.
101 Similarly, what experiments there had been in integrating humanitarian and political responses in Serbia, Sierra Leone and North Korea did not show that integration or co-ordination could not contribute to peaceful conflict resolution.
102 Paul D. Williams and Alex J. Bellamy, 'The responsibility to protect and the crisis in Darfur', in *Security Dialogue,* vol. 36, no. 1 (2005), p. 40.

CHAPTER 6 Conclusion

1 As the veteran political adviser to Garang and former foreign minister under Nimeiri, Mansour Khalid, put it to the author, 'No, I shouldn't blame them [the mediators]. It is 50 years of conflict, with 200 years behind it.' Interview with Mansour Khalid, Naivasha.
2 I. William Zartman, *Cowardly Lions: Missed Opportunities to Prevent Deadly Conflict and State Collapse* (Boulder, CO: Lynne Rienner, 2005), p. 201.
3 Each option meets at least one of Zartman's four criteria for 'moments of opportunity'. Broadly they also meet more formal criteria for judging counterfactual arguments or proposals, such as the 'minimum re-write' rule. Ibid., p. 9; and Philip E. Tetlock and Aaron Belkin (eds.), *Counterfactual Thought Experiments in World Politics: Logical, Methodological, and Psychological Perspectives* (Princeton: Princeton University Press, 1996), p. 18.
4 See, for example, David Keen, *The Economic Functions of Violence in Civil Wars* (Oxford: Oxford University Press, 1998); Paul Collier and Anke Hoeffler, 'On economic causes of civil war', in *Oxford Economic Papers,* vol. 50, no. 4 (1998); Paul Collier and Anke Hoeffler, *Greed and Grievance in Civil War* (Oxford: Centre for the Study of African Economies, 2002); Karen Ballentine and Jake Sherman (eds.), *The Political Economy of Armed Conflict: Beyond Greed and Grievance* (Boulder, Colorado: Lynne Rienner, 2003); Michael L. Ross, 'How do natural resources influence civil war? Evidence from thirteen cases', in *International Organization,* vol. 58, no. 1 (2004); James D. Fearon, 'Why do some civil wars last so much longer than others?', in *Journal of Peace Research,* vol. 41, no. 3 (2004).
5 To some extent the variation reflects the country's social and political complexity, which tends to defy simplification and produces combinations which may surprise outsiders – such as a conservative Muslim southerner, who is a Nuer woman and member of the PCP, saying 'I am closer to Garang than Bashir. He [Garang] is fighting to liberate Sudan. I am too.' Interview with Haggar Gai Rer, PCP official and former MP for Bentiu (1971–99); Khartoum, 30 March 2004.
6 Interview with Tigani el-Seisi, Umma Party official and former governor of Darfur; London, 5 February 2004.
7 Interview with Ahmed Hussain, London.
8 Interview with Guma Kunda, Khartoum.
9 Interview with Ateem Yac Ateem, journalist and former member of SPLM; Naivasha, Kenya, 20 April 2004.
10 Interview with Balqis Badri, Khartoum.
11 Johnson, *The Root Causes,* p. 180.

12 This point was widely made, by interviewees and by Sudanese more generally. It was even said by one of the government delegation at Naivasha. Interview with Joseph Duer Jakok, Naivasha.
13 Joel Stettenheim, 'The Arusha Accords and the failure of international intervention in Rwanda', in *Words over War: Mediation and Arbitration to Prevent Deadly Conflict*, edited by Greenberg, Barton and McGuiness (Lanham: Rowman & Littlefield, 2000), p. 224.
14 Kathleen Collins, 'Tajikistan: bad peace agreements and prolonged conflict', in *From Promise to Practice: Strengthening UN Capacities for the Prevention of Violent Conflict*, edited by Sriram and Wermester (Boulder, Colorado: Lynne Rienner, 2003), p. 292.
15 George Klay Kieh Jr., 'Liberia: legacies and leaders', in *From Promise to Practice: Strengthening UN Capacities for the Prevention of Violent Conflict*, edited by Sriram and Wermester (Boulder, Colorado: Lynne Rienner, 2003), p.322.
16 As a Tanzanian diplomat, Maundi participated in the talks. Mohammed Omar Maundi, 'Preventing conflict escalation in Burundi', in *From Promise to Practice: Strengthening UN Capacities for the Prevention of Violent Conflict*, edited by Sriram and Wermester (Boulder, Colorado: Lynne Rienner, 2003), p. 346.
17 Richard Barltrop, *The Negotiation of Security Issues in the Burundi Peace Talks* (Geneva: Centre for Humanitarian Dialogue, 2008), pp. 16–21.
18 Tatiana Carayannis and Herbert F. Weiss, 'The Democratic Republic of Congo, 1996–2002', in *Dealing with Conflict in Africa: the United Nations and Regional Organizations*, edited by Boulden (Basingstoke: Palgrave Macmillan, 2003), p. 266, 276 and passim.
19 International Crisis Group, *Biting the Somali Bullet?* (Nairobi/Brussels: ICG, 2004a), p. ii and *passim*.
20 Kieh Jr., 'Liberia: legacies and leaders', p. 322.
21 Stettenheim, 'The Arusha Accords and the failure of international intervention in Rwanda', p. 224.
22 Barbara F. Walter, *Committing to Peace: The Successful Settlement of Civil Wars* (Princeton: Princeton University Press, 2002), pp. 150–52 and 158–59.
23 Maundi, 'Preventing conflict escalation in Burundi', p. 346.
24 Virginia Gamba, 'Managing violence: disarmament and demobilization', in *Contemporary Peacemaking: Conflict, Violence and Peace Processes*, edited by Darby and MacGinty (Basingstoke: Palgrave Macmillan, 2003), pp. 130–31.
25 Collins, 'Tajikistan: bad peace agreements and prolonged conflict', p. 293.
26 Reilly's choice of examples is not convincing, but he is not alone in making this argument. Ben Reilly, 'Democratic validation', in *Contemporary Peacemaking: Conflict, Violence and Peace Processes*, edited by Darby and MacGinty (Basingstoke: Palgrave Macmillan, 2003), pp. 176–77.
27 See for example Adam Roberts, *Humanitarian Action in War: Aid Protection and Impartiality in a Policy Vacuum* (Oxford: Oxford University Press, 1996), p. 80; Kent, 'International humanitarian crises', p. 856; David Rieff, *A Bed for the Night: Humanitarianism in Crisis* (London: Vintage, 2002), p. 131.
28 See for example de Waal (ed.), *Food and Power in Sudan*; de Waal, *Famine Crimes*; and the argument for domestic 'humanitarian accountability' in Alex de Waal (ed.), *Who Fights? Who Cares? War and Humanitarian Action in Africa* (Trenton, NJ: Africa World Press, 2000), pp. 227–39.
29 Zartman, *Cowardly Lions*.
30 Kenneth Menkhaus and Louis Ortmayer, 'Somalia: misread crises and missed opportunities', in *Opportunities Missed, Opportunities Seized: Preventive*

Diplomacy in the Post-Cold War World, edited by Jentleson (Lanham: Rowman and Littlefield, 2000), p. 213.
31 Walter, 'The critical barrier', p. 363.
32 Zartman, *Cowardly Lions*, p. 16.
33 Zartman, *Ripe for Resolution*, p. 276.

APPENDIX

INTERVIEWS BY THE AUTHOR

Abd al-Aziz al-Hilu, SPLM/A commander and delegate at peace talks; Naivasha, Kenya, 14 April 2004

Abd al-Nabi Ali Ahmed, Umma Party secretary-general and former governor of Darfur; Khartoum, 20 March 2004

Abd al-Rahim Ali, academic and member of NCP council who mediated in NCP split in 1999; Khartoum, 31 March 2004

Abdullah Hasan Ahmed, PCP deputy secretary-general and former minister of finance (1993–6); Khartoum, 17 March 2004

Abdel Latif Ismael, SLM/A representative in Britain; London, 19 March 2005

Ahmed Hussain, member of JEM delegation to Darfur peace talks and JEM representative in Britain; London, 19 March 2005

Aldo Ajo Deng, cabinet minister under Sadiq and political adviser to Bashir on peace and dialogue on the south (1989–1993); London, 5 February 2004

Ali Mahmoud Hassanein, DUP secretary-general; Khartoum, 9 March 2004

Anne Itto, SPLM agriculture and natural-resource development adviser and delegate at peace talks; Naivasha, Kenya, 13 April 2004

Anonymous; Khartoum, 29 March and 5 May 2004

Ateem Yac Ateem, journalist and former member of SPLM; Naivasha, Kenya, 20 April 2004

Badr el-Din Suleiman, economic adviser to President Bashir and former minister of finance under Nimeiri; Khartoum, 6 April 2004

Balqis Badri, director of Institute of Women, Gender and Development Studies, Ahfad University, and member of women's delegation to Naivasha talks; Khartoum, 9 March 2004

Busho Ndinyenka, Ugandan diplomat and special envoy for Sudan peace talks; Naivasha, Kenya, 16 April 2004

Christoph Jaeger, former UN and UNDP head for Sudan (1994–8); Juba, Sudan, 26 October 2005

Cirino Hiteng, SPLM/A delegate at peace talks; Naivasha, Kenya, 13 April 2004

Conversations with various UN staff; Khartoum, March and October 2004

David Rhoad, USAID liaison official at US State Department 'Sudan Programs Group'; Washington DC, 30 March 2005

Deng Alor, SPLM/A delegate to peace talks (1989–2004); Naivasha, Kenya, 22 April 2004

Elijah Malok, director of SRRC; Naivasha, Kenya, 13 April 2004

Emmanuel Jay Prakash, official from US-based missionary organisation; Khartoum, 18 October 2004

Faruq Kaduda, Sudan Communist Party member; Khartoum, 13 March 2004

Fatma Ahmed Ibrahim, president of Sudanese Women's Union and former MP; Khartoum, 4 April 2004

George Garang, journalist and editor of SPLM Update; Naivasha, Kenya, 15 April 2004

Ghazi Salah al-Din Atabani, former lead Sudanese government negotiator at peace talks (1994–2003); Khartoum, 4 May 2004

Guma Kunda, Sudanese inter-faith peace activist; Khartoum, 13 March 2004

Hafiz Mohammed, Justice Africa staff member; London, 18 March 2005

Haggar Gai Rer, PCP official and former MP for Bentiu (1971–99); Khartoum, 30 March 2004

Hashim Muhammed Ahmed, member of NDA leadership council and former president of National Union of Engineering and Trades Unions; Oxford, 17 December 2003

Hassan Abdelgadir Hilal, DUP official and businessman; Khartoum, 14 and 20 March 2004

Haydar Ibrahim, director of Sudan Studies Centre and former member of NDA; Khartoum, 6 April 2004

Hussain Musharrafa, former Egyptian ambassador to Sudan (1985–9); Cairo, 11 May 2004

Hussein Abu Saleh, former foreign minister of Sudan (1988 and 1993–5); Khartoum, 7 April 2004

Jake Hamm, UN field co-ordinator for Nuba Mountains and aid worker in Sudan since 1989; Khartoum, 22 October 2004

Jeremiah Swaka, SCC national coordinator for peace and advocacy; Khartoum, 23 March 2004

Jeremy Brickhill, member of IGAD secretariat resource staff for Sudan talks; Naivasha, Kenya, 16 April 2005

John Andruga Duku, SPLM/A representative to the EU and Scandinavia; Naivasha, Kenya, 16 April 2004

Joseph Duer Jakok, Sudanese government delegate at peace talks; Naivasha, Kenya, 16 April 2004

Joseph Lagu, former leader of SSLM and former vice-president for the south under Nimeiri; London, 9 December 2003

Joseph Ukel Abango, secretary-general of NDA and chairman of USAP; Naivasha, Kenya, 19 April 2004

Kjell Hødnebø, representative of Norway at the peace talks in Kenya; Naivasha, Kenya, 20 April 2004

Lam Akol, former leader of SPLM/A breakaway faction and successor groups; Nairobi, 28 April 2004

Lazaro Sumbeiywo, chair of the IGAD peace talks for Sudan (2001–5); Naivasha,

Kenya, 16 April 2004

Mahjoub Mohammed Salih, editor of *Al-Ayaam* newspaper; Khartoum, 11 March 2004

Malik Agar, SPLM/A commander and delegate at peace talks; Naivasha, Kenya, 11 April 2004

Mansour Khalid, senior political adviser to Garang and formerly foreign minister under Nimeiri; Naivasha, Kenya, 12 April 2004

Mansour al-Agab; DUP politician; London, 18 December 2003

Martin Lomuro, chairman of South Sudan Civic Forum; London, 5 February 2004

Maxwell Gaylard, former head of UN OCHA Sudan; Nairobi, 23 April 2004

Member of troika; Naivasha, Kenya, 20 April 2004

Michael Ouko, New Sudan Council of Churches peace advocacy co-ordinator; Nairobi, 29 April 2004

Mohammed el-Amin Khalifa, former government negotiator and PCP official; Khartoum, 16 March 2004

Mohammed Qasim, head of the Sudan desk at the Egyptian Ministry of Foreign Affairs; Cairo, 10 May 2004

Mohammed Zain Osman, DUP political affairs officer; Khartoum, 5 March 2004

Mudawwi Turabi, assistant secretary-general of DUP-Hindi faction; Khartoum, 6 March 2004

Musa al-Mak, PCP assistant secretary-general; Khartoum, 30 March 2004

Nasr Mohammed, Islamic Call Society official and personal secretary to General Sawar al-Dhahab; Khartoum, 5 May 2004

Nhial Bol, Sudanese journalist; Nairobi, 24 April 2004

Nicholas 'Fink' Haysom, member of IGAD secretariat resource staff for Sudan talks; Naivasha, Kenya, 15 April 2004

Pagan Amum, SPLM/A commander and delegate at peace talks and former secretary for trade and aid; Naivasha, Kenya, 14 April 2004

Peter Marwa, member of IGAD secretariat resource staff for Sudan talks; Naivasha, Kenya, 12 April 2004

Peter Nyaba, former captain in the SPLA; Nairobi, 26 April 2004

Riek Machar, former leader of SPLM/A breakaway faction and successor groups; Nairobi, 28 April 2004

Roger Winter, USAID assistant administrator responsible for DCHA bureau; Naivasha, Kenya, 20 April 2004

Sadiq al-Mahdi, Umma Party leader; Khartoum, 15 March 2004

Samson Kwaje, SPLM/A spokesman and delegate at peace talks; Naivasha, Kenya, 12 April 2004

Sayyid el-Khatib, Sudanese government delegate at peace talks and director of Centre for Strategic Studies; Naivasha, Kenya, 12 April 2004

Southern Blue Nile delegation, including Stephen Missa, Elhadi Eltinjour (Chairman of North and South Funj Union), and others; Naivasha, Kenya, 19 April 2004

Suleiman Musa Rahhal, director of Nuba Survival (NGO); London, 18 December 2003

Tigani el-Seisi, Umma Party official and former governor of Darfur; London,

5 February 2004
Various; Rubkona, Unity State, Southern Sudan, 24 March 2004
William, Sudanese oil worker; Khartoum, 29 March 2004
William Patey, British ambassador to Sudan (2002–5); Khartoum, 1 April 2004
Winston Simon, former military police general; Khartoum, 21 March 2004
Yasser Arman, SPLM/A spokesman and delegate at peace talks; Naivasha, Kenya, 11 April 2004

BIBLIOGRAPHY

PRESS AND MEDIA

Africa Confidential (London: Asempa)
BBC Summary of World Broadcasts (Reading: BBC Monitoring)
Integrated Relief Information Networks (IRIN) news briefs: Sudan (UN OCHA)
Al-Inqadh al-Watani (Khartoum, Sudan)
Al-Sudan al-Hadith (Khartoum, Sudan)
International Herald Tribune (Paris, France)
Sudan Times (Khartoum, Sudan)
Sudan United News Agency (Khartoum, Sudan: SUNA)
Washington Post (Washington DC, USA)

DOCUMENTS, REPORTS AND SECONDARY SOURCES

9/11 Commission, *The 9/11 Commission Report: Final Report of the National Commission on Terrorist Attacks upon the United States* (New York: WW Norton, 2004)
Abuelbashar, Abaker Mohamed, 'On the failure of Darfur peace talks in Abuja', *Sudan Tribune*, 25 August 2006
Ali, Hasan Hajj, *'Al-Siyasa al-Kharijiyya l-il-Inqadh tujah Duwal al-Jiwar al-Ifriqi'* ('The Foreign Policy of the Salvation towards Neighbouring African States'), paper read at 'Erkowit conference', at Erkowit, Sudan, 2000
Alier, Abel, *Southern Sudan: Too Many Agreements Dishonoured* (Exeter: Ithaca, 1990)
Amnesty International, *The Human Price of Oil* (New York: Amnesty International, May 2000)
Anderson, G. Norman, *Sudan in Crisis: The Failure of Democracy* (Gainesville: University of Florida Press, 1999)
Applied Science and Analysis Inc., 'Analysis of samples from Sudan', *The ASA Newsletter*, no. 79 (2000)

AU, 'Report of the Chairperson of the Commission on the Situation in the Darfur Region of the Sudan', AU Peace and Security Council document PSC/PR/2(XXVIII), Addis Ababa, 28 April 2005

AU and UN, 'The Chairmen's conclusions from the Arusha consultations', Arusha, Tanzania, 6 August 2007

Ballentine, Karen and Jake Sherman (eds.), *The Political Economy of Armed Conflict: Beyond Greed and Grievance* (Boulder, Colorado: Lynne Rienner, 2003)

Barltrop, Richard, *The Negotiation of Security Issues in the Burundi Peace Talks*, Country Study no. 1 (Geneva: Centre for Humanitarian Dialogue, 2008)

BBC, '"Never Again"', edited transcript of interview with John Danforth, Panorama television programme, 3 July 2005

Beshir, Mohamed Omer, *The Southern Sudan: From Conflict to Peace* (London: C. Hurst, 1975)

Bleuchot, Hervé, Christian Delmet and Derek Hopwood (eds.), *Sudan: History, Identity, Ideology* (Reading: Ithaca Press, 1991)

Bowyer Bell, J., 'The Sudan's Africa policy: problems and prospects', *Africa Today*, vol. 20, no. 3 (1973)

Boyce, James K., *Investing in Peace: Aid and Conditionality after Civil Wars*, Adelphi Paper no. 351 (Oxford: Oxford University Press, 2002)

Bradbury, M., 'Normalising the crisis in Africa', *Disasters*, vol. 22, no. 4 (1998)

Bradbury, Mark, Nicholas Leader and Kate Mackintosh, *The 'Agreement on Ground Rules' in South Sudan*, Humanitarian Policy Group report no. 4 (London: Overseas Development Institute, March 2000)

Brickhill, Jeremy, *Protecting Civilians through Peace Agreements: Challenges and Lessons of the Darfur Peace Agreement*, ISS paper no. 138 (Pretoria: Institute for Security Studies, May 2007)

Brown, Michael E. (ed.), *The International Dimensions of Internal Conflict* (Cambridge: MIT Press, 1996)

Brusset, Emery, 'Sudan's foreign policy environment: some implications for humanitarian assistance', in *The Wider Impact of Humanitarian Assistance: The Case of Sudan and the Implications for European Union Policy*, edited by G. Loane and T. Schümer (Baden-Baden: Nomos Verlagsgesellschaft, 2000)

Burr, Millard, *Quantifying Genocide in the Southern Sudan, 1983–1993*, working paper (Washington DC: US Committee for Refugees, 1993)

---, *Quantifying Genocide in Southern Sudan and the Nuba Mountains, 1983–1998*, working paper (Washington DC: US Committee for Refugees, 1998)

Burr, Millard and Robert O. Collins, *Requiem for the Sudan: War, Drought, and Disaster Relief on the Nile* (Boulder: Westview, 1995)

Carayannis, Tatiana and Herbert F. Weiss, 'The Democratic Republic of Congo, 1996–2002', in *Dealing with Conflict in Africa: the United Nations and Regional Organizations*, edited by J. Boulden (Basingstoke: Palgrave Macmillan, 2003)

CARE, Christian Aid, International Rescue Committee (IRC), Oxfam et al., *The Key to Peace: Unlocking the Human Potential of Sudan*, inter-agency paper (London: CARE et al., May 2002)

Center for Strategic and International Studies, *US Policy to End Sudan's War: Report*

of the CSIS Task Force on US–Sudan Policy (Washington: CSIS, February 2001)
Christian Aid, *The Scorched Earth: Oil and War in Sudan* (London: Christian Aid, March 2001)
Civilian Protection Monitoring Team, 'CPMT Final Report: Military Events in Western Upper Nile, 31 December 2002 to 30 January 2003', Khartoum, Sudan, 2003
Clapham, Christopher S., *Africa and the International System: The Politics of State Survival* (Cambridge: Cambridge University Press, 1996)
Cohen, Herman J., *Intervening in Africa: Superpower Peacemaking in a Troubled Continent* (Basingstoke: Macmillan, 2000)
Collier, Paul and Anke Hoeffler, 'On economic causes of civil war', *Oxford Economic Papers,* vol. 50, no. 4 (1998)
---, *Greed and Grievance in Civil War,* CSAE Working Paper (Oxford: Centre for the Study of African Economies, 2002)
Collins, Kathleen, 'Tajikistan: bad peace agreements and prolonged conflict', in *From Promise to Practice: Strengthening UN Capacities for the Prevention of Violent Conflict,* edited by C. L. Sriram and K. Wermester (Boulder, Colorado: Lynne Rienner, 2003)
Danforth, John C., *Report to the President of the United States on the Outlook for Peace in Sudan,* report from John C. Danforth, Special Envoy for Peace in Sudan (Washington DC 26 April 2002)
Danida and Overseas Development Institute, *Evaluation of Danish Humanitarian Assistance to Sudan,* 1992–98 (Copenhagen: Ministry of Foreign Affairs / Danida, 1999)
de Waal, Alex, 'Starving out the South', in *Civil War in the Sudan,* edited by M. W. Daly and A. A. Sikainga (London: British Academic Press, 1992)
---, *Famine Crimes: Politics and the Disaster Relief Industry in Africa* (Oxford: James Currey, 1997a)
--- (ed.), *Food and Power in Sudan: A Critique of Humanitarianism* (London: African Rights, 1997b)
--- (ed.), *Who Fights? Who Cares? War and Humanitarian Action in Africa* (Trenton, NJ: Africa World Press, 2000)
--- (ed.), *Islamism and its Enemies in the Horn of Africa* (London: Hurst, 2004)
---, *Famine that Kills: Darfur, Sudan,* revised edn. (Oxford: Oxford University Press, 2005)
---, '"I will not sign"', *London Review of Books,* 30 November 2006
Deng, Francis Mading, *War of Visions: Conflict of Identities in the Sudan* (Washington DC: Brookings Institution, 1995)
Department for International Development (DFID), 'Sudan: Country Engagement Plan', London, 2004
Department for International Development (DFID), Foreign and Commonwealth Office (FCO) and Ministry of Defence (MOD), *The Global Conflict Prevention Pool: A Joint UK Government Approach to Reducing Conflict* (London: FCO, August 2003)
Duffield, Mark, *'Humanitarian conditionality: origins, consequences and implications*

of the pursuit of development in conflict', in *The Wider Impact of Humanitarian Assistance: The Case of Sudan and the Implications for European Union Policy*, edited by G. Loane and T. Schümer (Baden-Baden: Nomos Verlagsgesellschaft, 2000)

Duffield, Mark, Jok Madut Jok, David Keen, Geoff Loane et al., *Sudan: Unintended Consequences of Humanitarian Assistance*, field evaluation study for the European Commission Humanitarian Affairs Office (Dublin: Trinity College, University of Dublin, April 2000)

Economist Intelligence Unit, *Country Profile: Sudan, 1986–87* (London: EIU, 1986)

---, *Country Report: Sudan, June 2002* (London: EIU, 2002)

---, *Country Profile: Sudan, 2004* (London: EIU, 2004a)

---, *Country Report: Sudan, March 2004* (London: EIU, 2004b)

el-Affendi, Abdelwahab, 'The impasse in the IGAD peace process for Sudan: the limits of regional peacemaking?', *African Affairs*, vol. 100, no. 401 (2001)

Eprile, Cecil, *War and Peace in the Sudan, 1955–1972* (Newton Abbot: David & Charles, 1974)

European Coalition on Oil in Sudan, 'Statement of background', 2001, www.ecosonline.org/back/history.html (accessed on 20 January 2004)

Fearon, James D., 'Why do some civil wars last so much longer than others?', *Journal of Peace Research*, vol. 41, no. 3 (2004)

Flint, Julie and Alex de Waal, *Darfur: A Short History of a Long War* (London: Zed Books, 2005)

Gamba, Virginia, 'Managing violence: disarmament and demobilization', in *Contemporary Peacemaking: Conflict, Violence and Peace Processes,* edited by J. Darby and R. MacGinty (Basingstoke: Palgrave Macmillan, 2003)

Garang, John, *John Garang Speaks*, edited and introduced by Mansour Khalid (London: Kegan Paul, 1987)

---, *The Call for Democracy in Sudan*, 2nd edn., edited by Mansour Khalid (London: Kegan Paul International, 1992)

Government of Kenya, 'Agreement on Operation Lifeline Sudan (OLS) Corridors for Relief Supplies and Humanitarian Assistance to War Affected Areas', Nairobi, 17 May 1994a

---, 'Relief Supplies and Humanitarian Assistance to the War Affected Areas', Nairobi, 23 March 1994b

Government of Sudan, 'The Attitude of the Government Delegation towards the SPLM-Main Stream Proposal', Nairobi, November 1997

---, 'Updated Sudan Government Position', Nairobi, May 1998

---, *Al-Taqrir al-Istratigi al-Sudani, 1999* ('The Sudan Strategic Report, 1999') (Khartoum: Centre for Strategic Studies, 1999)

Government of Sudan, SLM/A and JEM, 'Humanitarian Ceasefire Agreement on the Conflict in Darfur', N'djamena, Chad, 8 April 2004

Government of Sudan and SPLM/A, 'Machakos Protocol', Machakos, Kenya, 20 July 2002a

---, 'Memorandum of Understanding on Cessation of Hostilities', Kenya, 15 October 2002b

---, 'Nuba Mountains Cease-Fire Agreement', Bürgenstock, Switzerland, 19 January 2002c

Government of Sudan and SSIM/A, 'Political Charter', Khartoum, 10 April 1996

Government of Sudan and UDSF, 'Sudan Peace Agreement', Khartoum, 21 April 1997

Guha-Sapir, Debarati and Olivier Degomme, *Darfur: Counting the Deaths. Mortality Estimates from Multiple Survey Data*, Centre for Research on the Epidemiology of Disasters (CRED) report (Brussels: University of Louvain, May 2005)

Harker, John, *Human Security in Sudan: The Report of a Canadian Assessment Mission*, report prepared for the Canadian Department of Foreign Affairs and International Trade (Ottawa January 2000)

Human Rights Watch, *Sudan, Oil, and Human Rights* (New York: HRW, 2003)

IGAD, 'The Proceedings of the Summit of Heads of State and Government of IGAD Member States for the Launching of Revitalized IGAD', Djibouti, 25–26 November 1996

---, 'Proceedings of the 6th Ordinary IGAD Summit of Heads of State and Government', Djibouti, 16 March 1998

---, 'Declaration of the 7th IGAD Summit of Heads of State and Government', Djibouti, 26 November 1999

---, 'Proceedings of the 8th Ordinary IGAD Summit of Heads of State and Government', Djibouti, November 2000a

---, 'Resolution on the Sudan Peace Process', Khartoum, 23 November 2000b

---, 'Proceedings of the 9th Summit of the Assembly of Heads of State and Government of IGAD', Khartoum, 10–11 January 2002

IGAD Ministerial Subcommittee, 'Communiqué issued at Addis Ababa on 7 August 1998', Addis Ababa, 7 August 1998a

---, 'Communiqué issued in Nairobi on 6 May 1998', Nairobi, 6 May 1998b

IGAD Partners Forum, 'First Ministerial Meeting of the Joint IGAD Partners Forum', Rome, 19–20 January 1998

---, *Facing up to the Realities of Future Peace: First Outline of the Integrated Planning for Peace (PfP) Framework*, three-volume report produced for the IPF (Rome: IPF, March 2002)

International Crisis Group, *Capturing the Moment: Sudan's Peace Process in the Balance*, ICG Africa Report no. 42 (Nairobi/Brussels: ICG, 3 April 2002a)

---, *Ending Starvation as a Weapon of War in Sudan*, ICG Africa Report no. 54 (Nairobi/Brussels: ICG, 14 November 2002b)

---, *God, Oil and Country: Changing the Logic of War in Sudan,* ICG Africa Report no. 39 (Nairobi/Brussels: ICG, 28 January 2002c)

---, *Sudan: Towards an Incomplete Peace,* ICG Africa Report no. 73 (Nairobi/Brussels: ICG, 11 December 2003)

---, *Biting the Somali Bullet?*, ICG Africa Report no. 79 (Nairobi/Brussels: ICG, 4 May 2004a)

---, *Darfur Rising: Sudan's New Crisis*, ICG Africa Report no. 76 (Nairobi/Brussels: ICG, 25 March 2004b)

---, *Darfur: Revitalising the Peace Process*, ICG Africa Report no. 125 (Nairobi/Brussels: ICG, 30 April 2007)

Johnson, Douglas H., *The Root Causes of Sudan's Civil Wars* (Oxford: James Currey, 2003)

Joint Military Commission, 'Facts and figures', information on the JMC in the Nuba Mountains, including data on ceasefire violations, www.jmc.nu/en/0302.htm (accessed on 23 October 2004)

---, 'The Nuba Mountains Experience', report by Brigadier General Jan Erik Wilhelmsen, Chairman of the JMC, in 2004, www.jmc.nu/en/0301.htm (accessed on 23 October 2004)

Karim, Ataul, Mark Duffield, Susanne Jaspars, Aldo Benini et al., *Operation Lifeline Sudan (OLS): A Review* (Geneva: UN Department of Humanitarian Affairs, July 1996)

Keen, David, *The Benefits of Famine: A Political Economy of Famine and Relief in Southwestern Sudan, 1983–1989* (Princeton: Princeton University Press, 1994)

---, *The Economic Functions of Violence in Civil Wars*, Adelphi Paper no. 320 (Oxford: Oxford University Press, 1998)

Kent, Randolph C., 'International humanitarian crises: two decades before and two decades beyond', *International Affairs*, vol. 80, no. 5 (2004)

Kevane, Michael and Leslie Gray, 'Darfur: rainfall and conflict', *Environmental Research Letters*, no. 3 (2008)

Khalid, Mansour, *War and Peace in Sudan: A Tale of Two Countries* (London: Kegan Paul, 2003)

Khalifa, Mohammed el-Amin, *Ten Years of Peace Making in Sudan, 1989–1999: Documents and Facts*. Translated by G. G. A. el-Julla (Khartoum: COFPA, 2003)

Kieh Jr., George Klay, 'Liberia: legacies and leaders', in *From Promise to Practice: Strengthening UN Capacities for the Prevention of Violent Conflict*, edited by C. L. Sriram and K. Wermester (Boulder, Colorado: Lynne Rienner, 2003)

Kleiboer, Marieke, 'Understanding success and failure of international mediation', *Journal of Conflict Resolution*, vol. 40, no. 2 (1996)

Large, Dan, 'From non-interference to constructive engagement? China's evolving relations with Sudan', in *China Returns to Africa: A Rising Power and a Continent Embrace*, edited by C. Alden, D. Large and R. Soares de Oliveira (London: Hurst, 2008)

Lesch, Ann Mosely, 'Sudan's foreign policy: in search of arms, aid and allies', in *Sudan: State and Society in Crisis*, edited by J. O. Voll (Bloomington, Ind.: Indiana University Press, 1991)

---, *The Sudan: Contested National Identities* (Bloomington: Indiana University Press, 1998)

Licklider, Roy E., 'The consequences of negotiated settlements in civil wars, 1945–1993', *American Political Science Review*, vol. 89, no. 3 (1995)

Loane, Geoff and Tanja Schümer (eds.), *The Wider Impact of Humanitarian Assistance: The Case of Sudan and the Implications for European Union Policy* (Baden-Baden: Nomos Verlagsgesellschaft, 2000)

MacFarlane, S. Neil, *Humanitarian Action: The Conflict Connection*, Thomas J.

Watson Jr. Institute for International Studies and the United Nations University Occasional Paper no. 43 (Providence RI: Watson Institute, 2000)

Macrae, Joanna, *The New Humanitarianisms: A Review of Global Trends in Humanitarian Action*, Humanitarian Policy Group report no. 11 (London: Overseas Development Institute, April 2002)

Macrae, Joanna, Susanne Jaspars, Mark Duffield, Mark Bradbury et al., 'Conflict, the continuum and chronic emergencies: a critical analysis of the scope for linking relief, rehabilitation and development planning in Sudan', *Disasters*, vol. 21, no. 3 (1997)

Macrae, Joanna and Nicholas Leader, *Shifting Sands: The Search for 'Coherence' between Political and Humanitarian Responses to Complex Emergencies*, Humanitarian Policy Group report no. 8 (London: Overseas Development Institute, August 2000)

Mamdani, Mahmood, *Saviors and Survivors: Darfur, Politics, and the War on Terror* (London: Verso, 2008)

Maundi, Mohammed Omar, 'Preventing conflict escalation in Burundi', in *From Promise to Practice: Strengthening UN Capacities for the Prevention of Violent Conflict*, edited by C. L. Sriram and K. Wermester (Boulder, Colorado: Lynne Rienner, 2003)

Medley, Michael, 'Humanitarian assistance in Sudan: a chronological analysis of shifting mandates', in *The Wider Impact of Humanitarian Assistance: The Case of Sudan and the Implications for European Union Policy*, edited by G. Loane and T. Schümer (Baden-Baden: Nomos Verlagsgesellschaft, 2000)

Menkhaus, Kenneth and Louis Ortmayer, 'Somalia: misread crises and missed opportunities', in *Opportunities Missed, Opportunities Seized: Preventive Diplomacy in the Post-Cold War World*, edited by B. W. Jentleson (Lanham: Rowman and Littlefield, 2000)

Minear, Larry, 'Time to pull the plug on Operation Lifeline Sudan?', *Crosslines Global Report* (1997)

Minear, Larry and Thomas G. Weiss, *Mercy under Fire: War and the Global Humanitarian Community* (Boulder: Westview, 1995)

Nathan, Laurie, *No Ownership, No Peace: The Darfur Peace Agreement*, Crisis States Research Centre working paper no. 5 (London: LSE, September 2006)

Nyaba, Peter Adwok, *The Politics of Liberation in South Sudan: An Insider's View* (Kampala, Uganda: Fountain Publishers, 1997)

O'Ballance, Edgar, *The Secret War in the Sudan, 1955–1972* (London: Faber, 1977)

---, *Sudan: Civil War and Terrorism, 1956–99* (Basingstoke: Macmillan Press, 2000)

O'Fahey, R. S., *The Darfur Sultanate: A History* (London: Hurst, 2008)

Petterson, Don, *Inside Sudan: Political Islam, Conflict, and Catastrophe*, 2nd (revised and updated) edn. (Boulder: Westview, 2003)

Prunier, Gérard, 'Rebel movements and proxy warfare: Uganda, Sudan and the Congo (1986–99)', *African Affairs*, vol. 103, no. 412 (2004)

---, *Darfur: The Ambiguous Genocide* (London: Hurst, 2005)

Randel, Judith and Tony German, 'Trends in the financing of humanitarian assistance', in *The New Humanitarianisms: A Review of Global Trends in*

Humanitarian Action, edited by J. Macrae (London: Overseas Development Institute, 2002)

Reilly, Ben, 'Democratic validation', in *Contemporary Peacemaking: Conflict, Violence and Peace Processes*, edited by J. Darby and R. MacGinty (Basingstoke: Palgrave Macmillan, 2003)

Rieff, David, *A Bed for the Night: Humanitarianism in Crisis* (London: Vintage, 2002)

Roberts, Adam, *Humanitarian Action in War: Aid Protection and Impartiality in a Policy Vacuum*, Adelphi Paper no. 305 (Oxford: Oxford University Press, 1996)

Rose, David, 'The Osama files', *Vanity Fair*, January 2002, pp. 50–56

Ross, Michael L., 'How do natural resources influence civil war? Evidence from thirteen cases', *International Organization*, vol. 58, no. 1 (2004)

Save Darfur Coalition, *Annual Report 2008* (Washington DC: SDC, 2008)

SLM/A and JEM, 'Joint Statement', Abuja, 14 April 2006

Smith, Gayle, 'George Bush in Khartoum', *MERIP Reports*, no. 135, 'Sudan's Revolutionary Spring' (1985)

SPLM/A, 'Resolutions of the SPLM/SPLA Torit Conference, 1991', Sudan, SPLM/A 1991

Srinivasan, Sharath, *Minority Rights, Early Warning and Conflict Prevention: Lessons from Darfur*, Minority Rights Group micro study (London: Minority Rights Group, September 2006)

Stedman, Stephen J., 'Negotiation and mediation in internal conflict', in *The International Dimensions of Internal Conflict*, edited by M. E. Brown (Cambridge: MIT Press, 1996)

---, 'Spoiler problems in peace processes', *International Security*, vol. 22, no. 2 (1997)

Stettenheim, Joel, 'The Arusha Accords and the failure of international intervention in Rwanda', in *Words over War: Mediation and Arbitration to Prevent Deadly Conflict*, edited by M. C. Greenberg, J. H. Barton and M. E. McGuiness (Lanham: Rowman & Littlefield, 2000)

Stoddard, Abby, 'Trends in US humanitarian policy', in *The New Humanitarianisms: A Review of Trends in Global Humanitarian Action*, edited by J. Macrae (London: ODI, 2002)

Tetlock, Philip E. and Aaron Belkin (eds.), *Counterfactual Thought Experiments in World Politics: Logical, Methodological, and Psychological Perspectives* (Princeton: Princeton University Press, 1996)

UK International Development Committee, 'Darfur, Sudan: Crisis, Response and Lessons', minutes of evidence taken before the House of Commons International Development Committee, 21 December 2004 (London: The Stationery Office, 2004)

---, 'Darfur, Sudan: Crisis, Response and Lessons', minutes of evidence taken before the House of Commons International Development Committee, 23 February 2005 (London: The Stationery Office, 2005a)

---, 'Darfur, Sudan: Crisis, Response and Lessons', minutes of evidence taken before the House of Commons International Development Committee, 22 February 2005 (London: The Stationery Office, 2005b)

UK Minister of State for Defence Procurement, 'Regarding the testing of Sudan samples at the Chemical and Biological Defence Agency', letter to the President of CSI, Baroness Cox, from the UK Minister of State for Defence Procurement, Baroness Symons, 5 June 2000

Umma Party, 'Message to Co-Chairman and Honorable Members of IPF Conference', Rome, 18 October 1999

UN, 'Situation of Refugees in the Sudan: Report of the Secretary-General', New York, 8 April 1986

---, 'Emergency Assistance to the Sudan: Summary of Urgent Humanitarian Requirements. Report of the Secretary-General', New York, 27 October 1988a

---, 'Situation of Refugees in the Sudan: Report of the Secretary-General', New York, 29 August 1988b

---, 'Emergency Assistance to the Sudan: Operation Lifeline Sudan. Report of the Secretary-General', New York, 27 September 1989a

---, 'Plan of Action: Sudan Emergency Relief Operations', Khartoum, 14 March 1989b

---, 'Operation Lifeline Sudan: Draft Plan of Action', Khartoum, 28 March 1990

---, 'Emergency Assistance to the Sudan: Report of the Secretary-General', New York, 12 September 1994a

---, 'Situation of Human Rights in the Sudan', A/49/539, interim report prepared by Gaspar Biro (Special Rapporteur of the UN Human Rights Commission), New York, 19 October 1994b

---, 'Emergency Assistance to the Sudan: Report of the Secretary-General', New York, 22 September 1995

---, 'Emergency Assistance to the Sudan: Report of the Secretary-General', New York, 4 September 1996

---, 'Emergency Assistance to the Sudan: Report of the Secretary-General', New York, 24 October 1997

---, 'Emergency Assistance to the Sudan: Report of the Secretary-General', New York, 4 September 1998

---, 'Emergency Assistance to the Sudan: Report of the Secretary-General', New York, 31 August 1999a

---, *Report of the Panel on United Nations Peace Operations* (New York: UN, 1999b)

---, 'Humanitarian Assistance to the Sudan: Report of the Secretary-General', New York, 27 September 2001

---, 'Situation of Human Rights in the Sudan', New York, 20 August 2002

---, *Darfur Humanitarian Profile no. 7* (Khartoum: Office of the UN Resident and Humanitarian Co-ordinator, October 2004)

---, *Darfur Humanitarian Profile no. 10* (Khartoum: Office of the UN Resident and Humanitarian Co-ordinator, January 2005a)

---, 'Monthly Report of the Secretary-General on Darfur', S/2005/825, New York, 23 December 2005b

---, 'Monthly Report of the Secretary-General on Darfur', S/2005/240, New York, 12 April 2005c

---, *Report of the International Commission of Inquiry on Darfur to the United Nations Secretary-General* (Geneva: UN, 25 January 2005d)

---, 'Report of the Secretary-General on the Sudan Pursuant to Paragraphs 6, 13 and 16 of Security Council Resolution 1556 (2004), Paragraph 15 of Security Council Resolution 1564 (2004) and Paragraph 17 of Security Council Resolution 1574 (2004)', S/2005/68, New York, 4 February 2005e

---, 'Monthly Report of the Secretary-General on Darfur', S/2006/870, New York, 8 November 2006a

---, 'Monthly Report of the Secretary-General on Darfur', S/2006/430, New York, 21 June 2006b

---, 'Report of the Panel of Experts Established Pursuant to Paragraph 3 of Resolution 1591 (2005) Concerning the Sudan', S/2006/65, New York, January 2006c

---, 'Report of the Secretary-General on the Deployment of the African Union–United Nations Hybrid Operation in Darfur', S/2007/759, New York, 24 December 2007

---, 'Report of the Secretary-General on the Deployment of the African Union–United Nations Hybrid Operation in Darfur', S/2008/781, New York, 12 December 2008

---, 'Report of the Secretary-General on the Deployment of the African Union–United Nations Hybrid Operation in Darfur', S/2009/201, New York, 14 April 2009

UN Country Team Sudan, *The Common Country Assessment for the Sudan*, 1999 (Sudan: UN, 1999)

UN Office for the Coordination of Humanitarian Affairs, *Consolidated UN Inter-Agency Appeal for Sudan, January–December 1996* (Geneva: UN OCHA, 1995)

---, *Consolidated Inter-Agency Appeal 2003: Sudan* (Geneva: UN OCHA, 2002)

---, *Sudan 2004: Consolidated Appeal for the Sudan Assistance Programme* (Geneva: UN OCHA, November 2003a)

---, *Sudan: Mid-year Review* (Geneva/New York: UN OCHA, May 2003b)

---, *United Nations and Partners 2005 Work Plan for the Sudan* (Geneva: UN OCHA, 2004)

---, *United Nations and Partners 2006 Work Plan for Sudan* (Geneva: UN OCHA, 2005)

---, *United Nations and Partners 2008 Work Plan for Sudan* (Geneva: UN OCHA, 2007)

---, *United Nations and Partners 2009 Work Plan for Sudan* (Geneva: UN OCHA, 2008)

UN Resident Co-ordinator in Sudan, *Annual Report 2000* (Khartoum: Office of the UN RC in Sudan, 2001)

UN Security Council, 'Resolution 1556', New York, 30 July 2004a

---, 'Resolution 1564', New York, 18 September 2004b

---, 'Resolution 1590', New York, 24 March 2005

UNICEF, 'Country Note: Sudan', New York, 20 November 2000

US Agency for International Development, 'Interim Strategic Plan for Sudan,

2004–2006', Washington DC, June 2003
US Commission on International Religious Freedom, *Annual Report 2000* (Washington DC: US CIRF, May 2000)
US Congress, 'Emergency Famine Relief Needs in Ethiopia and Sudan', hearing before the Subcommittee on Africa of the Committee on Foreign Affairs, House of Representatives, 99th Congress, first session, 19 September 1985 (Washington DC: US GPO, 1985)
---, 'Ethiopia and Sudan: Warfare, Politics, and Famine', hearing before the Select Committee on Hunger, House of Representatives, 100th Congress, second session, 14 July 1988 (Washington DC: US GPO, 1988)
---, 'Politics of Hunger in the Sudan', joint hearing before the Select Committee on Hunger and the Subcommittee on Africa of the Committee on Foreign Affairs, House of Representatives, 101st Congress, first session, 2 March 1989 (Washington DC: US GPO, 1989)
---, 'Impending Famine and Recent Political Developments in the Sudan', hearing before the Subcommittee on Africa of the Committee on Foreign Affairs, House of Representatives, 101st Congress, second session, 25 October 1990 (Washington DC: US GPO, 1990)
---, 'The Crisis in Sudan', hearing before the Subcommittee on Africa of the Committee on International Relations, House of Representatives, 104th Congress, first session, 22 March 1995 (Washington DC: US GPO, 1995)
---, 'Terrorism and Sudan', hearing before the Subcommittee on African Affairs of the Committee on Foreign Relations, United States Senate, 105th Congress, first session, 15 May 1997 (Washington DC: US GPO, 1997)
---, 'Crimes against Humanity in Sudan', joint hearing before the Subcommittee on International Operations and Human Rights and Subcommittee on Africa, 106th Congress, 27 May 1999 (Washington DC: US GPO, 1999)
---, 'House Resolution 2906: To Facilitate Famine Relief Efforts and a Comprehensive Solution to the War in Sudan', mark-up before the Sub-committee on Africa of the Committee on Foreign Relations, 106th Congress, first session (Washington DC: US GPO, 2000)
---, 'America's Sudan Policy: A New direction?', joint hearing before House Committee on International Relations, Subcommittee on Africa and Subcommittee on International Operations and Human Rights, 28 March 2001 (Washington DC: US GPO, 2001)
---, 'Implementing US Policy in Sudan', hearing before the Subcommittee on African Affairs of the Committee on Foreign Relations, 107th Congress (Washington DC: US GPO, 2002)
---, 'The Crisis in Darfur: A New Front in Sudan's Bloody War', hearing and mark-up before the Committee on International Relations, House of Representatives, 108th Congress, second session (Washington DC: US GPO, 2004a)
---, 'Sudan: Peace Agreement Around the Corner?', hearing before the Subcommittee on Africa of the Committee on International Relations, House of Representatives, 108th Congress, second session (Washington DC: US GPO, 2004b)
US Congressional Research Service, *Sudan: Humanitarian Crisis, Peace Talks, Terrorism, and US Policy,* Congressional Research Service (CRS) issue brief

(Washington DC: CRS, May 2002)

---, *Sudan: Humanitarian Crisis, Peace Talks, Terrorism, and US Policy*, Congressional Research Service (CRS) issue brief (Washington DC: CRS, September 2004)

---, *Sudan: Economic Sanctions*, Congressional Research Service (CRS) report for Congress (Washington DC: CRS, October 2005)

US Government Accountability Office (GAO), *Darfur Crisis: Death Estimates Demonstrate Severity of Crisis, but Their Accuracy and Credibility Could be Enhanced*, report to congressional requesters (Washington DC: GAO, November 2006)

US Library of Congress Federal Research Division, *Sudan: A Country Study* (Washington DC: Library of Congress, June 1991)

Verney, Peter, *Raising the Stakes: Oil and Conflict in Sudan* (Hebden Bridge, England: Sudan Update, December 1999)

Walter, Barbara F., 'The critical barrier to civil war settlement', *International Organization*, vol. 51, no. 3 (1997)

---, *Committing to Peace: The Successful Settlement of Civil Wars* (Princeton: Princeton University Press, 2002)

Walter, Barbara F. and Jack L. Snyder (eds.), *Civil Wars, Insecurity, and Intervention* (New York: Columbia University Press, 1999)

Williams, Paul D. and Alex J. Bellamy, 'The responsibility to protect and the crisis in Darfur', *Security Dialogue*, vol. 36, no. 1 (2005)

Wondu, Steven and Ann Mosely Lesch, *Battle for Peace in Sudan: An Analysis of the Abuja Conferences, 1992–1993* (Lanham: University Press of America, 2000)

Woodward, Peter (ed.), *Sudan after Nimeiri* (London: Routledge, 1991)

---, *The Horn of Africa: Politics and International Relations*, 2nd edn. (London: I.B. Tauris, 2003)

World Food Programme, *WFP in Sudan: Emergency Food Assistance to War and Drought Affected Populations – Monthly Overview* (Khartoum: WFP, December 1998)

---, *Full Report of the Evaluation of EMOP 10339.0/1: Assistance to Populations Affected by Conflict in Greater Darfur, West Sudan*, a report from the Office of Evaluation (Rome: WFP, December 2006)

Young, Helen and Daniel Maxwell, *Targeting in Complex Emergencies: Darfur Case Study* (Medford, MA: Feinstein International Center, April 2009)

Young, John, *The Eastern Front and the Struggle Against Marginalization*, Sudan Human Security Baseline Assessment working paper no. 3 (Geneva: Small Arms Survey, May 2007)

Zartman, I. William, *Ripe for Resolution: Conflict and Intervention in Africa*, updated edn. (Oxford: Oxford University Press, 1989)

---, *Cowardly Lions: Missed Opportunities to Prevent Deadly Conflict and State Collapse* (Boulder, CO: Lynne Rienner, 2005)

INDEX

Abu Saleh, Hussein 38
Abuelbashar, Abaker Mohamed 63–4
Abuja peace conferences
   civil war 5, 40–43, 139
   Darfur 62–4
Abyei 34, 46–7, 54, 144
Action Contre la Faim 81
Addis Ababa Agreement (1972) 4, 16–19, 140
Africa, front-line states 114, 116
African Union (AU)
   AMIS 33, 34, 66, 127, 133, 135
   UNAMID 34, 66, 133, 135
   see also Abuja peace conferences
aid see development aid; military aid; relief aid
airlifts, Operation Rainbow 72
Akol, Lam 27, 40, 45–6, 75, 78
Al-Shifa bombing 116–17
Albright, Madeleine 117
Algeria 111
Ali, Mutrif Siddig 53
Alier, Abel 16, 18
AMIS (African Union Mission in Sudan) 33, 34, 66, 127, 133, 135
Amum, Pagan 142
Angola 178, 179
Anyanya 15–16, 17, 19, 84, 91
Arab League 48
Arab states 23–4, 114–15
Arab-African divide 13–14
Arabisation 30, 31, 110–111, 113
Atabani, Ghazi Salah al-Din 42, 44, 124, 142
Aweil 82, 87

Babangida, Ibrahim 40, 42

Badri, Balqis 141
Bahr el-Ghazal
   famine 27, 87
   fighting in 21, 28
   flight bans 81, 87, 95
   security incidents 80
Barre, Mohammed Siad 179
al-Bashir, Omar
   9/11 attacks 124
   autocratic government 29
   ICC charges against 66, 99, 134
   Islamist ideology 110
   OLS relief operations 75–6
   peace talks 25, 36–7, 38–40, 57
   takes power 20
Bassolé, Djibril 66
Baum, Gerhart 145–6
Beja Congress 26, 30, 58, 67
Belgium 179
Benn, Hilary 63, 145
Beshir, Mohamed Omer 17
Biafran war 8
bin Laden, Osama 8, 50, 111, 113, 115, 116, 124
Biro, Gaspar 28
Black Book, The 31–2
Blue Nile 21, 26, 54, 144
Bol, Kerubino Kuanyin 45, 86–7
Bolad, Daud 26
Boma 21
Bor 19, 21, 81, 82
Bosnia 163
Bradbury, Mark 154
Brickhill, Jeremy 64
Britain
   debt relief 129
   Global Conflict Prevention Pool 9

IPF/troika member 52
peace processes 127, 130, 144, 145
relief aid 120
sanctions 114
Sudan Unit policy co-ordination 129, 165, 185
Burr, Millard 75, 77, 83
Burundi 177, 178, 179
Bush, George W. 122

Cameroun 98
Canada, oil 118
Care International 88
Carlos the Jackal 111, 113
Carter peace initiative (1989) 5, 36–8, 76
Caryannis, Tatiana 177
ceasefire agreements
  allowed troop redeployment 55, 162–3
  civil war 41–2, 85, 87
  Darfur 58, 62, 127
  Nuba Mountains 50, 53–4, 55, 131, 161–2
  Southern Sudan, violations 55–6, 60
Chad
  agreements with Sudan 66
  conflict in 31, 134
  Darfurian refugees 31, 32, 97
  Libyan war 105, 109
  peace talks in 34–5, 58
Cheek, James 120
Chevron 104
children 55–6, 79
China 110, 128, 131, 132, 185, 188
China National Petroleum Corporation (CNPC) 117
Christian Aid 60
Christian charities 88
Christian Solidarity International 117
Christianity 14
civil wars
  background 4–5, 13–15
  costs, human and economic 17, 21–2, 27–8
  duration, reasons for 172–4
  economic dimensions 173
  first 15–16
  international comparisons 175–80

international dimensions 3
  as *jihad* 29
  Nuer civil war 46
  second 20–21, 26–7
civilian killings 27–8, 32–3, 56
Civilian Protection Monitoring Team (CPMT) 55–6
clientelism 103–5, 108–9, 179
Cohen, Herman 5, 38–9, 108, 111–12
Collins, Kathleen 176
Collins, Robert 75, 77, 83
Comprehensive Peace Agreement (CPA)
  exclusions 183
  implementation 34, 134–5
  international support for 134–5, 169
  liberal peace provisions 187
  progress towards 174–5
  prospects for 6, 61, 180–81, 188
  signature 1, 54
  see also Kenya peace talks (2002-5)
conflict resolution
  conditions for success 62, 68, 177–8, 183, 188
  grassroots 10, 163, 186
  initiatives 9
  international comparisons 175–80
  mutually hurting stalemate 138, 141–3, 182
  outside states' interest 185–6
  and relief aid 90–91, 101–2, 163
  ripeness for resolution 10, 61–2, 68, 138, 141–3
  theories 10
  see also peace processes
Congo, Democratic Republic of (DRC) 163–4, 177, 179
coups d'état 16, 17, 20, 23, 25, 29, 114
CPA *see* Comprehensive Peace Agreement (CPA)
Cuba 108

Danforth, John
  Nuba Mountains agreement 50, 90, 161
  US ambassador to UN 128
  US role in negotiations 51–2, 53, 124

INDEX

US special envoy 123
Darfur
   Darfur Joint Assessment Mission 98
   famines 22
   political movements 31–2
Darfur conflict
   background 30–31
   Darfur Liberation Front 32
   deaths 5, 27, 32–3, 56
   displaced persons 31, 32, 34, 56, 94, 97
   escalation 32, 55, 126
   international attention 33–4, 60–61
   lower priority than Kenya peace talks 126–8
   missed opportunities 171–2
   separate from north-south framework 146
   SLM/A 32, 58, 63–4, 141
   SPLM/A operations 26, 30–31, 32, 95
   UN International Commission of Inquiry 32, 133
   UNAMID 34, 66, 133, 135
Darfur peace process
   Abuja talks 62–4
   ceasefire agreements 58, 62, 127
   Darfur Peace Agreement (DPA) 34, 63–5, 134, 135, 141
   exclusion of minor parties from 63, 65–6, 141, 183
   limitations 67–8, 141, 183
   stalemate 143
   weakness of 183
Darfur relief aid
   depoliticising effects of 101–2
   distribution and funding 97–8
   obstruction and diversion 97–8, 99
   programmes 94–5, 96–9, 181
   UN Greater Darfur initiative 94, 97
de Waal, Alex 7–8, 71, 74, 82–3
deaths
   civil war 21–2, 27–8, 70
   Darfur conflict 5, 27, 32–3, 56
   relief workers 80–81
Deby, Idris 134
Declaration of Principles (DOP, 1994) 43–4, 45, 46–7
Democratic Republic of Congo (DRC) 163–4, 177, 179

Democratic Unionist Party (DUP) 23, 48, 58
democratisation 145–6, 178
Deng, Aldo Ajo 42–3
Deng, Francis 23, 38
Deng, Gatluak 83
development aid 104, 119, 134, 153–5, 183–4
al-Dhahab, Sawar 20, 22–3, 105
displaced persons
   civil wars 21–2
   Darfur conflict 31, 32, 34, 56, 94, 97
   numbers 5
   to Chad 31, 97
DPA (Darfur Peace Agreement) 34, 63–5, 134, 135, 141
Duffield, Mark 154
DUP (Democratic Unionist Party) 74, 140–41
DUP-SPLM accord (1988) 23, 25, 74, 140

East Germany 108
Eastern Equatoria 21, 26, 81, 82, 95
Eastern Front 67, 146
Eastern Sudan 4, 146
Eastern Sudan Peace Agreement (ESPA) 6, 67
economy
   breadbasket vision 104
   debt relief offer 129, 175
   growth 100
   US disinvestment campaign 132
   see also oil; sanctions
Egypt
   Darfur talks 66
   disinformation campaign 112
   military aid 106, 107
   opposition groups 111, 115
   peace negotiations 37
   relations with Sudan 19, 24, 104, 105, 118
Egyptian-Libyan peace initiative 5, 47–9, 183
El Fasher 97
El Gineina 97
El Obeid 77
elections
   and democracy 178

Sudan 29, 146
Elgabid, Hamid 62
Eliasson, Jan 65
Equatoria
   Eastern Equatoria 21, 26, 81, 82, 95
   Western Equatoria 28, 95
Equatoria Defence Force (EDF) 45
Eritrea 44, 114, 116
Eritrean Islamic Jihad 111
Eritrean People's Liberation Front (EPLF) 25, 83
Eritrean People's Revolutionary Democratic Front (EPRDF) 83–4
Ethiopia
   Addis Ababa talks 16–17, 23, 37
   foreign policy towards 104
   front-line state 114
   Operation Moses 105
   support for opposition groups 19, 21, 25, 26, 108, 116
   ethnic cleansing 28, 127
   see also genocide
European Community Humanitarian Aid Office (ECHO) 120
European Union 34, 119, 121

factionalism 14–15, 45, 65
failed state, prevention 125, 166
famine 22, 27, 70, 71–2, 77–8, 107
Fashoda Agreement (1997) 25, 45–6
flight bans 77, 78, 80, 81, 85, 86–7, 95
food aid 70, 99, 119, 120
foreign policy
   clientelism 103–5, 108–9, 179
   containment 109–122
   engagement in peace process 122–31
   front-line states 114, 116
   and humanitarian policy 9, 129–30, 163–7, 184–5
   shortcomings 170–71
   strategies 8–9, 103, 159
   of Sudan 110–111, 118
   see also relief aid
France 114, 134, 179
Frankfurt Agreement (1992) 40–41
front-line states 114, 116
Frontline Fellowship 88

Fur tribe 30, 31

Gaddafi, Muammar 20
Garang, John
   death 34, 135
   and food supplies 71–2
   forms SPLM/A 19–20
   'New Sudan' 30, 75
   peace negotiations 23, 38, 40, 57
genocide
   Rwanda 176
   Sudan 28, 117, 129, 133
al-Ghannoushi, Rashid 111
Gogrial 87
Gosh, Salah Abdallah 66, 134
Goulty, Alan 129
Government of National Unity (GONU) 34, 180–81
Government of Southern Sudan (GOSS) 34, 134–5, 180
Grant, James 75
grassroots conflict resolution 10, 163, 186
Great Lakes 120, 164, 179
Gulf States 24, 106
Gulf war 39, 110, 112, 114–15

al-Hag, Ali 41, 44
Hagen, Egil 89
Haile Selassie, Emperor 16
Hamesh Koraib 26
Haroun, Ahmed 134
Haroun el-Din, Mohammed 45
el-Hilu, Abd al-Aziz 53
al-Hindi, Sharif Zain al-Abdin 48
history, Sudan 13–14
hostage-taking 80
hudud punishments 19, 105
human rights 28–9, 84, 117
humanitarian action see relief aid
humanitarian armed intervention 166
humanitarian crises
   international 175–80
   political causes of 73–4, 102, 156–7, 158
   see also Darfur relief aid; relief aid

Ibok, Sam 62–3
identity 14–15, 30, 41
IDPs (internally displaced persons) *see*

displaced persons
IGAD (Intergovernmental Authority on Development)
   and Egyptian-Libyan initiative 48–9
   funding 51
   internationalisation of peace talks 50–52, 143
   peace talks 5, 43–7
   secretariat 52, 54
   Technical Committee on Humanitarian Assistance 87
   US and Western engagement 121
   see also Kenya peace talks (2002-5)
IGAD Partners Forum (IPF) 47, 48–9, 51–2, 60–61
INGOs 52, 60, 88–9
internal conflicts *see* civil wars
international actors
   Darfur 33–4, 60–61
   failures 170
   IGAD peace talks 50–52, 143
   importance of 61–2, 135–6, 147–8, 149
   Kenya peace talks 5–6, 52, 53, 62, 123, 124–5, 143
International Criminal Court (ICC) 66, 133–4
International Crisis Group 51, 52, 59–60, 93, 126
Iran 24, 106, 110–111
Iraq 24, 39, 114–15, 129
Islam 14
   sharia 19, 23, 25, 37–8, 105
Islamic Charter Front (ICF) 18–19, 23
Islamism 29–30, 105, 110–111
Israel 104, 105

Jaeger, Christoph 90
Janjawid 32–3, 133–4
Al-Jazuli, Dafallah 23
jihad 29
Johnson, Douglas 7, 8, 16, 43, 45, 46, 49, 161
Johnson, Hilde 50–51, 130
Johnstone, Harry 118–19
Joint Assessment Mission (JAM) 98, 100, 148
Joint Military Commission (JMC) 55, 63–4

Jonglei 82
Jonglei Canal 18, 24
Jordan 107
Juba 28, 81, 82
Juba agreement 186
Justice Africa 59, 60
Justice and Equality Movement (JEM)
   attacks 66
   exclusion from Darfur peace talks 63, 65–6, 141
   formation 32
   motivation 30
   and relief aid 95–6

Kajo-Keji 28
Kapila, Mukesh 92, 126–7, 155, 159
Kapoeta 21
Karim, Ataul 78, 79, 83
Kass 97
Kebkabiya 97
Keen, David 71
Kenya, Turkana 163
Kenya peace talks (2002-5)
   exclusion of smaller groups 59–60, 140–41
   internationalisation of 5–6, 52, 53, 62, 123, 124–5, 143
   limitations 56–9
   oil 174
   priority over Darfur conflict 126–8
   successful outcome 52–4, 61–2
Khalifa, Mohammed el-Amin 38, 44, 77
Khartoum Peace Agreement (1997) 25, 45–6, 140
Kieh, George 176–7, 177
Koka Dam declaration 23, 25
Kongor 82
Kordofan 22, 54, 144
Kurmuk 21
Kushayb, Ali 134
Kutum 97
Kwaje, Samson 142

Lagu, Joseph 16, 17, 18
land, access to 31
languages 17
Lara 55, 56
Lebanon 111
Leel 55

legal system (*sharia*) 19, 23, 25, 37–8, 105
Lesch, Ann Mosely 6, 37, 39, 40, 41, 42
liberal peace 187
Liberia 176–7, 177
Libya
   Darfur talks 66
   and Egypt 24
   foreign policy 104, 105, 106, 107
   relief aid through 98
   and Sudan 20, 22–3, 23, 37, 105
Licklider, Roy 3
Loane, Geoff 161
Lokichokio 76, 77, 95
looting 56, 82, 82–3, 84–5, 99
Lotti, Theophilus Ochang 45

MacFarlane, Neil 163
Machakos Protocol 25–6, 52, 53–4, 57, 144
Machar, Riek 27, 40, 45, 78, 143, 147
MacRae, Joanna 166
al-Mahdi, Sadiq *see* Sadiq al-Mahdi
Malakal 81, 83
Malaysia, oil 117
Mankien 55, 56
Masalit tribe 30, 31
Maundi, Mohammed 177, 178
Mayom 55, 56
mediation *see* peace processes
Medley, Michael 83, 88
Meiram 82
Mengistu, Haile Mariam 26
military aid 104–5, 106–7, 110–111, 144
military coups 16, 17, 20, 23, 25, 29, 114
militia
   Arab 31
   Janjawid 32–3, 133–4
   negotiations 45–6
   Popular Defence Forces (PDF) 29–30
   raiding and looting 70
   training camps 110, 112, 113
   tribal 21
Millington, Jeff 130
Minear, Larry 86

Minnawi, Minni 63, 65
al-Mirghani, Mohammed Othman 58
Moi, Daniel Arap 43
Mubarak, Hosni 111, 114, 115
Muglad 82
Murahilin ('nomads') 21
Museveni, Yoweri 25
Muslim Brotherhood 18
mutually hurting stalemate 138, 141–3, 182

Nafi, Nafi Ali 66, 118
Naivasha protocols 58, 128
Nakuru document 57
Nasir 21
Nathan, Laurie 64
National Congress Party (NCP) 29, 180
National Democratic Alliance (NDA) 26, 48, 49, 58, 116, 119
national identity *see* identity
National Islamic Front (NIF) 23, 29, 110–111
National Redemption Front 65
natural resources 31, 186–7
   see also oil
'New Sudan' 30, 75, 144
NGOs 70, 72, 77, 98–9, 118
Nigeria, mediation efforts 40–43
Nimeiri, Ja'far
   Addis Ababa Agreement 17, 18–20
   attempted coups against 18
   external military assistance 20
   foreign policy 104–5
   introduction of September (*sharia*) laws 19, 105
   military coup of 16
   overthrow of 20, 24, 70, 105
North Korea 166
Norway 5–6, 39, 50–51, 52, 130
Norwegian People's Aid (NPA) 88–9
Nuba Mountains
   conflict 26, 45
   genocide accusations 28
   Programme for Advancing Conflict Transformation (NMPACT) 93, 162
   relief aid 81, 89, 92–3, 130
Nuba Mountains ceasefire agreement 50, 53–4, 55, 131, 161–2

Nuer civil war 46
al-Nur, Abdul Wahid Mohammed
   63–4, 134
Nyaba, Peter 83, 84
Nyala 97
Nyuon, William 82

Obasanjo, Olusegun 23, 38
Obote, Milton 16
Ocampo, Luis Moreno 66
Occidental 116
oil
   European Coalition on Oil in Sudan (ECOS) 118
   exploration 87, 104, 116, 117–18
   exports 117–18
   imports from Libya 106
   in negotiations 174–5
   not primary cause of conflict 173–4
   revenues 100, 174
oil fields, conflict in 27, 55, 186
Olagunju, Tunji 41
OLS (Operation Lifeline Sudan)
   depoliticisation of the crisis 90–91, 155–6
   government view of 77–8
   Ground Rules 79, 151–2, 161
   legal basis of operation 88
   origins 74–6
   problems of access and security 80–85, 86–9
   relief-development continuum 153–5, 184
   review of failings 85–6
   SPLM/A view of 78–80
   structure and operation 7, 76–7, 92, 96, 153
Operation Bright Star 104–5, 105
Operation Moses 105
Operation Rainbow 72
Organisation for Security and Co-operation in Europe (OSCE) 176
Oxfam 72, 88

Palestinian groups 111, 112, 125
peace agreements
   Addis Ababa Agreement (1972) 4, 16–19, 140
   Darfur Peace Agreement (DPA) 34, 63–5, 134, 135, 141
   DUP-SPLM accord (1988) 23, 25, 74
   Eastern Sudan Peace Agreement (ESPA) 6, 67
   Fashoda Agreement (1997) 25, 45–6
   Frankfurt Agreement (1992) 40–41
   Khartoum Peace Agreement (1997) 25, 45–6, 140
   Koka Dam declaration (1986) 23
   see also ceasefire agreements; Comprehensive Peace Agreement (CPA)
peace processes
   Addis Ababa (1989) 37
   carrot and stick incentives 123–4, 125, 128, 129, 148, 175
   Carter initiative 5, 36–8, 76
   categories 36
   in civil war 23
   commitment 62, 146–7, 147–8, 182
   determinants of mediation outcomes 137–8
   Egyptian-Libyan 5, 47–9, 183
   exclusion of minor parties 59–60, 63, 65–6, 139–41, 145, 176–7, 183
   failures 6, 55–9, 139–40, 170, 187–8
   good offices and eminent persons 36–40
   international actors, importance of 61–2, 135–6, 147–8, 149
   liberal peace 187
   mutually hurting stalemate 138, 141–3, 182
   and NDA 58–9
   north-south framework 144–6, 183
   'Peace from within' strategy 45–6
   regional initiatives 40–50
   and relief 93–4, 108–9, 136
   slow pace of 56–8
   success, reasons for 54
   summary 5–6, 34–5
   see also Abuja peace conferences; conflict resolution; Darfur peace process; IGAD (Intergovernmental Authority on Development); Kenya peace talks (2002-5)

peacebuilding strategies, UN 9, 89–90
peacekeeping missions 3, 10, 62, 127, 131, 133, 148, 170, 178
Petronas 117
Petterson, Don 51, 112–13, 120
Popular Congress Party (PCP) 29, 30–31
Popular Defence Forces (PDF) 29–30, 110
Port Sudan 76, 81, 104
Powell, Colin 57, 122, 124
Prattley, Winston 72
Priestley, Michael 75
Pronk, Jan 133

Qadhafi, Muammar 20
Qaissan 21
Qatar, Darfur talks 66

Rafsanjani, Ali Akbar 110
Raga 82
Rashaida Free Lions 30, 58, 67
refugees
  from Ethiopia 22, 107
  Sudanese 22, 32
  see also displaced persons
relief agencies 88–9, 102
relief aid
  anti-democratic effects of 91, 184
  conditionality 161
  and conflict resolution 2, 73–4, 90–91, 96, 101–2, 150, 163, 183
  consequences of prolonged relief 149–50
  Darfur *see* Darfur relief aid
  dependency 152–3, 157
  distribution of 77, 79, 81, 86–7
  see also flight bans
  exaggerated claims for 157, 184
  expenditure 2, 70, 100, 154
  and foreign policy 129–30, 163–7, 184–5
  obstruction and diversion 71–2, 80–85, 87–8, 95, 120, 151
  operations 69–74
  and political action 101–2, 129–30, 131, 159–63, 178–80
  relief-development continuum 153–5, 183–4
  role of 7–8, 107–8

shortcomings 157–8, 170
Southern Sudan 38, 72, 99–100
Sudanese institutions 71
systematisation of 169–70
see also OLS (Operation Lifeline Sudan)
Relief and Rehabilitation Commission (RRC) 71
relief workers 80–81
relief-development continuum 153–5, 183–4
religion 14, 41, 117
Commission on International Religious Freedom (CIRF) 117, 122, 123
ripeness, for conflict resolution 10, 61–2, 68, 138, 141–3
Round Table Conference (1965) 17
Rwanda 114, 163–4, 176, 177–8, 179

Sadiq al-Mahdi
  foreign policy 24, 105–7
  government 20, 22, 48
  leaves Nimeiri government 18
  peace process 48, 59
  and relief supplies 71–2
  and SPLM/A 23
Salim, Salim Ahmed 63, 65
Samaritan's Purse 88
Sanchez, Ilich Ramirez (Carlos the Jackal) 111, 113
sanctions
  UN 46, 114, 115, 124, 128
  US 114, 116, 124
Saudi Arabia 24, 106, 107, 114, 115
Save the Children 88
Save Darfur Coalition (SDC) 132
Schümer, Tanja 161
September 2001 terrorist attacks 50, 123, 123–5
September laws 19, 23
sharia 19, 23, 25, 37–8, 105
Sierra Leone 166
slave trade 117, 123
SLM-Abdul Wahid 63–4, 65, 66, 95–6, 134
SLM/A 32, 58, 63–4, 141
SLM/A-Minnawi 33, 63
Somalia 177, 179, 180
sources 9–10
South Sudan Independence Movement/

Army (SSIM/A) 45, 79
South Yemen 104
Southern Blue Nile 4, 25–6, 46–7, 54, 89
  self-determination 46–7
Southern Kordofan 54, 144
Southern Sudan
  ceasefire violations 55–6, 60
  discontent 19
  see also civil wars
  Nimeiri's division 18
  relief operations 38, 72, 99–100
  security incidents 80
  self-determination 40–41, 43, 44–5, 46–7, 53, 145, 181
Southern Sudan Liberation Movement (SSLM) 16
Soviet Union 17, 104
SPLM/A (Sudan People's Liberation Movement/Army)
  aims and formation 4, 19–20, 30
  alliance with NDA 26
  Carter initiative 37
  in Darfur 30–31, 32, 95
  Declaration of Principles (DOP, 1994) 43
  Egyptian-Libyan initiative 48
  external support for 20–21, 25, 108, 115–16
  human rights record 84
  implementation of the CPA 180
  internal factions 26, 27, 40–41, 78
  loses Ethiopian support 26
  OLS relief operations 71–2, 78–80
  operations 21, 27–8, 75, 79, 106–7
  peace talks 25, 38–9, 41–2, 46–7, 52–4, 139–40
  relief obstruction 82–3, 85, 95
  relief requests 74, 95–6
  SPLM Bahr el-Ghazal 45
  SPLM/A-Nasir 27, 28, 40–41, 78
  SRRA 71, 72, 79, 83, 88, 120
  and US 114, 119, 120
  weakness in mobilising popular support 83–4
  willingness to continue fighting 143
  see also Garang, John
SSIM/A (South Sudan Independence Movement/Army) 45, 79
Stedman, Stephen 6, 139

Stettenheim, Joel 177–8
Sudan
  African-Arab identity 14
  'failed state', prevention 125, 166
  foreign policy 110–111, 118
  history 13–14
  religion 14, 41, 117
Sudan African Nationalist Union 15
Sudan Armed Forces (SAF) 28, 32–3, 34, 100, 135, 143
Sudan Council of Churches (SCC) 72
Sudan Federal Democratic Alliance 30
Sudan People's Liberation Movement/Army *see* SPLM/A (Sudan People's Liberation Movement/Army)
Sudan Relief and Rehabilitation Association (SRRA) 71, 72, 79, 83, 88, 120
Sudan Relief and Rehabilitation Commission (SRRC) 79
Sudanaid 72
Sudanese Allied Forces 26
Sumbeiywo, Lazaro 52, 56–7, 147
Sweden, oil 118
Switzerland, peace agreement 53

Taha, Ali Uthman Mohammed 118
Taha, Mahmoud Mohammed 105
Tajikistan 176, 178
Tam 55
Tawila 97
terrorism
  allegations of Sudanese involvement 50, 112, 113, 118, 119
  US counter-terrorism 123–4, 125, 130–31, 134
Toposa 163
Torit 21, 28
Transitional Military Council (TMC) 20, 24
Traxler, Vieiri 86
tribal groupings 14–15, 45, 65
Tunis 111
al-Turabi, Hasan 18–19, 29, 30–31, 110, 118, 139

Uganda 16, 17, 22, 25, 39, 114, 116
Umma militia 26
Umma Party
  and Arab states 24

Darfur 31
government 20
and Nimeiri 18
peace negotiations 23, 48, 58–9, 140
UNICEF 72, 76, 79, 88
United Kingdom *see* Britain
United Nations
  Brahimi report 165
  Children's Fund (UNICEF) 72, 76, 79, 88
  Convention of the Rights of the Child 79
  Department of Peacekeeping Operations 9
  Department of Political Affairs (DPA) 9, 165
  Greater Darfur initiative 94, 97
  Human Rights Commission 123
  International Commission of Inquiry on Darfur 32, 133
  Mediation Support Unit 165
  need for neutrality 151
  Office for Emergency Operations in Sudan 70
  Operation Lifeline Sudan (OLS) 7
  peace process 9, 66, 89–90, 165
  peacebuilding strategies 9, 89–90
  peacekeeping 34, 133
  preoccupation with humanitarian response 165, 166
  relief activities 72–3, 151–2
  Resident Co-ordinator 76
  sanctions 46, 114, 115, 124, 128
  Security Council resolutions 33, 63, 128, 133
  and SPLM/A 74
  Tajikistan 176
  UNAMID (AU-UN Hybrid Operation in Darfur) 34, 66, 133, 135
  UNMIS (Mission in Sudan) 62, 135
United States
  Al-Shifa bombing 116–17
  Centre for Strategic and International Studies (CSIS) 122–3
  civil war, view 144
  Commission on International Religious Freedom (CIRF) 117, 122, 123
  foreign policy 104–6, 111–14, 122–5, 179
  Khartoum embassy 112, 114
  military aid 106
  and Nimeiri 17, 19, 105
  peace process 5–6, 36–9, 50–52, 54, 119
  relief aid 107–8, 119–20
  relief and political co-ordination 129, 165, 185
  sanctions 114, 116, 124
  Save Darfur Coalition (SDC) 132
  and Somalia 180
  and SPLM/A 120
  Sudan Peace Act 61, 117
  terrorism concerns 112, 118, 119, 123–4, 125, 134
  USAID 9, 112, 119–20, 121, 129–30, 161–2, 165
Upper Nile 28, 80, 87

van Shaik, Robert 86

Walter, Barbara 148, 178, 182
Wau 81, 82, 87
Weiss, Herbert 177
Wells, Melissa 113
Western Equatoria 28, 95
Western Upper Nile 55, 87, 95
Winter, Roger 130
women 55–6, 141, 145
Wondu, Stephen 6, 37, 39, 41, 42
World Council of Churches 16
World Food Programme (WFP) 76, 77, 80, 81, 82, 83, 84, 88, 98
World Trade Center bombing 112
World Vision 72, 88
Wunlit Agreement (1999) 163, 186

Yirol 21
Yugoslavia 178–9, 179

Zaghawa 14, 31
Zaire 163–4, 177
Zartman, William 10, 142, 171, 179–80
Zoellick, Robert 63